LE CORBUSIER'S
AHMEDABAD MILLOWNERS'
ASSOCIATION BUILDING

MEHRDAD HADIGHI

LE CORBUSIER'S AHMEDABAD MILLOWNERS' ASSOCIATION BUILDING

BETWEEN THE BEAUTIFUL AND THE SUBLIME

BIRKHÄUSER

For Shadi and Dara

CONTENTS

FOREWORD
KENNETH FRAMPTON

Every architect in their maturity has a singular building with which they are destined to be preoccupied throughout their lives. In this fixation the building assumes the form of an archetypal image, embodying all the attributes of a fundamental gestalt capable of inspiring a sequence of projects to which the architect repeatedly returns in vain pursuit of an inaccessible ideal.

For Hadighi, this is evidently Le Corbusier's Millowners' Building designed for Ahmedabad, India in 1954. This work is indisputably the most integral, free-standing civic monument that Le Corbusier would realize in India during the last fifteen years of his life. It would attain a level of compact monumentality unmatched by any other structure of his consummate Indian career when he worked, as a singular archetypal modern architect, for the Nehru government as part of the welfare state project that characterized the first years of Indian independence.

A striking characteristic of this work is its use of full-height, fixed, monumental brise-soleil in reinforced concrete of such a depth and scale as to be incorporated into the cubic volume of the work itself. Equally conspicuous is the articulation of the enclosed volume so as to accord with Le Corbusier's concept of the so-called "promenade architecturale," which, as Hadighi observes, has its origin in the Socratic dialogue of a Greek architect named Eupalinos as he was imagined by Paul Valéry in his book of that title, expressly annotated by Le Corbusier in this particular respect when it first came out in 1923.

The Millowners' Building is characteristic of Le Corbusier's Purist Mediterranean parasol house type as this was first projected for Carthage in Tunisia in 1928. The reappearance of this type in Le Corbusier's Indian work would seem to echo spontaneously the monumental open-air pavilion that was so characteristic of Akbar Shah's ill-fated city of Fatehpur Sikri, thereby combining Le Corbusier's Purist *palazzetto* type with a trope from the neglected Mughal architectural tradition. This is characteristic of Hadighi's aperçus in his exhaustive analysis of this singular paradigm.

By focusing on a single work, Hadighi follows in the footsteps of generations of Le Corbusier scholars in his rigorous analysis of the most compact civic building of Le Corbusier's Indian career. In so doing, he inevitably interprets the work as a layered overlay of interrelated dualities, much like the Engineer's Aesthetic and Architecture, which structured Le Corbusier's *Vers Une Architecture* credo of 1923. Assuming this as his parti, Hadighi proceeds to analyze this work, the single most compact and elegant building of Le Corbusier's Indian career in terms of circulation, proportion, servicing, orientation, and structural consistency plus the subtle experiential social narrative built into its volumetric organization. He also shows at the end of his analysis the way in which the introduction of a riverfront autoroute and the totally anti-ecological subsequent canalization of the Sabarmati River has totally destroyed the once hypersensitive relationship between the building and the river.

London, January 2025

EUPALINOS

OU L'ARCHITECTE

précédé de

L'AME ET LA DANSE

par

PAUL VALÉRY

PARIS

Éditions de la

NOUVELLE REVUE FRANÇAISE

3, Rue de Grenelle

MCMXXIII

INTRODUCTION: LE CORBUSIER AND VALÉRY

← Front matter of Le Corbusier's copy of Paul Valéry's *Eupalinos ou L'Architecte.*

"Talking about Geometry" writes Le Corbusier in pencil script on page 90 of a 1923 edition of Paul Valéry's *Eupalinos ou L'Architecte.*[1] He inscribes this phrase next to a dialogue between Phaedrus and Socrates, two figures from the Platonic dialogues who appear as the interlocutors in Valéry's *Eupalinos.* They are both dead and appear as "shades" of themselves. The two converse about architecture, Phaedrus paraphrasing Eupalinos, an architect whom he had met when he was alive. The larger topic is that of reality. Whether the physical world and acting in it (constructing) is the ultimate reality, or the world of thought. Already in the set-up of the dialogue, Valéry is suggesting that this "dim habitation" of the souls where the dead appear as "shades" of themselves, where no action and only thought is possible, is the environment of ideality, which in this dialogue is portrayed as the environment of death. Life, he says, which is mortal, is the only place for beauty to exist.

The entire dialogue circles around questions of the ideality of thought and the reality of construction. It compares "acting" as required for construction with "thinking."[2] In this rich topic of extreme relevance to architecture, Le Corbusier marks three pages in the book, none focused on the main topic: an annotation on page 87 that refers to the aforementioned note on page 90, and a paragraph marked on page 100.

Pages 87–90 refer to a section of the dialogue that focuses on geometry, hence Le Corbusier's note: "Talking about Geometry." Socrates describes to Phaedrus what he means when he says, "I call 'geometric' those figures which are records of the movements we can express in few words."[3] He explains:

1 Paul Valéry, *Eupalinos ou L'Architecte* (Paris: Éditions de la Nouvelle Revue française, 1923), 90.
2 Paul Valéry, "Eupalinos or the Architect," in *Dialogues* (Princeton, New Jersey: Princeton University Press, 1989), 75.
3 Valéry, "Eupalinos or the Architect," 103.

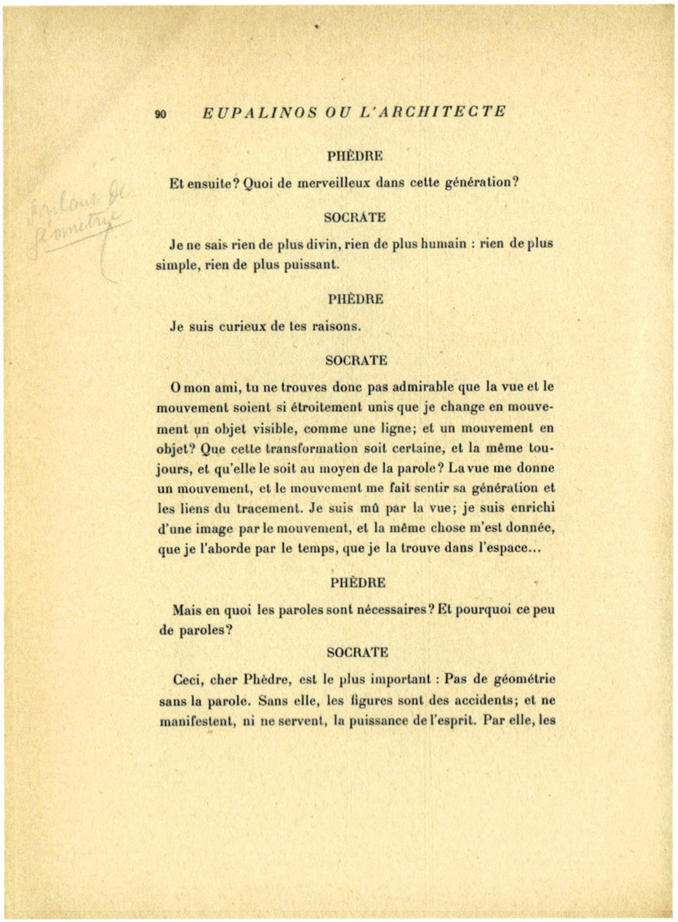

90 *EUPALINOS OU L'ARCHITECTE*

PHÈDRE

Et ensuite? Quoi de merveilleux dans cette génération?

SOCRATE

Je ne sais rien de plus divin, rien de plus humain : rien de plus simple, rien de plus puissant.

PHÈDRE

Je suis curieux de tes raisons.

SOCRATE

O mon ami, tu ne trouves donc pas admirable que la vue et le mouvement soient si étroitement unis que je change en mouvement un objet visible, comme une ligne; et un mouvement en objet? Que cette transformation soit certaine, et la même toujours, et qu'elle le soit au moyen de la parole? La vue me donne un mouvement, et le mouvement me fait sentir sa génération et les liens du tracement. Je suis mû par la vue; je suis enrichi d'une image par le mouvement, et la même chose m'est donnée, que je l'aborde par le temps, que je la trouve dans l'espace...

PHÈDRE

Mais en quoi les paroles sont nécessaires? Et pourquoi ce peu de paroles?

SOCRATE

Ceci, cher Phèdre, est le plus important : Pas de géométrie sans la parole. Sans elle, les figures sont des accidents; et ne manifestent, ni ne servent, la puissance de l'esprit. Par elle, les

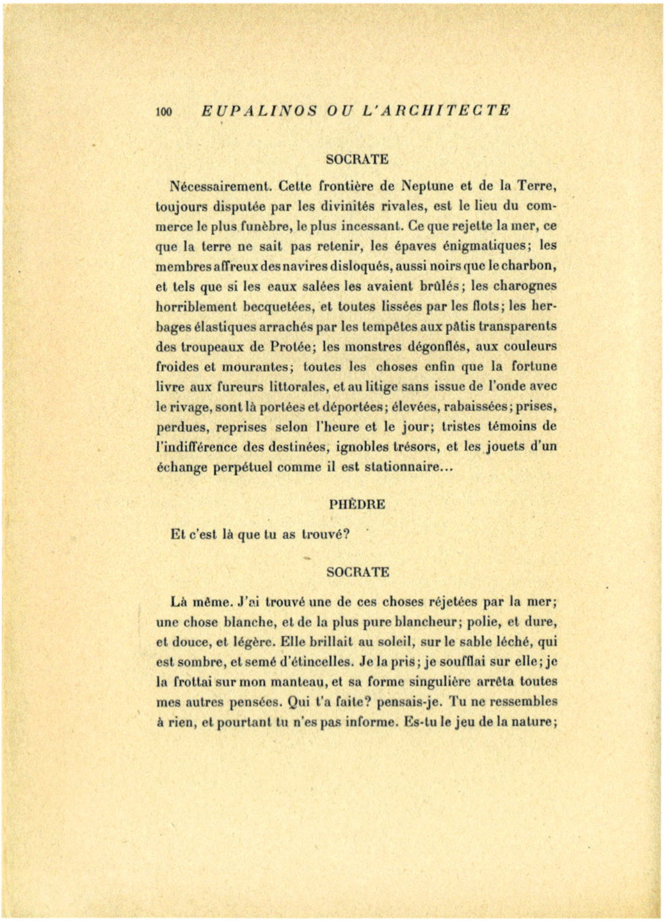

100 *EUPALINOS OU L'ARCHITECTE*

SOCRATE

Nécessairement. Cette frontière de Neptune et de la Terre, toujours disputée par les divinités rivales, est le lieu du commerce le plus funèbre, le plus incessant. Ce que rejette la mer, ce que la terre ne sait pas retenir, les épaves énigmatiques; les membres affreux des navires disloqués, aussi noirs que le charbon, et tels que si les eaux salées les avaient brûlés; les charognes horriblement becquetées, et toutes lissées par les flots; les herbages élastiques arrachés par les tempêtes aux pâtis transparents des troupeaux de Protée; les monstres dégonflés, aux couleurs froides et mourantes; toutes les choses enfin que la fortune livre aux fureurs littorales, et au litige sans issue de l'onde avec le rivage, sont là portées et déportées; élevées, rabaissées; prises, perdues, reprises selon l'heure et le jour; tristes témoins de l'indifférence des destinées, ignobles trésors, et les jouets d'un échange perpétuel comme il est stationnaire...

PHÈDRE

Et c'est là que tu as trouvé?

SOCRATE

Là même. J'ai trouvé une de ces choses réjetées par la mer; une chose blanche, et de la plus pure blancheur; polie, et dure, et douce, et légère. Elle brillait au soleil, sur le sable léché, qui est sombre, et semé d'étincelles. Je la pris; je soufflai sur elle; je la frottai sur mon manteau, et sa forme singulière arrêta toutes mes autres pensées. Qui t'a faite? pensais-je. Tu ne ressembles à rien, et pourtant tu n'es pas informe. Es-tu le jeu de la nature;

Pages 90 and 100 of Le Corbusier's copy of Valéry's *Eupalinos ou L'Architecte*, where he has annotated the discussion of geometry and the significance of found objects.

> What is necessary is that, by a single proposition, the movement should be defined so precisely that there remains no other liberty to the body in motion but to follow it, and it alone. And this proposition must be obeyed by each instant of this movement, so that all the parts of the figure may be one identical thing in thought, though different in extension. If then I tell you to walk remaining always at an equal distance from two trees, you will engender one of those figures, provided that in your movement you observe the condition that I have set.[4]

The succinctness and exactitude of geometric forms attract Le Corbusier, as is evidenced by his annotation of this section of Valéry's dialogue. Similarly, the prescription of bodily movement forecasts his later "promenade architecturale." This attraction also exists towards indescribable qualities of mysterious artifacts such as that mentioned on page 100: something washed up on the beach, what the sea has refused. He marks the related paragraph, the only other marking in the book:

> I found one of those things cast up by the sea; a white thing of the most pure whiteness; polished and hard and smooth and light. It shone in the sun on the licked sand, that is somber and spark-bestrewn. I took it up; I blew upon it;

4 Valéry, "Eupalinos or the Architect," 103–104.

Le Corbusier's hands, holding an object found at the seaside. Photograph taken by Lucien Hervé at Le Corbusier's summer cabin, Le Cabanon in Roquebrune-Cap-Martin, France, 1950. Lucien Hervé photographs of architecture and artworks by Le Corbusier, 1949–1965.

> I rubbed it against my cloak, and its singular shape suspended all my other thoughts. Who made thee? I pondered. Thou resembles nothing, and yet thou art not shapeless. Art thou a sport of nature, O nameless thing, that art come to me by the will of gods, in the midst of the refuse that the sea this night has flung from her?[5]

The two paragraphs marked/annotated by Le Corbusier point to the two extremes of form that held his attention in architecture: ones that belonged to a family of geometric shapes that had not changed since time immemorial and could be defined today as they had been 2500 years prior with few words, and the other: singular forms that "resemble nothing," yet captivate us. Le Corbusier collected and documented objects "washed up by the sea" that belong to the family of these "mysterious" objects.

PLASTIC EXPERIENCES

Le Corbusier completed more than fifty buildings between 1906 and 1965, when he drowned swimming off the shores of his summer cabin at Roquebrune. Architectural historians have pointed to the many "periods" of his architecture: the very early years in La Chaux-de-Fonds, his seminal buildings from the 1920s through the 1930s mostly in and around Paris, his large-scale buildings and urban proposals of the pre-Second World War era, and his post-Second World War buildings. Although these "periods" are justified and do, in fact, present different sensibilities, they share an adherence to principles of geometry and also to singular formal and spatial experiences. The adherence to these dual, apparently contradictory desires in architecture remained with him throughout his career.

Le Corbusier's buildings have left an indelible mark on the psyche of architects all around the world and, most importantly, on our contemporary conception of architectural forms and spaces. Fans and foes will agree that his formal inventions, architecturally and in relation to landscapes and urban conditions, are unparalleled. A 2013 exhibition of his work at the Museum of Modern Art in New York, titled *An Atlas of Modern Landscapes,* curated by the late Jean-Louis Cohen, architect, historian, and member of the Committee of Experts for the Architectural Work of the Fondation Le Corbusier, outlines how the idea of landscape was addressed in the exhibition, "both in its accepted sense as well as in terms of what it meant for Le Corbusier. The term 'landscape,' in use in the Anglophone world since the end of the sixteenth century, denotes both the physical and visible form of a specific outdoor space and its graphic, pictorial, or photographic representation; it was strictly rural in origin but today it is understood to be nonspecific."[6] I would add that Le Corbusier was interested in more than recording or creating already known

5 Valéry, "Eupalinos or the Architect," 114.
6 Jean-Louis Cohen, "In the Cause of Landscape," in *Le Corbusier: An Atlas of Modern Landscapes* (New York: Museum of Modern Art, 2013), 24–25.

concepts of landscapes; rather, he was interested in inventing new ones never before thought of. In fact, the exhibition records visions of "modern" landscapes never before conceived. The "Atlas" not only records Le Corbusier's care for and interest in natural and urban landscapes as they relate to buildings, but also, and most importantly, invents a landscape of heretofore unknown architecture. Le Corbusier invented the language of modern architectural landscapes.[7]

Although these architectural landscapes are most visible in his buildings, Le Corbusier was also a prolific writer and presented his ideas of modernity in architecture through books, essays, lectures, journals he edited, and much more. His writings generally did not present theories or arguments, nor did they reference histories or other writers. They had the tone of proclamations and prescriptions. They were declarative, which made them easy to dismiss. In the words of Caroline Constant, an architectural historian, "his utopian urban pronouncements had a militant tone."[8] This has led most architects either to agree with him or to disagree with him, but not to read him as closely as he warranted. My contention in the following work is that behind these dogmatic masks, created by Le Corbusier and maintained by architects and historians, the buildings speak differently. His built work, analyzed through a close reading, speaks of the architect's struggle to make manifest singular formal and spatial experiences using the geometry of rationalized building systems. He created singular plastic experiences impossible to imagine within the confines of the geometry of a building's technical systems. He worked the components of these two architectural conditions (technical building systems and singular forms and experiences) in order both to resolve systemic technical concerns and to heighten plastic spatial and formal experiences. As much as Le Corbusier was wedded to the ideal of the rationality of building systems and their geometric order, he had a more complex agenda in his work, which was to create singular plastic experiences of spaces and forms through the manipulation of a geometrically and systemically conceived architecture. His work was created through a constant tension between these two realms: the systematicity and geometric organization of building systems (such as structural, plumbing, sun-shading, and circulatory ones) and the singularity of spatial experience achieved through movement in space.

TRAINING

Le Corbusier's training as a young artist and craftsman at the Municipal Art School of La Chaux-de-Fonds under the tutelage of Charles L'Eplattenier provides a source for his interest in geometry. The Art School in the Jura Mountain watch-making town in western Switzerland trained pupils in watch-engraving, for which nature served as the

7 Here, I am referring to an even wider meaning of landscape to include the built environment of architecture. Of course, there were others with an interest in landscape, such as Ludwig Mies van der Rohe and Frank Lloyd Wright. In my view, however, none reached the complexity or the extent of invention apparent in Le Corbusier's work.

8 Caroline Constant, *The Modern Architectural Landscape* (Minneapolis: University of Minnesota Press, 2012), 20.

Charles-Édouard Jeanneret, *Study of Pine Trees*, 1905–1906, black gouache and pencil on paper (top); *Pine Forest Ornament*, 1911, gouache on paper (bottom).

source of all content. All ornamentation would be derivative of a geometrized abstraction of nature. Le Corbusier's 1905–1906 *Study of Pine Trees* presents a "sapin" forest (Swiss pine or fir forest) in geometric form, from which ornamental geometries were derived for watch engravings. Even as late as 1911, we see gouache illustrations of abstracted *Pine Forest Ornament* by Le Corbusier. Many of these ornaments, drawn for watch cases, find their way into his early La Chaux-de-Fonds houses. Although the ornaments stay in his hometown when he moves to Paris, the geometries remain with him for the rest of his career.

Another part of his training in the Municipal Art School that stayed with him throughout his career was the teachings of John Ruskin. L'Eplattenier was a devout reader of Ruskin and had developed an entire curriculum based on his writings at the school, where he also ensured that the library would house the French translations of the same. Le Corbusier eventually parted ways with L'Eplattenier and his teachings, yet he remained wedded to Ruskin's theories. Not only did he adhere to Ruskin's ideas about the relationship of geometry, nature, and beauty, but he was also inspired by his ideas of a higher order of beauty that could only be reached through "truth." Le Corbusier wrote in 1925, "Ruskin spoke of spirituality. In his *The Seven Lamps of Architecture* shone the Lamp of Sacrifice, the Lamp of Truth, the Lamp of Humility."[9] It was not surprising, then, that he found an affinity with Amédée Ozenfant when they met in Paris in 1918 and later co-edited the journal they founded, *L'Esprit Nouveau*.

Ozenfant and Ruskin shared roots in Plato and the relationship of beauty and geometry, but also the search for "truth." Ozenfant introduced Le Corbusier to the cultural and artistic world of Paris and the two began exhibiting paintings together under the "Purism" banner.[10] The compositional strategies developed in this period in line with ideas of fragmentation and collage played a central role in Le Corbusier's architecture for the remainder of his life, as did studies of transparency – initially, of the bottle subjects of the painted still lives, later turned into architectural transparency.

TRAVELS

Beginning in 1907, Le Corbusier embarked on a series of travels – first to Italy and Vienna, and then to Paris in March 1908. There, he made a decisive move to work for the brothers Auguste and Gustave Perret, architectural reinforced-concrete pioneers. Their office was at 25 bis rue Franklin in Paris, an apartment building the Perrets had designed and constructed. As pioneers of reinforced concrete in architecture, the brothers had been unable to secure a bank loan for the construction of the apartment building, as the banks were unsure of the new material's structural capabilities. The Perret brothers financed the construction themselves and, once complete, estab-

9 Le Corbusier, *The Decorative Art of Today.* Translated by James Dunnett (Cambridge, Massachusetts: The MIT Press, 1987), 132.

10 On Le Corbusier's artistic activities in the 1930s, see Tim Benton, *The Painter Le Corbusier. Eileen Gray's Villa E 1027 and Le Cabanon* (Basel: Birkhäuser, 2023), 26–31.

L'ESPRIT NOUVEAU

REVUE INTERNATIONALE D'ESTHÉTIQUE

PARAISSANT LE 15 DE CHAQUE MOIS

DIRECTEUR : PAUL DERMÉE

ESTHÉTIQUE EXPÉRIMENTALE
PEINTURE SCULPTURE ARCHITECTURE
LITTÉRATURE MUSIQUE
ESTHÉTIQUE DE L'INGÉNIEUR
LE THÉATRE LE MUSIC-HALL LE CINÉMA LE CIRQUE LES SPORTS
LE COSTUME LE LIVRE LE MEUBLE
ESTHÉTIQUE DE LA VIE MODERNE

N° 1

DANS CE NUMÉRO

50 photogravures et deux reproductions aux trois couleurs,

SOMMAIRE

Voir au dos les avantages et les primes réservés aux Abonnés.

PRIX NET : 6 francs français POUR TOUS PAYS

ÉDITIONS DE L'ESPRIT NOUVEAU
SOCIÉTÉ ANONYME AU CAPITAL DE 100.000 FRANCS
13, QUAI DE CONTI
PARIS (VIe)

↑ Cover of *L'Esprit Nouveau 1*, a journal founded in 1920 by Le Corbusier, Ozenfant, and Dermée. Twenty-eight issues were published between 1920 and 1925.

← Le Corbusier, *Vertical Still Life*, 1922, oil on canvas, 146.3 × 89.3 centimeters, Kunstmuseum, Basel.

lished their office in the same building. Kenneth Frampton, architect and historian, describes the rue Franklin apartments as seminal, both for the Perrets and for the history of modern architecture:

> Perret … regarded the structural frame as the quintessential expression of built form. The ferro-concrete frame of the Rue Franklin block was tiled in such a way as to suggest post and lintel construction in wood – the remainder being either windows or solid panels faced in ceramic mosaic. While the tessellated sunflowers of the latter gave the building that quality of fossilized Art

→ Auguste and Gustave Perret, 25 bis rue Franklin, Paris, 1903, elevation, section, and exterior view. An early reinforced concrete building.

> Nouveau so peculiar to the end of the Belle Epoque, the frame itself, and the open planning it permitted, pointed towards Le Corbusier's later development of the free plan.[11]

Working in the Perret building with such minimal structural frame components made Le Corbusier recognize the possibility of an efficient structural system, open plan, and large expanses of glass.

We know now that the use of reinforced concrete and the structural frame became central to Le Corbusier's architecture for the rest of his career. The structural frame was both pure geometry and efficient structure that led to open plan and expansive strip windows, free façade, pilotis, and the roof garden – the five elements of Le Corbusier's "Five Points of Architecture."[12]

In 1910, Le Corbusier traveled to Germany and worked in Peter Behrens's office, where Ludwig Mies van der Rohe was also working. Behrens was one of the founding members of the Deutsche Werkbund, a group of twelve designers and twelve craft firms whose aim was to coalesce the arts with production and craft techniques, making design available to the masses. Behrens had been appointed as the architect and designer for AEG (the Allgemeine Elektricitäts Gesellschaft – General Electric Company) to work on a house type that included not only the dwelling, but also everything from graphics to product design – and, most importantly, their industrial production. The Deutsche Werkbund and one of its original founders Hermann Muthesius were focused on several ideas that appear in later Le Corbusier doctrines: the refinement over time of everyday objects: the "standard" (Le Corbusier's *objet-type*); the refinement of these types towards mass production; and the availability of great design and production techniques to the masses through mass-produced, industrialized artifacts.

The travels continued from Germany to Eastern Europe, Greece, and Turkey – known as the "Voyage d'Orient" – with impres-

11 Kenneth Frampton, *Modern Architecture: A Critical History* (London: Thames & Hudson, 2007), 106.

12 Charles-Édouard Jeanneret (Le Corbusier), *Le Corbusier 1910–1965*. Edited by Willy Besiger and Hans Girsberger (Zurich: Les Éditions d'Architecture Zurich, 1967), 44–45.

sions and sketches published, exhibited, and discussed in lectures. The Parthenon of the Acropolis of Athens consumed Le Corbusier for the remainder of his life and is a subject that reappeared in many essays, including multiple chapters of his seminal book *Towards a New Architecture*.[13] At the time of his visit to the Parthenon in 1911, the columns of the north façade were still lying on the ground and the Acropolis was not yet the tourist mecca that it is today. He was able to spend time with the columns, in diameter as tall as he was, touch them and assess their proportions, lying on the ground, with sections reasonably aligned as they would have been, standing. Their formal and proportional refinement and the exactitude of their making brought a nuanced awareness of the "standard," the "*objet-type*." It need not be mass-producible but designed and refined over time and made precisely.

In 1917, he moved to Paris, where he met Ozenfant and began painting in parallel with architecture, a practice he maintained throughout his life. In fact, his daily routine, often mentioned by the architects who worked with him much later in his architecture atelier, always included painting in the morning and atelier in the afternoon. These bits and pieces, fragments collaged together as a life's experiences give us a window into the workings of Le Corbusier's architecture. It was wedded to the geometry and regularity of the building systems, structural and otherwise, and also in search of an indescribable sense of beauty and truth, which were rarely found but when found, in exemplary objects such as the Parthenon, would move us: they would "affect our senses acutely," they would produce "plastic emotion."[14]

Le Corbusier did not point to these two conditions as simultaneous in his writings. He did, however, focus on them in his buildings. In writing, he outlined the two conditions independently, describing each separately. The separation would make sense if we were discussing his paintings; however, in architecture, technical systems are a fundamental part of the inception and the execution of every building and are inseparable from the experience of architecture. Firmness, commodity, and delight have been written as the three foundations of architecture since the first-century-CE treatise of Vitruvius, *On Architecture* (also casually known as the *Ten Books on Architecture*.)[15] Both firmness and commodity relate directly to the building systems and would not exist without them.[16] Delight, for Le Corbusier, came from "plastic emotion," the singular spatial experience that affects our senses acutely.

Le Corbusier at the Acropolis of Athens, standing next to a column from the Parthenon as it lay on the ground, 1911.

13 Charles-Édouard Jeanneret (Le Corbusier), *Towards a New Architecture*. Translated by Frederick Etchells (New York, Toronto, London, Sydney: Holt, Reinhart and Winston, 1960).

14 Le Corbusier, *Towards a New Architecture*, 7.

15 Marcus V. Pollio Vitruvius, *On Architecture*. Translated by Frank Granger (Cambridge, Massachusetts, and London: Harvard University Press, 1998).

16 "Building systems" belong to a contemporary language referring to structural, mechanical, electrical, environmental, circulatory, envelope, assembly, and more. Clearly, our understanding of these has evolved throughout history and many have become "systems" as specialization has taken hold.

THE DUAL CONDITION: THE BOOK AND THE BUILDING

To gain a more precise understanding of Le Corbusier's work both as an architect and as a writer, I will explore, in parallel, his writings in his seminal 1923 book *Towards a New Architecture (Vers Une Architecture),* and one of his late buildings, the Millowners' Association Building in Ahmedabad, India, 1951–1954. Why these two? It is easy to select the book, as it is the best-known, most taught, most referenced, and the closest thing to an overall architectural theory by Le Corbusier. It would have made sense to select a building from the same era as the book, the era that Charles Jencks called the "Heroic Period" of 1917–1928.[17] However, my argument here is not about a particular period in which the theories promulgated in *Towards a New Architecture* were instilled but rather a constant architectural struggle between the two conditions mentioned above, and, most importantly, the presentation of the two conditions in a state of tension, where both are present simultaneously: elements belonging to different modalities forming a spatial collage. In this model, any of his buildings may have been analyzed comparatively with the text of the book.

I selected the Millowners' Association Building, first and foremost, as an architect who has been awed by it for decades, a building that truly uplifts the spirit. It is also one that has not been well documented. There is a single duograph (half-)dedicated to this building, published in 1975 by *Global Architecture,* containing a very insightful but brief essay by Kenneth Frampton with thirteen images by Yukio Futagawa. The building, of course, is mentioned in almost every book on Le Corbusier, and on his work in India. The books that concentrate on India are mostly dedicated to Chandigarh but also include the buildings in Ahmedabad, however briefly. So, in the end, there is no thorough study and documentation of the building. A part of the current endeavor has been to "preserve" the building through a set of precise drawings of the existing structure, a three-dimensional computational model, and a physical model, as well as documenting the alterations to the building over time. Fondation Le Corbusier listed this building as "not visitable," perhaps due to its private ownership. I found that the Millowners' Association welcomed visitors with open arms, no doubt in part to encourage a better understanding of the building and to promote its recognition on the world stage.

When it was initially built, there were sixty-four thriving mills in Ahmedabad, whose leadership constituted the board of the Association and also guaranteed its financial health. Currently, there are four mills left and the Association and its future financial stability have come into question. Although there is a robust presidential infrastructure for the Association, much depends on future financing,

17 Charles Jencks, *Le Corbusier and the Tragic View of Architecture* (Cambridge, Massachusetts: Harvard University Press, 1973), 47.

which may also invite doubts about the building's maintenance and preservation. One hope for this study is to record this remarkable building as one of the most influential and theoretically precise later works of Le Corbusier, highlighting its worthiness of attention, visitation, and preservation. The Ahmedabad Millowners' Association Building is a calculated and precise materialization of Le Corbusier's constant struggle to give shape to the regular geometry of the building's technical systems in tension with a series of singular spatial and formal experiences.

Cover of Le Corbusier's 1923 *Vers Une Architecture*, Éditions G. Crès, Collection de "L'Esprit Nouveau", Paris.

I
LEGACY CREATED: ARCHIVING LE CORBUSIER

← The stairs, three-story cavity, and brise-soleil of the west façade.

18 The Museum of Modern Art, "Le Corbusier: 5 Projects," press release, April 1987. https://assets.moma.org/documents/moma_press-release_327453.pdf?_ga=2.144888822.311536638.1612405102-1048391941.1612405102 (accessed June 28, 2024).
19 The Museum of Modern Art, "Symposium to Complement Le Corbusier Exhibition," press release, April 1987. https://assets.moma.org/documents/moma_press-release_327452.pdf?_ga=2.116504388.311536638.1612405102-1048391941.1612405102 (accessed June 28, 2024).
20 Cohen later curated another seminal exhibition on the work of Le Corbusier at the Museum of Modern Art in New York, titled: *Le Corbusier: An Atlas of Modern Landscapes*, June 15 to September 23, 2013.
21 Charles-Édouard Jeanneret (Le Corbusier) and Fondation Le Corbusier, *Le Corbusier Archive* (New York and London: Garland Publishing, 1983–1984). The *Le Corbusier Archive* was imagined and published by the Fondation Le Corbusier after his death as an archival tool of more than 20,000 pages that documented all records for each project. It thus presented process, changes, and edits not visible in the final artifact.

Earlier, Le Corbusier had already imagined and prepared for the publication of the *Œuvre Complète*, an eight-volume record with approximately 1700 pages of all of the final products of his architectural and urban projects. These volumes had been published between 1929 and 1970, originally by Les Editions d'Architecture in Zurich, and later by Birkhäuser. Edited by Willy Boesiger, Oscar Stonorov, and Max Bill. *Le Corbusier. Œuvre Complète* (Basel: Birkhäuser, 2013).

The year 1987 marked the one hundredth anniversary of the birth of Charles-Édouard Jeanneret-Gris, better known to the world as Le Corbusier. There were many celebrations around the world prepared for this date. The Museum of Modern Art in New York (MoMA) planned an exhibition of *Le Corbusier: Five Projects* in its architecture gallery that was exhibited between March 26 and May 26, 1987. The press release noted, "The Museum of Modern Art presents a modest tribute commemorating the centennial of the birth of Le Corbusier (1887–1965), one of the seminal figures of twentieth-century architecture."[18] The exhibition focused on five of his buildings – four built, one a competition entry – all executed between 1926 and 1933. MoMA also planned a symposium during the exhibition entitled "Le Corbusier Between the Wars: Architecture and Ideology."[19] The symposium was organized by Stuart Wrede of MoMA and Kenneth Frampton. Other participants included Tim Benton, Le Corbusier scholar, and Jean-Louis Cohen, then a member of the Committee of Experts for the Architectural Works of the Fondation Le Corbusier, among a handful of others. Cohen was at the same time curating the centennial celebration exhibition *L'aventure Le Corbusier* at the Centre Georges Pompidou in Paris.[20] The Fondation Le Corbusier, in its turn, had planned the largest publication project of Le Corbusier documents ever undertaken by any entity: the *Le Corbusier Archive*.[21] The Fondation Le Corbusier would publish thirty-two volumes covering Le Corbusier's work from 1912 to 1965, the year of his death. Each volume of more than five hundred large-format pages (23 × 31 centime-

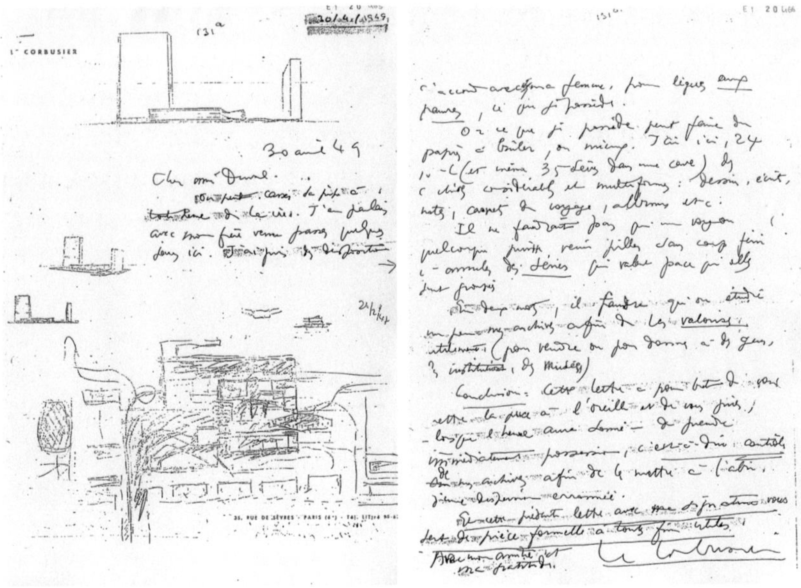
30 avril 49

Cher ami Duval

← Le Corbusier's April 30, 1949 letter to Jean-Jacques Duval, prompting the idea of a foundation to preserve his work.

ters) would present complete drawings in the Fondation's holdings of a set of chronologically organized building documents totaling 32,000 drawings in its entirety. Each drawing is reproduced in black and white, numbered both by Atelier Le Corbusier and the Fondation's archival cataloging system. Also included are the Fondation's catalogue entries for each drawing, which include typical archival data such as title, description, scale, signature, date, medium, material, dimension, and the Fondation's archival number. There was a collection of sixteen essays, edited by H. Allen Brooks, accompanying the thirty-two volumes. Fifteen of the essays were commissioned to bring diverse analytical views to the work presented, and thus included work by renowned architectural historians, scholars, biographers, critics, and architects that had worked in Le Corbusier's atelier. The remaining essay was one already published and selected by Brooks for inclusion. About this non-linear organization of essays, Brooks writes in his foreword:

> I must have been thinking, to use an architectural analogy, of an axonometric projection wherein one sees various faces simultaneously rather than viewing only one thing at a time. I wanted to contrast articles that were broad against those that were narrow and deep, with obvious overlaps serving to stimulate the reader's mind. I sought to juxtapose different views rather than avoid them.[22]

THE FONDATION LE CORBUSIER

The thirty-two volume *Le Corbusier Archive* was only possible because the Fondation Le Corbusier existed and held all of Le Corbusier's drawings. It is important to note that the Fondation was Le Corbusier's brainchild. As early as 1949, he documented this idea in a

22 H. Allen Brooks, ed., *Le Corbusier* (Princeton, New Jersey: Princeton University Press, 1987), ix.
Fifteen of the sixteen essays that were originally published in the Garland 32-volume *Le Corbusier Archive* were republished in a hard-bound volume, also edited by H. Allen Brooks, in 1987 by Garland Publishing, and a soft-bound version by Princeton University Press. The sixteenth essay, by James Stirling, titled "Garches to Jaoul: Le Corbusier as Domestic Architect in 1927 and 1953," had appeared in Volume 20 of the *Le Corbusier Archive*. This essay was, however, not a commissioned essay; it was reprinted from an original September 1955 *Architectural Review* issue and was therefore not republished in the referenced book.

letter to Jean-Jacques Duval, a trusted friend for whom he designed the Duval factory.[23] Le Corbusier wrote to Duval about the establishment of a foundation to preserve and maintain his life's work in a complete set of documents and "to protect them from being wrongfully scattered."[24] In the letter, Le Corbusier documents his intention to give his personal belongings to the poor. However, he recognizes the significance of his work and that part of the maintenance of its future significance relies precisely on the establishment of the foundation: a place where all his drawings, writings, books, notes, and sketchbooks would be preserved as a complete collection. He writes, "I don't want some hooligan happily pillaging it all and destroying series whose value depends on their being complete."[25] From this point on, during the last fifteen years of his life, Le Corbusier decidedly organized his work, classified, and recorded towards the eventual establishment of the Fondation Le Corbusier. Finally, on January 13, 1960, he formalized the foundation by writing, "I hereby declare, in any case, to bequeath all that I possess in favor of an administrative being, the 'Foundation Le Corbusier,' or any other useful form, which will become a spiritual being, that is to say a continuation of the effort pursued during a lifetime."[26] The Fondation Le Corbusier was legally established on July 24, 1968, after his death.

The Fondation has played an enormous role in archiving the work of Le Corbusier impeccably and providing it to researchers and the public in an organized and accessible fashion. Most importantly, it has also played an important role in preserving, or perhaps even accelerating, a legacy. Clearly, without substance, there can be no legacy. However, substance alone does not guarantee a legacy. Le Corbusier was well aware of this and insisted on creating and maintaining his legacy through as many avenues as possible, one of which was the establishment of the Fondation Le Corbusier.

THE SKETCHBOOKS

Another was consistently maintaining a sketchbook. He kept a small sketchbook, sometimes two, roughly between 10 × 15 centimeters and 11 × 18 centimeters, in his coat pocket along with a drawing implement. These served as a repository, a place to record thoughts in writing, in numbers, or drawings. He sketched places, landscapes, objects, and nascent ideas; wrote reminder notes, travel itineraries, and calculations, starting in 1907 and transitioning to the sketchbooks in 1914, and maintaining those to his death in 1965. He rarely shared these sketchbooks with anyone. If Le Corbusier ever shared one of the notes or sketches from them with one of the architects in the atelier, it would be a privilege to have seen it. The sketchbooks were hardly the kind of thing that would require post-rationalization and organization beyond what they were, a way of working through ideas before they were ready to be drawn or presented to the public.

23 The Claude and Duval factory (1947–1951) is the only industrial building designed by Le Corbusier. It is located in Saint Dié des Vosges in France and was designed for Jean-Jacques Duval, an admirer of Le Corbusier whose hosiery factory had been demolished during the war.

24 "Histoire de la Fondation." https://www.fondationlecorbusier.fr/lafondation/fondation/histoire/ (accessed June 28, 2024). FLC E1(20)465–466. The original quote from Le Corbusier's letter is: "c'est-à-dire contrôle de mes archives afin de les mettre à l'abri d'une dispersion erronée."

25 "Histoire de la Fondation." https://www.fondationlecorbusier.fr/la-fondation/fondation/histoire/ (accessed July 10, 2024). FLC E1(20)465–466. The original quote reads: "Il ne faudrait pas qu'un voyou quelconque puisse venir piller sans coup férir, et annuler des séries qui valent parce qu'elles sont groupées."

26 Le Corbusier, note of January 13, 1960. https://www.fondationlecorbusier.fr/en/the-foundation/foundation/history/ (accessed August 24, 2024). FLC E1(20)465–466.

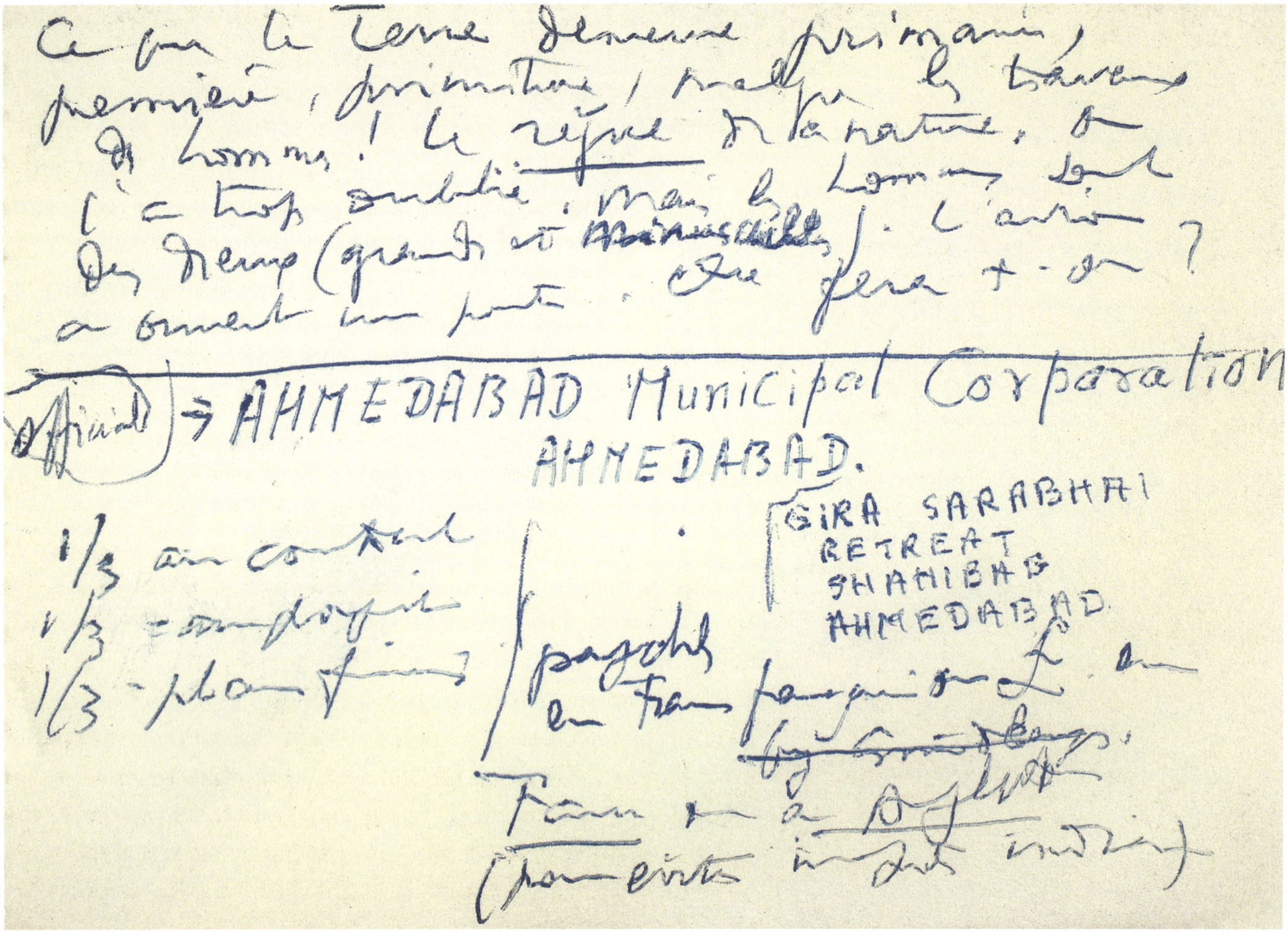

Le Corbusier's note in his sketchbook E18 from Ahmedabad. He writes about the primacy of earth and nature, noting men as gods, the plane opens a door! He writes contractual and financial notes, getting paid in French francs to avoid Indian taxes.

For a period of almost fifty years, they were kept private and were only found after Le Corbusier's death – in a leather suitcase, meticulously numbered and organized, in a locked closet at his apartment. When the sketchbooks were finally retrieved and examined, several organizational problems surfaced that Le Corbusier appears to have deliberately overlooked. He established a cataloging system for the sketchbooks, which are in series from "A" through "T." Within each series, there are numbered volumes, such as A1, A2, A3...; B4, B5...; to T69, and T70. These numbers were stenciled on the cover of each sketchbook at a point of time after their initiation, along with a date. Altogether, seventy-three of them were found in the leather suitcase. The Fondation Le Corbusier decided to publish the sketchbooks in a four-volume set, each containing roughly five hundred 26 × 26 centimeter pages. The black-and-white sketches were reproduced in monochrome and the color sketches in full color. Each of the four volumes begins with the covers of all the sketchbooks contained in that volume and includes a translation of all the text found on the pages of each. Also included are explanatory notes for each sketchbook. At the end of each volume, there is a section devoted to the technical data for each sketchbook: the size of the original, the size of the reproduction, the cover and page material, type of binding, and a numbered set of all the sketches and their corresponding pages in each sketchbook.

THE THEATRICS OF SYSTEMATICITY

Maurice Besset, Le Corbusier's literary executor, in his introduction to the four-volume *Le Corbusier Sketchbooks,* outlines the problems with the cataloging system.[27] First, since Le Corbusier established the numbering and dating system for the sketchbooks post facto, they do not align with the actual dates in the sketchbooks. Although the sketchbooks themselves are serial, as they were naturally filled page by page, the numbering system on the cover defies the logic of the content. Second, this consecutive numbering system ignores two major gaps in the series, the periods 1919–1929 and 1936–1945. Third, the series is incomplete for the periods 1914–1919, 1932–1936, and 1945–1950. Le Corbusier was certainly aware of these gaps and claimed that those sketchbooks had been lost during a move. For others, he did not have an explanation. Nonetheless, he maintained the regular sequence of numbers as if the sketchbooks were in a continuous series. Fourth, there were five additional sketchbooks that were not in the suitcase that Le Corbusier had intentionally not included in the series. Four of them "appear to have been used sporadically for fairly long periods of time, no doubt concurrently with other sketchbooks that are now lost. Possibly it was the marginal and discontinuous aspect of these five sketchbooks that prompted Le Corbusier to separate them from the body of his work."[28]

We sense here a penchant for regularity and systematicity, and also control – not only in the case of his own legacy but even in the numbering and dating of the sketchbooks to make them appear sequential, regardless of their internal dates and major gaps in sequence. Also, the separation of the aforementioned five sketchbooks because they did not share the rhythm of the others points to the same penchant for organization – perhaps, more precisely, the *appearance* of order and organization – even when the content is about spontaneity and spur-of-the-moment sketches and notes. The appearance of organization and its related theatrics were further fortified by the organized arrangement of the sketchbooks in a leather suitcase that was maintained in a locked closet.

This tension between systematicity and organization, on the one hand, and spontaneity and improvisation, on the other, is, I will argue, at the core of Le Corbusier's life-work. His formation of plastic experience by molding space, form, movement, and texture within a structure organized by the regularity of the building systems is at the core of his work. The two cannot be separated from one another, just as the spontaneity of the sketchbooks and their chronologic sequence cannot be separated. Moreover, it is not simply that they cannot be separated; rather, they thrive in a state of tension, a constant push and pull between the two states. Each sketch, due to its place in a sketchbook, immediately after and before other sketches,

27 Charles-Édouard Jeanneret (Le Corbusier) and Fondation Le Corbusier, *Le Corbusier Sketchbooks* (New York: The Architectural History Foundation and Cambridge, Massachusetts: The MIT Press, 1981).

28 Maurice Besset, introduction to Le Corbusier and Fondation Le Corbusier, *Le Corbusier Sketchbooks,* xii.

notes, dates, sets of numbers, etc., belongs to a particular time and space. Yet, each sketch, due to its spontaneity, interconnects with hundreds of other sketches, ideas, places, buildings, and thoughts. The sketch is fixed, on the one hand, in space and time to where and when it was made, and, on the other, to a part of non-chronological time and non-metric space where it can intermingle with many other sketches.

THE FIVE POINTS

This penchant for the appearance of organization and systematicity is not unique to the sketchbooks and can be found in Le Corbusier's writings as well – most distinctly, his identification of the "Five Points of Architecture."[29] These were initially sporadically mentioned as ideas in his essays in *L'Esprit Nouveau*[30] and were developed through the lecture "The New Spirit in Architecture," which was given at a conference at the Sorbonne on June 12, 1921, then published in *Almanach d'Architecture moderne,*[31] and later brought together in the *Œuvre Complète*. The "five points," like the theatrics of the packaging of the sketchbooks in a suitcase, convey an astute sensibility and sensitivity towards the packaging of the foundational problems of architecture in the 1920s. They accumulate and fortify what others had discovered as the material and structural system of the age, reinforced concrete, and give it architectural expression. On the surface, the "five points" appear as dogmatic proclamations. Upon close reading, however, they are about concretizing the architectural and aesthetic possibilities embedded within reinforced concrete, the structural system that was promoted and refined by the Perret brothers, Auguste and Gustave.

The "five points" and Le Corbusier's other proclamations manifest, for a cursory reader, an architect who works with prescriptions based on the geometry of structural, mechanical, and constructional building systems. For the most part, in his practice, he engaged with the "five points" and their consequences. In fact, a cursory "read" of many of his buildings throughout his career confirms that he was wedded to the proclamations, to the building systems, and their mathematical precision and geometric underpinning. However, a detailed study of any of his buildings – and for me, a particular one: the Millowners' Association Building of Ahmedabad, India (1951–1954) – paints a different picture and makes possible a different hypothesis – namely, that Le Corbusier abided by the prescriptions of these proclamations of a systemic approach to architecture only so long as the formal result served his aesthetic sensibility. Yet, he always reconsidered the prescriptions in the context of plastic experiences – spaces and forms that he desired aesthetically to "affect our senses to an acute degree and provoke plastic emotions"[32] – that only partially belonged to the prescriptions of the building systems, and that at times interrupted essential building organization.

29 Le Corbusier, *Le Corbusier 1910–1965,* 44–45.
30 *L'Esprit Nouveau* was a journal founded in 1920 by Le Corbusier, painter Amédée Ozenfant, and poet Paul Dermée. Twenty-eight issues of *L'Esprit Nouveau* were published between 1920 and 1925.
31 Charles-Édouard Jeanneret (Le Corbusier), "L'Esprit Nouveau en Architecture," in *Almanach d'architecture moderne* (Paris: Éditions Crès, 1925).
32 Le Corbusier, *Towards a New Architecture,* 7.

THE DUAL CONDITION

As outlined in the introduction, my contention is that as much as Le Corbusier was wedded to the ideal of the geometric order of building systems, he had a more complex agenda, which was to create singular plastic experiences of spaces and forms within a systemically conceived architecture. His work was created through a constant tension between these two realms: the systematicity and rationality of building systems (such as structural, plumbing, sun-shading, and circulatory ones) and the plasticity and malleability of space and form in light, shadow, color, and texture, experienced through movement.

Despite Le Corbusier's renown, and over 1200 writings on his work by significant scholars and historians, few have approached his work from the vantage point of this particular tension between these dual conditions, and most have fallen on one side or the other of the binary. He is often referred to as an architect of the "International Style" due to his interest in the mass production of buildings and building systems. He is also often called a functionalist because he referred to the house as a machine for living in. Vincent Scully has referred to him as a "prescriptive prophet,"[33] and elsewhere as a "conceptual artist."[34] Kenneth Frampton, who has written extensively on the binary nature of Le Corbusier's work, highlights his "decidedly organized ... monumental systems of order and control ..." in the context of his urban-scale proposals.[35] Peter Reyner Banham, in describing Le Corbusier's "Dom-ino" system, asks if this is a "continuous architectural system that can be divided into single units, or a unit that could be conjoined with others to form a continuous architecture?"[36] Danièle Pauly speaks of Le Corbusier's "immediate intuition" that finds answers to complex problems of site and building.[37] Many of these readings are, in fact, popularized by Le Corbusier himself in his lectures and writings. My contention is that behind these masks, created by Le Corbusier and maintained by historians and scholars, the buildings speak differently. His built architecture, when analyzed carefully through close reading, speaks of the architect's constant struggle made visible through the manipulation of rationalized building systems in order to reach a plastic experience which cannot immediately be projected by those same systems. He worked the components of these dual conditions on both sides to resolve systemic technical concerns as well as plastic spatial and formal ones. Le Corbusier pointed to this interplay between the two poles of the dual condition in *La Ville Radieuse (The Radiant City)* of 1933, when he wrote, "this prodigious spectacle has been produced by the interplay of two elements, one male, one female: sun and water. Two contradictory elements that both need the other in order to exist."[38] It is not simply that there is a dual condition, but rather that the terms are contradictory and that they are in an interplay where each needs the other in order to exist. This points to a resolution which is far from privileging one side over the other or fusing the two or neutralizing

33 Vincent Scully, "Le Corbusier 1922–1965," in H. Allen Brooks, ed., *Le Corbusier* (Princeton, New Jersey: Princeton University Press, 1987), 50.
34 Scully, "Le Corbusier 1922–1965," 50.
35 Kenneth Frampton, "Le Corbusier's Designs for the League of Nations, The Centrosoyus, and the Palace of the Soviets, 1926–1931," in H. Allen Brooks, ed., *Le Corbusier* (Princeton, New Jersey: Princeton University Press, 1987), 57.
36 Peter Reyner Banham, "*La Maison des hommes* and *La Misère des villes:* Le Corbusier and the Architecture of Mass Housing," in H. Allen Brooks, ed., *Le Corbusier* (Princeton, New Jersey: Princeton University Press, 1987), 109.
37 Danièle Pauly, "The Chapel of Ronchamp as an Example of Le Corbusier's Creative Process," in H. Allen Brooks, ed., *Le Corbusier* (Princeton, New Jersey: Princeton University Press, 1987), 128.
38 Charles-Édouard Jeanneret (Le Corbusier), *The Radiant City* (New York: The Orion Press, 1967), 78 (originally published as *La Ville Radieuse* in 1933).

their differences. The dual condition is intentionally oppositional and intentionally maintained as such, in a state of tension. The plasticity of space and form is decidedly maintained in tension with the systematicity of the buildings' technical apparatus.

ART AND SCIENCE

In this context, and to provide a reasonable explanation of the use of the terms "system" and "systemic" as they apply to architecture, it is necessary to briefly describe what an architect does, and in that environment to describe the term "system" more precisely. Dictionaries define architecture as the art and science of designing a building, and the architect as the person involved in this endeavor. This dictionary definition is both comprehensive and vacuous. It positions architecture between its two poles, art and science; it does not, however, provide any clues for how it relates to the two poles.

In the work of an architect, the artistic and the scientific are never separate, nor separable. There is no scientific decision without an accompanying aesthetic consequence, and no aesthetic decision without an accompanying scientific consequence. In fact, the two poles of scientific and artistic, though acceptable common descriptions, present a reductive view of architecture. Architects design to create spaces that acutely affect our senses. That is and has always been the ultimate goal of architecture. From the very early Greek temples that were erected for the "gods" to contemporary architectural artifacts that house different human endeavors, architects have always been in search of that acute sensory experience of form and space. Yet, creating an experience, be it ordinary or extra-ordinary, is not the sole purpose of architects. For architecture to be possible, architects must address a multitude of problems, concerns, and issues. There is usually a client with programmatic desires, financial limitations, and particular taste. Moreover, there are usually zoning and code restrictions, along with the accompanying building regulations. The building must have structural stability in all different axes, vertically and laterally, as well as resistance to movement, such as would occur with wind and earthquakes. It must have suitable environmental conditions, air movement, heat and cold, sun and shade, and humidity management/control – for its occupants as well as for the preservation of the structure itself. Those environmental conditions must also address both daylighting and artificial lighting so that occupants may partake in the experience and perform their necessary tasks. There are also other building services and mechanical systems, such as plumbing and waste, which must be considered – from the source of clean, pure water to the release of waste. The building's relationship to the surrounding landscape, both near and far, is paramount, as well as the type of soil, site, and building access. There are material concerns that limit the selection, detailing, and use of building materials. Available construction technologies suitable for the specific building play into this complexity. Add to this brief listing the public, social, cultural, urban, and economic determinants and consequences of building and it is clear that the number of variables in an architectural project is vast. Even more important than the quantity of variables is the fact that they are incongruent, meaning that addressing one of them does not necessarily address others. In fact, most often, addressing one of the issues/solving one of the problems undermines a multitude of others.

It would not be fair to say that engineers (building scientists) most often have singular problems, as anyone involved in design has complex ones. However, their problems are more interrelated and congruent than the architects'. A structural engineer will design the most elegant and efficient solution for a structural problem based on the length of span, the possible depth of members, available and prudent materials, the technology of assembly, cost, and the structural system. But, for an architect, that same structural system must foreground the architectural and material expression of the project and accommodate the other building systems. This may suggest, in fact, that what is most efficient structurally may not be suitable architecturally. Building scientists are great problem-solvers. They will find the most elegant and efficient solution to building problems. Architects have a different aim: to design forms and spaces that acutely affect the human sensory experience. In achieving that goal, architects end up not being the best, most efficient, problem-solvers. However, if they do not address the multitude of concerns/problems/issues within a building, they will not be able to build. It is imperative for architects to address the complex set of incongruent, variable requirements and systems while at the same time designing to acutely affect the human senses. This duality marks architecture at its core and Le Corbusier recognized this.

Even the most unusual architectural form must be rationalized if it is to be built. In other words, every form must be dissected to its material, constructional, and geometric components, and its reassembly configured in such a way that the logic of its form, material, and assembly may be documented and made visible and comprehensible to others who build it. Architecture is thus submitted to a certain geometric and systemic rationalization in order for it to be built. Architecture is therefore always already on the side of the rationalized, simply because it engages with the process of construction in a systemic manner.

But what must be, in the end, rationalized to be constructed does not necessarily have to be prescriptive or systemic in its conception. Architects map geometries of delineations in space, which generally demarcate the building systems and requirements. Whether these systems are aligned and unified remains open to inquiry. Moreover, whether forms, spaces, movements, and enclosures reaffirm the building systems – i.e. belong to their geometric logic – or maintain a different sensory/material/experiential tendency also remains open to inquiry. Architects, then, can decisively make possible the projection of spaces that are at once within the delineations of the building systems and, at the same time, defy being shaped by the geometric delineations of the same systems. Yet, by necessity, all forms must be constructed within the limits of geometry and constructability, but those limits may be redrawn with each projection. This is the paradox of great architecture: to be within the demarcated geometry of constructable objects yet to redraw the limits of the possible within that geometry, in order to "affect our senses to an acute degree and provoke plastic emotions."[39] It is in this complex sense that the word "system" is being used here, in relation to necessarily rationalized building systems within an aspiration to affect human senses with the plasticity of the built environment.

THE *LE CORBUSIER ARCHIVE*

To assess how Le Corbusier's work, both as an architect and writer, has been received in the context of my hypothesis, i.e., the tension that Le Corbusier maintains in the dual condition – the utility and necessity of the building systems and the sculpting of form and space to affect our senses acutely – relevant essays commissioned for the thirty-two volumes of the *Le Corbusier Archive* will be reviewed. Many of the authors have also published widely on Le Corbusier elsewhere: some in multiple books, others in essay form. To maintain the spirit of Brooks's axonometric projection as a mode of organization of the essays that would permit multiple vantage points simultaneously, it is more fruitful not to follow the chronology of the volumes and associated essays. Rather, I will examine them within types. The first are essays written by architects who apprenticed in Le Corbusier's atelier at 35 rue de Sèvres in Paris.

APPRENTICES

What stands out most clearly in the context of my hypothesis is recorded anecdotes from the atelier. André Wogenscky, with the longest tenure in the atelier, notes,

> He [Le Corbusier] always insisted that the Modulor be taken as a tool and not as a machine for the manufacturing of beauty … Having become accustomed to the Modulor at the rue de Sèvres workshop, we would often respond, when Le Corbusier criticized our drawings, by saying "But it's done according to the Modulor." And then Le Corbusier would answer: "To hell with the Modulor! When it doesn't work you shouldn't use it."[40]

39 Le Corbusier, *Towards a New Architecture*, 7.
40 André Wogenscky, "Unité d'Habitation at Marseille". Translated by Stephen Sartarelli, in H. Allen Brooks, ed., *Le Corbusier* (Princeton, New Jersey: Princeton University Press, 1987), 125.

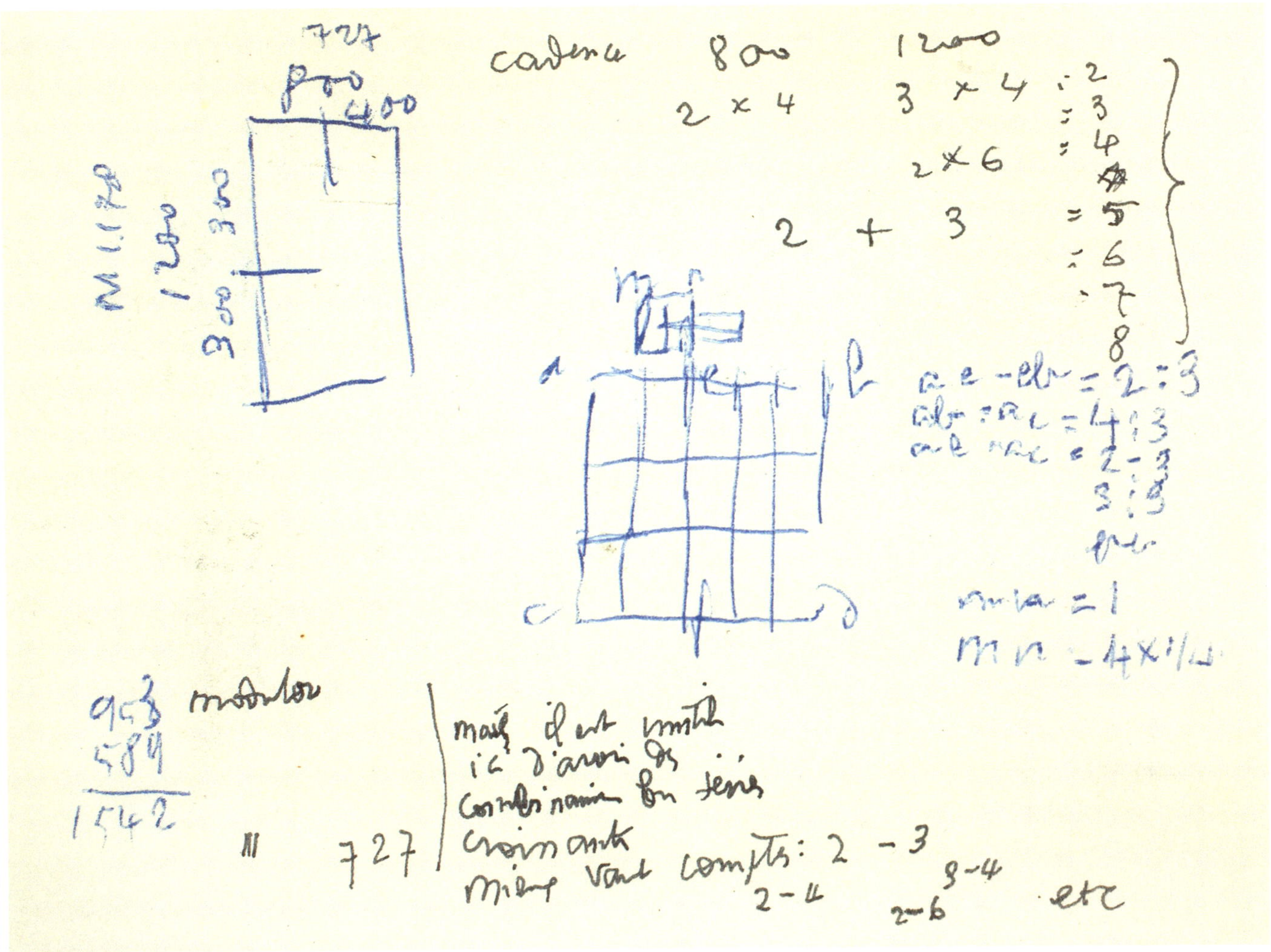

Le Corbusier's sketch of the Modulor in the context of Ahmedabad, sketchbook E18. He writes: "Rhythm, Modulor // but here it is useless to have combinations in increasing series. Better to count: 2–3 // 2–4 / 3–4 // 2–6 / etc. Adapting the rule to the context."

Having spent his entire career developing a proportional system, which he documented in the two-volume book *The Modulor 1 and 2*, Le Corbusier simply responded "to hell with it" when the resultant drawing was aesthetically unsatisfactory to him.[41] Modulor was only used to refine already visually (to Le Corbusier) beautiful forms and to place them in context and proportion to other forms. Without the genius of the artist, the proportioning system was of little use. The proportioning system that took Le Corbusier more than half his life to develop is yet another sign of the appearance of systematicity; Le Corbusier, not the system, is the real judge of proportional beauty.

The second anecdote is from Jerzy Sołtan, who worked in Le Corbusier's atelier from 1945 to 1949. He writes:

> It was not long after I settled into my work routine that I received one of my most intense Corbusierian shocks. To appreciate its intensity, one has to remember my own background. From a provincial school of architecture, I had brought with me to Paris the "form-follows-function" and *neue Sachlichkeit* spirit. In my earlier milieu, discussions of aesthetics were simply missing; visual concerns were smuggled in as afterthoughts, if they appeared at all. Such considerations were not becoming to a serious,

41 Charles-Édouard Jeanneret (Le Corbusier), *The Modulor 1 and 2* (Cambridge, Massachusetts: Harvard University Press, 1958). In 2000 and 2004 reprinted as *The Modulor and Modulor 2* by Birkhäuser, Basel, in cooperation with Fondation Le Corbusier.

> socially minded architect. Imagine my amazement, then, when during an argument with Corbu about the final permutations of the St.-Dié project, he turned to me and said "Mais mon cher Sołtan, il faut que ce soit beau." This remark, of course, destroyed my argument. I was demolished, demolished but also delighted: Le Corbusier had offered me, openly, aboveboard, a marvelous gift that for years I had been eyeing secretly, from a distance. "Il faut que ce soit beau" – it has to be beautiful. To have the guts not only to speak of visual quality but to put one's thought so bluntly.[42]

Sołtan's anecdote not only provides a flavor of the office but also highlights Le Corbusier's foremost interest in beauty above all else, beauty as judged by the eye of the artist. In a different context, Sołtan notes that "Le Modulor – the Golden Module" reveals something important about the dual nature of its author's personality, as it was "conceived to unify the world's technology" yet bring about a "certain humanistic quality that technology lacked." "On the one side, it used mathematics in an attempt to operate on the objective, quantifiable level; on the other, it attested to romantic, lyrical longings to capture beauty."[43] On the one hand, we see an absolute privileging of beauty, and, on the other, a battle for primacy in a dual condition between beauty and things quantifiable. Elsewhere, Sołtan describes another dual condition in Le Corbusier's work whereby he stressed the simultaneity of the two processes involved in architectural research: "from general to particular and from particular to general."[44] If we were to draw any conclusion from these anecdotes, it would be that Le Corbusier concerned himself with dual conditions and their relationships in cases where he was engaged in long-term research and building projects. In the day-to-day practice of painting and architecture, however, he privileged beauty as perceived by the judgment of the artist. So much for the functionalist aesthetics with which he has been associated. But there is more, and it is more complicated.

URBAN PROJECTS

Next are a set of essays that engage with Le Corbusier's urban projects and ideas, documented in volumes 10 through 15 of the *Le Corbusier Archive*. These essays do not shed light on his architectural work or process and concentrate on urban concerns. One of the authors, Stanislaus von Moos, in his seminal book on Le Corbusier, *Elements of a Synthesis,*[45] accounts for the role of the dual condition. In it, he traces the roots of Le Corbusier's interest in dual conditions to his earlier studies of nature with L'Eplattenier, who, in turn, was influenced by Ruskin; and soon thereafter, his being influenced by his *L'Esprit Nouveau* partner Ozenfant's deep knowledge of Plato

42 Jerzy Sołtan, "Working with Le Corbusier," in H. Allen Brooks, ed., *Le Corbusier* (Princeton, New Jersey: Princeton University Press, 1987), 2.
43 Sołtan, "Working with Le Corbusier," 11.
44 Sołtan, "Working with Le Corbusier," 9.
45 Stanislaus von Moos, *Le Corbusier: Elements of a Synthesis.* Translated by Beatrice Mock, Joseph Stein, and Maureen Oberil (Cambridge, Massachusetts, and London: The MIT Press, 1980).

and interest in mechanics. Von Moos sets up the dual condition as an essential struggle between the eternal and the material, the ideal and the real. From these roots, Le Corbusier developed a view of contemporary engineering technology and its ability to refine artifacts to the point of a mass-producible "standard" as parallel to a "rationalist cosmology," in which nature is a "logical machine whose adherence to physical laws is the very reason for its beauty."[46] He saw nature as both a material machine and a manifestation of the eternal order. Despite the potential parity between idea and material, von Moos argues that the dual condition for Le Corbusier is one where idea and concept are privileged over the material. He attributes this privileging in Le Corbusier to Alberti, writing, "it is possible to create either in thought or imagination perfect forms of buildings without paying any attention to the material."[47]

Although von Moos sets up the dual condition and its roots, the equity, and the potential tension between the two sides is dismissed in favor of a privileged reading towards the ideal and the eternal. Synthesis, in the title of his book, is much more connected to a synthetic view of the arts and engineering, a total work of art where painting, sculpture, and architecture relate to engineering in a synthetic manner because they all strive for the universal laws of nature and towards the eternal. The synthesis is not an equilibrium between the ideal and the real, but rather a striving by the material condition towards the ideal and the eternal.

There are two other essays that concern urban issues, each about a particular project that had an urban scale. One concentrates on Chandigarh and the other on mass housing. The first is Charles Correa's "Chandigarh: The View from Benares,"[48] which analyzes Chandigarh in the Indian context and from the Indian point of view. Benares, also known as Varanasi, is one of India's holiest cities on the banks of the Ganges River. The city hosts annual bathing rituals. It is said that Buddha found Buddhism in Benares around the sixth century BCE. Correa's use of Benares in the title clearly provokes questions about a Western architect building in an Eastern cultural, climatic, and socio-political environment. Correa praises Le Corbusier's modern vocabulary in concrete and writes that "[o]vernight the things we couldn't possibly build in our climate and within the constraints of our economy (i.e., paper-thin Miesian glass boxes) were OUT. What was IN was exactly what we could do best: in situ concrete, handcrafted form work, an architecture of hot, vivid color, deep shadow, and tropical sun."[49] But praise quickly turns to sharp critique and shifts to Le Corbusier's failings in India. Correa likens Le Corbusier to a child playing with cardboard boxes and calling the result a motorcar. He believes that Le Corbusier was more interested in the theatrics of climate and environmental concerns than actually dealing with them, "assuming the heroic pose – of addressing it."[50] Although Correa's essay is in relation to Chandigarh, it can also apply to the buildings in Ahmedabad – including the one under consid-

46 Von Moos, *Le Corbusier: Elements of a Synthesis,* 39.
47 Von Moos, *Le Corbusier: Elements of a Synthesis,* 299. Quoted by von Moos from Leon Battista Alberti, *On the Art of Building in Ten Books.* Translated by Joseph Rykwert, Neil Leach, and Robert Tavernor (Cambridge, Massachusetts, and London: The MIT Press, 1988), Book 1, 1.
48 Charles Correa, "Chandigarh: The View from Benares," in H. Allen Brooks, ed., *Le Corbusier* (Princeton, New Jersey: Princeton University Press, 1987), 197–202.
49 Correa, "Chandigarh: The View from Benares," 197.
50 Correa, "Chandigarh: The View from Benares," 198.

eration here. We will explore this very issue later in Chapter III. The dual condition, here, has been figured under the opposition of Western and local.

The essay concerning mass housing is Peter Reyner Banham's "*La Maison des hommes* and *La Misère des villes:* Le Corbusier and the Architecture of Mass Housing,"[51] which examines unit vs. whole, repetition, prefabrication, and the mass production of units. Banham had already devoted a significant section of his book *Theory and Design in the First Machine Age* to Le Corbusier.[52] So, he came to the topic with a vast knowledge and a particular view of Le Corbusier's entire career. The question that Banham poses in the final part of the essay is the same question with which he starts: "is it a continuous architectural system that can be divided into single units, or a single unit that could be conjoined with others to form a continuous architecture?"[53] The potential for the legibility of two simultaneous yet incongruent conditions is at the core of Banham's analysis of Le Corbusier. In his *Theory and Design in the First Machine Age,* Banham analyzes *Towards a New Architecture* and argues that Le Corbusier was working on two fronts – mechanistic and academic[54] – yet another dual condition. He divides the chapters of the book between the two categories and, despite his desire to see the two brought together – especially in the final chapter – Banham finds that Le Corbusier does not make any attempt at synthesis. The chapters in the book were produced by Le Corbusier as separate and independent essays for the journal issues of *L'Esprit Nouveau* and they remained as such, separate and independent. Even with the final chapter, "Architecture or Revolution," which Le Corbusier wrote specifically for the book and where he did indeed have a chance to relate the two conditions, he did not.

Almost in passing, in *A Concrete Atlantis,*[55] a book published in 1989, a year after Banham's death but clearly under consideration as he was working on the essay for the *Le Corbusier Archive,* Banham mentions a "dialectic" in Le Corbusier's work in the context of an observation about defunct industrial artifacts and buildings, abandoned tanks, and a concrete frame on Cannery Row in the Monterey Bay fisheries. He writes:

> But, looking through the open spaces defined by its square members to the closed bulks of the cylinders behind, I seemed to be seeing something else, equally familiar, but not observed in so perfectly abstracted a form before: the very essentials; the "ultimate metaphysic of form" of the high period of the International Style around 1930, as summed up in the "Two Geometries" of Le Corbusier; the "dialectical confrontation between sculptural forms and gridded space" of which Richard Etlin has spoken and which I suggest is a European derivative of the closed forms of American industrial storage containers and of the openly gridded loft space of regular American factories.[56]

51 Peter Reyner Banham, "*La Maison des hommes* and *La Misère des villes:* Le Corbusier and the Architecture of Mass Housing," in H. Allen Brooks, ed., *Le Corbusier* (Princeton, New Jersey: Princeton University Press, 1987), 107–16.

52 Peter Reyner Banham, *Theory and Design in the First Machine Age* (Cambridge, Massachusetts: The MIT Press, 1980).

53 Banham, "*La Maison des hommes* and *La Misère des villes,*" 109.

54 Banham, *Theory and Design in the First Machine Age,* 223.

55 Peter Reyner Banham, *A Concrete Atlantis* (Cambridge, Massachusetts: The MIT Press, 1989). In the context of the current set of essays, which were published in 1987, the research for this book started in 1976 while Banham was teaching in the Department of Architecture at SUNY Buffalo and continued through out his time teaching at UC Santa Cruz. The book was completed in 1988 when he became ill and was published a year after his death.

56 Banham, *A Concrete Atlantis,* 3. There is included in the book, on page 5 of the introduction, an image of this exact scene recorded by Banham. To Banham, this image clearly resembles Le Corbusier's architectural vocabulary.

Concrete frame and abandoned tanks, Cannery Row, Monterey, California, 1986. Peter Reyner Banham, *A Concrete Atlantis*, Introduction, 5. Banham suggests that the forms visible in this image of industrial storage and concrete structural frame present the dialectic found in Le Corbusier.

This statement records a keen observation but is not followed in any of Banham's essays on Le Corbusier. It is, clearly, of extreme interest to the current study. Richard Etlin's 1985 presentation at the annual meeting of the Society of Architectural Historians in Pittsburgh, mentioned as a source for the statement by Banham, is noted as an early version of an essay later published in *The Art Bulletin*. In the published version, Etlin attends to this dual condition in identifying Le Corbusier's links to nineteenth-century Romanticism and French Hellenism. He traces Le Corbusier's admiration of the Parthenon to French nineteenth-century Hellenism, and his use of the architectural promenade to the nineteenth-century "Picturesque." Etlin notes in the context of Villas Cook, Stein, and Savoye that "the regular grid of columns served as a foil to the organic shapes of the curved walls and stairs, which together combined to organize a picturesque architectural promenade with asymmetrically balanced views according to the lessons of Greek Architecture."[57] Etlin not only identifies the two conditions of the gridded field and the organic shapes, but also traces their historical roots in Le Corbusier's work. His use of the word "foil" suggests that he believes that the regular grid is the background to produce a contrast to the organic shapes. This implies a one-way concept: we need the gridded, neutral landscape as a backdrop and a contrast for the sculptural forms. The conversation between the two is linear and limited to one direction, defined by the sculpture in a gridded field. It is not conceived as a dialogue, but rather as a "one-way," a monologue. Nonetheless, Etlin's analysis is incisive and thorough, not only substantiating the dual condition but confirming its roots in nineteenth-century authoritative texts of architectural history with which Le Corbusier was familiar.

Clearly, the topic of "dual conditions" is central to the work of Le Corbusier in Banham's and Etlin's analyses. Banham discusses accident and type, unit and whole, mechanistic and academic, and gridded and sculptural, but he does not pursue these dual conditions as foundational concepts of Le Corbusier's architecture. They are mentioned in general reference and not as specific strategies or as major conceptual underpinnings of the work, yet Banham's insights are central to this study.

SEVEN BUILDINGS

Next in the *Le Corbusier Archive* study is a set of essays that engage with specific buildings of Le Corbusier in detail. Each author concentrates on an individual building and brings an intense level of study to our understanding of it. Addressing one of the early buildings, also one of the most iconic of Le Corbusier's work, is Tim Benton writing on the Villa Savoye.[58] In this essay, Benton notes that the "Villa Savoye was an unconstrained response to the dogmas of the Five Points."[59] The "five points" read like dogmas and prescriptions.

57 Richard A. Etlin, "Le Corbusier, Choisy, and French Hellenism: The Search for a New Architecture," *The Art Bulletin* 69, no. 2 (1987): 276.
58 Tim Benton, "Villa Savoye and the Architects' Practice," in H. Allen Brooks, ed., *Le Corbusier* (Princeton, New Jersey: Princeton University Press, 1987), 83–105.
59 Benton, "Villa Savoye and the Architects' Practice," 85.

Read carefully, they outline the architectural possibilities of reinforced-concrete framing as a structural system that had just become accepted by the building industry following the Perret Brothers' rue Franklin apartments.[60] In this context the "five points" are dogmas, but dogmas that open rather than fix architectural possibilities. To see the villa as an "unconstrained response" is quite astute. To be more precise, the villa is an unconstrained architectural response to the constraints of the "five points." The dual condition noted by Benton between unconstrained-ness and dogma finds its way into another statement where he suggests that a "tension between the ideal and the pragmatic runs through all of Le Corbusier's work and theory."[61] Benton notes that this tension reaches its height in the Villa Savoye, but many of Le Corbusier's other villas and houses of the period do not live up to Savoye. This statement is in stark contrast to the one with which he concludes the essay: "Art, for Le Corbusier, transcends reality." Here, Benton suggests clearly that art, the ideal, always wins over the pragmatics of reality.

Danièle Pauly writes on "The Chapel of Ronchamp as an Example of Le Corbusier's Creative Process,"[62] in an essay that appeared in Volume 20 of the *Le Corbusier Archive*. Pauly was one of the early examiners of the Ronchamp material and thus had a hand in organizing the unarchived material into what we know today, housed at the Fondation Le Corbusier. She was also instrumental in synthesizing the sketches, drawings, notes, and correspondences into a coherent story that captured the genesis of the project and documented its genealogy. As a result of this close reading, it is possible for Pauly to describe Le Corbusier's creative process as recorded in the work itself through its documents. Her deciphering of the work's genesis aligns with Le Corbusier's own description of how he went about starting a project. Le Corbusier had published some of the early sketches of Ronchamp in a pamphlet, *Textes et dessins pour Ronchamp,* accompanied by the following text, which is cited in Pauly's essay:

> When assigned a task, I am in the habit of storing it in my memory, that is, of not allowing myself to make any sketches for months. The human brain is made in such a way that it has a certain independence: it is a box into which one can pour in bulk the elements of a problem, and then let them float, simmer, ferment. Then, one day, a spontaneous initiative of one's inner being takes shape, something clicks; you pick up a pencil, a stick of charcoal, some colored pencils ..., and give birth onto the paper: out comes the idea ...[63]

Pauly confirms this "method" in her examination of the sketches and documents of the building and argues for two phases in the development of the project. First, as Le Corbusier described, after a period

60 The Perret brothers were unable to receive a bank loan for the apartment building they had designed because there were no structural precedents for the use of reinforced concrete in the building industry. They self-financed the building and, once completed, the building itself became a test of the structural system and henceforth the system became more accepted. Le Corbusier apprenticed for the Perret brothers while their office was in the 24 bis rue Franklin apartment building.

61 Benton, "Villa Savoye and the Architects' Practice," 85.

62 Danièle Pauly, "The Chapel of Ronchamp as an Example of Le Corbusier's Creative Process," in H. Allen Brooks, ed., *Le Corbusier* (Princeton, New Jersey: Princeton University Press, 1987), 127–140.

63 Le Corbusier, *Textes et dessins pour Ronchamp* (Paris: Forces-Vives, 1965), unpaginated. Cited in Pauly, "The Chapel of Ronchamp," 128.

of gestation a kind of "immediate intuition" produces the project in its entirety as an answer to all the project's concerns.[64] Second, is a long period of developing the full idea into a buildable project, documented fully in drawings, followed by the building process itself. Le Corbusier describes these two phases as three stages, with Pauly having compacted the first two into Phase One. Concerning the three phases, Pauly cites Le Corbusier from *Textes et dessins pour Ronchamp:*

> 1 Identifying with the site;
> 2 Spontaneous birth (after incubation) of the whole work, all at once, and all of a sudden;
> 3 The slow execution of the drawings, the purpose, the plans and the construction itself.[65]

Pauly confirms the assertion Le Corbusier made about his process, as he documented in notes on Ronchamp. This is particularly interesting in the context of *Towards a New Architecture,* where Le Corbusier has argued exactly the opposite: that the architect must efface the engineer and introduce art into what is engineering.[66] In other words, in the Ronchamp notes there is art first, the genius of the artist bursting out with the complete idea, and then the engineer begins work and starts the execution drawings and the construction. In *Towards a New Architecture,* a book published more than twenty years prior to Ronchamp, the engineer puts everything together, and then the architect sculpts the forms to artistic perfection.[67] In both cases, we have the dual condition of the artist and the engineer (or, as Frampton and Benton referred to them, pragmatics and intellectual nourishment). Although reversed in their chronological order within a project, the artist's priority is confirmed in both.

Peter Serenyi writes about Le Corbusier's five commissions (four built, one unbuilt)[68] in Ahmedabad, one of which is the focus of this study. His essay, "Timeless but of its Time: Le Corbusier's Architecture in India" appears in Volume 26 of the *Le Corbusier Archive,* titled *Ahmedabad, 1953–60,* which concentrates entirely on the buildings in Ahmedabad.[69] Serenyi starts the essay with a sharp focus on the "resolution of opposites" as a constant theme in Le Corbusier and other modern architects. For Le Corbusier, he argues, "the resolution of opposites was a deeply felt need that elicited some of his most heroic architectural responses."[70] Serenyi continues this line of thinking to include the work of Frank Lloyd Wright and Mies van der Rohe, two other twentieth-century giants of modern architecture. In the resolution of the opposites, Serenyi argues that "Wright fused," suggesting that although distinction and difference were maintained in the American master's work, the elements were fused in such a way as to create a state of interdependence and continuity of parts. Mies "neutralized a building's constituent parts" in favor of a neutral state, one of anonymity. Le Corbusier, Serenyi

64 Pauly, "The Chapel of Ronchamp," 128.
65 Le Corbusier, *Textes et dessins pour Ronchamp,* cited in Pauly, "The Chapel of Ronchamp," 130.
66 Le Corbusier, *Towards a New Architecture,* 202.
67 This will be discussed further in Chapter II of this book, in the Section titled "The Engineer and the Plastic Artist."
68 Ahmedabad Cultural Center, commissioned 1951, only the museum was built; Chinubhai house, commissioned 1951, not built; Millowners' Association Building, commissioned 1951, built; Hutheesing house, commissioned 1951, plans were sold to Shodhan and built as the Shodhan house; Sarabhai house, commissioned 1951, built.
69 Peter Serenyi, "Timeless but of its Time: Le Corbusier's Architecture in India," in H. Allen Brooks, ed., *Le Corbusier* (Princeton, New Jersey: Princeton University Press, 1987), 163–195.
70 Serenyi, "Timeless but of its Time," 163.

argues, "used juxtaposition as a means of attaining a resolution of opposites." Stemming largely from his work within the Purist circle of painters, where individual objects were juxtaposed in a still life as independent elements in a painting, Le Corbusier strategized similarly in architecture. "In so doing, he succeeded in preserving the identity and at times even the separateness of a building's constituent parts." Much in the spirit of Purist paintings, Le Corbusier would juxtapose multiple standard mass-produced objects, mostly glass objects, in one canvas, maintaining the individuality of each artifact while creating a tension between them that drew them together. This same strategy also served him as an architect and one could argue it was an obsession that drove his work. Serenyi contends that this juxtaposition of diverse and seemingly contradictory architectural elements "found its richest and most subtle realization in his late work, of which India received the largest share."[71] In other words, Chandigarh and the buildings in Ahmedabad, including the subject of this study, serve as the paradigm of this strategy of Le Corbusier.

Le Corbusier juxtaposing mass-produced figural objects, mostly glass bottles, on the field of the canvas. Le Corbusier, *Bottle of Red Wine*, oil on canvas, 1922, 60 × 73 centimeters.

HISTORY

Next, are a set of essays by historians and scholars of Le Corbusier contextualizing his work within a larger architectural framework and positioning it somewhere on the spectrum between the artist and the engineer. The first of these is H. Allen Brooks's essay in the opening volume of the series, outlining "Le Corbusier's Formative Years at La Chaux-de-Fonds."[72] Brooks argues that Charles L'Eplattenier's interest in nature and regionalism is the foundation of Le Corbusier's work.[73] He notes that L'Eplattenier believed that all historical styles were derived from nature. It was not so much about imitating the visual reality of nature but rather about drawing out its simplified geometric essence. This is most visible in Le Corbusier's work when he was under L'Eplattenier's tutelage. In addition, Brooks notes that L'Eplattenier believed that work must be symbolically appropriate to its region: a predecessor of the later arguments towards "regionalism." We can also see this in Le Corbusier's early houses in and near his hometown, and his later work in different parts of the world, appropriating regional materials and vocabulary.

Finally, Brooks suggests that "a single constant remained uppermost in [Le Corbusier's] mind: idealism (using the term in its nineteenth-century philosophical sense), wherein intellect, not materialistic or pragmatic concerns, remained the dominant mode."[74] Once again, hovering so close to the dual condition in Le Corbusier's work, Brooks tends to one side: that of the idealism of the intellect.

We see a similar pattern with Vincent Scully in his essay "Le Corbusier, 1922–1965," appearing in Volume 2 of the *Le Corbusier Archive*.[75] Scully describes Le Corbusier as someone who changed

71 Serenyi, "Timeless but of its Time," 163.

72 H. Allen Brooks, "Le Corbusier's Formative Years at La Chaux-de-Fonds," in H. Allen Brooks, ed., *Le Corbusier* (Princeton, New Jersey: Princeton University Press, 1987).

73 L'Eplattenier was Le Corbusier's tutor while he was studying as a teen at the Municipal Art School in his hometown in western Switzerland's Jura Mountains, La Chaux-de-Fonds.

74 Brooks, "Le Corbusier's Formative Years," 27.

75 Vincent Scully, "Le Corbusier 1922–1965," in H. Allen Brooks, ed., *Le Corbusier* (Princeton, New Jersey: Princeton University Press, 1987).

Charles-Édouard Jeanneret, *Stylized Ornaments*, black ink, gouache and pencil on paper, 24.3 × 31.7 centimeters, drawn at the Municipal Art School at La Chaux-de-Fonds, 1905.

with the times throughout his career. He anecdotally mentions the academics of his generation who "can vividly remember students of the late 1940s condemning Le Corbusier for what they regarded as his betrayal of the machine age and the machine aesthetic, indeed of everything in which he had professed to believe before." Certainly, Le Corbusier may be blamed for this, as he promoted a view of himself as someone who was constantly seeking innovation and thus susceptible to regular change. Scully notes that the mistake lies in "regarding him as primarily a conceptual artist and a prescriptive prophet. He was those things in part, and often pretended to be them wholly, but he was in fact an instinctive artist before everything else."[76] Scully, like Brooks, commits Le Corbusier to the artist – and an instinctive one, no less. The dual condition once again has been resolved, and only to one side.

The last of the essays in this grouping, and in the context of this study the most astute one, is Alan Colquhoun's "The Significance of Le Corbusier,"[77] which appears as the opening essay of the first volume in the series. Colquhoun argues for a "dialectic" reading of Le Corbusier and presents a forceful essay on this notion. He starts by painting him as more of an artist and writes:

> Le Corbusier, more than any other architect of the modern movement, insisted that architecture was the product of the individual creative intelligence. The order it created was ideal, not pragmatic. If he said, "The house is a machine for living in," it was not to annex architecture to a branch of empirical science, but to use the machine as a model for a work of art whose form and structure were determined by laws internal to itself.[78]

Colquhoun argues that at the foundation of the modern movement lies an idea of the "fusion" of art and technology and, further, that this idea is also the foundation of Le Corbusier's work. However, he adds that in Le Corbusier there is also a pull towards classicism, a pull towards the "standard," which is absolute and does not change with history. He describes Le Corbusier's writings in *L'Esprit Nouveau* as recording this dialectic but with an added complexity, that of trying to resolve two views of history: classicism, which he sees as absolute, and historicism, which he sees as relative. The absolute is wedded to "eternal principles and natural law,"[79] completely unaffected by history and advances in technology, and the other is a position relative to its place in history and its contemporary technology. In relation to architecture this difference can be monumental, as much of what is accomplished architecturally in any era is impossible to imagine as a built artifact outside of its contemporary technology. This is not to say that Le Corbusier believed that technology instigates or causes formal or stylistic change, rather than arguing that technology facilitates that change. He saw the architect as a "creative

76 Scully, "Le Corbusier 1922–1965," 50.
77 Alan Colquhoun, "The Significance of Le Corbusier," in H. Allen Brooks, ed., *Le Corbusier* (Princeton, New Jersey: Princeton University Press, 1987), 17–26.
78 Colquhoun, "The Significance of Le Corbusier," 17.
79 Colquhoun, "The Significance of Le Corbusier," 17.

subject who transforms technology into art, material production into ideology ... ." And in this dual condition that is set up by Le Corbusier, the architect is "to create an image of perfection,"[80] but is only able to accomplish this task through the engineer's reality. Out of all the essays in the thirty-two volumes, this is the place where the tension in the dual condition is recognized as a driving force in Le Corbusier's work. One does not serve the other, or win over the other; rather, each requires the other to work through and become what it is. Colquhoun lists a series of dialectical conditions that run "through all Le Corbusier's theory and practice, where a number of oppositions are either stated or implied: Order/Disorder; Platonic Harmony/Contingency; Mind/Organism; Form/Structure; Symmetry/Asymmetry."[81] In conclusion, Colquhoun refers to Le Corbusier's work as that of the "philosopher-architect for whom architecture, precisely because of the connection which it implies between the ideal and the real, was the expression of the profoundest truths"[82] – Le Corbusier as the philosopher-architect is in a constant tension between the ideal and the real.

CONCLUSION

Given the sixteen authors writing in the thirty-two volumes of the *Le Corbusier Archive* and their other writings on Le Corbusier, it is clear that the dual condition is central to Le Corbusier's thinking about architecture. It is also clear that the dual condition has not received an in-depth exploration as a defining conceptual paradigm for Le Corbusier's architecture. The next chapter will examine Le Corbusier's writings in *Towards a New Architecture* on the dual condition of the architect as engineer, producing technical building systems, and the architect as artist, producing plastic experiences.

80 Colquhoun, "The Significance of Le Corbusier," 18.
81 Colquhoun, "The Significance of Le Corbusier," 19.
82 Colquhoun, "The Significance of Le Corbusier," 25.

II
TRUTH, HARMONY, AND BEAUTY: LE CORBUSIER AND RUSKIN

← View of west façade with golden rectangle highlighted.

In his seminal book, *Towards a New Architecture,*[83] Le Corbusier does not reference other thinkers and theorists of architecture. There are no footnotes, endnotes, bibliography, glossary, or index. The English translation of the book ends on page 269 with an image of "a Briar Pipe," which concludes the last essay in the book, "Architecture or Revolution," as if Le Corbusier was working outside any intellectual context other than the book itself. He writes about and provides references for many artifacts, from airplanes and automobiles to the Parthenon entablatures and columns. But there is no reference to an intellectual context within which he writes. Why is this so? Is it for the writing to appear inventive and new? Is it to separate him from the past?

We can surmise from his writing, the topics, and his approach to those topics, a complete awareness of the issues with which architectural theory and discourse has struggled for centuries. In the built work, he is clearly interested in the past as a stage on which a new architecture may be set. In the written work, he distances himself from any reference to the discursive history of architecture. "If we set ourselves against the past, we are forced to the conclusion that the old architectural code, with its mass of rules and regulations evolved during four thousand years, is no longer of any interest; it no longer concerns us: all the values have been revised; there has been revolution in the conception of what Architecture is."[84]

Despite this announcement of divorce from history – a history which "no longer concerns us," which is "no longer of any interest"

83 Charles-Édouard Jeanneret (Le Corbusier), *Towards a New Architecture.* Translated by Frederick Etchells (New York, Toronto, London, Sydney: Holt, Reinhart and Winston, 1960). The English translation of the original French text was initially published by the Architectural Press of London in 1927. A newer translation was published as: *Le Corbusier. Toward an Architecture.* Introduction by Jean-Louis Cohen, translation by John Goodman (Santa Monica: Getty Research Institute, 2007). The original French text was published as *Vers Une Architecture* in 1923 by Éditions Crès. Six of the seven essays that appear in *Vers Une Architecture* had originally appeared in *L'Esprit Nouveau,* a journal founded in 1920 by Le Corbusier, painter Amédée Ozenfant, and poet Paul Dermée. Three of the essays each had three sections that appeared in different issues. Altogether, the essays published in *Vers Une Architecture* constituted the architecture section of twelve of the twenty-eight issues of *L'Esprit Nouveau* that were published between 1920 and 1925. The one remaining essay, "Architecture or Revolution," did not appear in the journal *L'Esprit Nouveau,* and its title – "Architecture ou Révolution" – was initially considered for the title of the book *Vers Une Architecture.*

84 Le Corbusier, *Towards a New Architecture,* 268.

to us – we find alignment between Le Corbusier's pronouncements about architecture and those of his predecessors, which go all the way back to the fifth century BCE. As much as he wants to divorce himself from the past, and his buildings, with their remarkable formal innovations, from any history, his writings and theories of harmony, truth, and beauty belong to the "old architectural code, with its mass of rules and regulations evolved during four thousand years." Their roots are in Ruskin pointing further back to Alberti and Vitruvius – pointing even further back and, most centrally, to Plato, to the classical period, and to the Greek philosophers whose contemporaries built the Parthenon of the Acropolis of Athens, which absolutely captured Le Corbusier's architectural imagination. During his second trip to the East, he visited the Acropolis at a time when "the columns of the north façade and the architrave of the Parthenon were still lying on the ground. *(ill. p. 44)* Touching them with his fingers,

↙ Perspective of the colonnade of the Parthenon of Athens with landscape beyond. Le Corbusier (Charles-Édouard Jeanneret). *The Parthenon,* Athens, 1911, watercolor and pencil on paper, 21 × 13.7 centimeters.

↘ John Ruskin, Part of Saint Mark's Basilica, Venice. "Sketch after Rain," 1846. *Stones of Venice*, title page.

caressing them, he grasps the proportions of the design. Amazement: reality has nothing in common with books of instruction. Here everything was a shout of inspiration, a dance in the sunlight … and a final and supreme warning: do not believe until you have seen and measured … and touched with your fingers."[85]

LE CORBUSIER'S LIBRARY

Le Corbusier maintained an extensive personal library, partially documented by Paul Turner in his PhD dissertation and now completed by the Fondation Le Corbusier, with approximately 1500 titles.[86] In this collection is a copy of Ruskin's *Mornings in Florence* that Le Corbusier owned already in 1906,[87] at the age of nineteen, while he was still studying at the Municipal Art School at La Chaux-de-Fonds. On one level, it is a travel book, one that describes six morning walks to sites of artistic and architectural import in Florence. On another,

85 Charles-Édouard Jeanneret (Le Corbusier), *My Work*. Translated by James Palmes (London: The Architectural Press, 1960), 21.
86 Paul Turner, "The Education of Le Corbusier – A Study of the Development of Le Corbusier's Thought, 1900–1920," unpublished PhD dissertation, Harvard University, April 1971.
87 The book remains in Le Corbusier's personal library maintained at the Fondation Le Corbusier.

it is a lesson in rigor and the precision of observation and studying artifacts in extreme detail. Le Corbusier carried this book in his knapsack during his first voyage to Italy in 1907 and continued studying it through 1909, the year he spent in the Jura Mountains. Most importantly, he learned from Ruskin that to understand art and architecture, one must be in its presence, studying it rigorously and precisely.

Like Ruskin, he began sketching during his travels in order to record, understand, and analyze.[88] Later, he wrote, "Our childhood was made of Ruskin's exhortations. A rich, complex, contradictory, paradoxical apostle."[89] These sketches and recordings were a part of his travels, but also of his daily walks into the Jura Mountains near La Chaux-de-Fonds. Le Corbusier's travel sketches have been recorded and published and their influence on his development is widely recognized. His daily sketches of nature, however, played as important a role as the travel sketches - especially in establishing the relationship of architecture to its environment. These sketches were maintained in sketchbooks, the first formalized version of which dates from 1914.[90]

At the Municipal Art School in La Chaux-de-Fonds, where he studied under L'Eplattenier, Le Corbusier was deeply embedded in Ruskinian thought. "L'Eplattenier stocked the school's Library with French translations of Ruskin and instituted a scheme of instruction based on Ruskin's precept of studying nature ... Not only did Le Corbusier study under this Ruskinian regime, but he imbibed from L'Eplattenier the devotion to Ruskin."[91] L'Eplattenier introduced Le Corbusier to Ruskin, but Le Corbusier remained tied to Ruskin long after his divergence from his former teacher.

RUSKIN

We know that Ruskin was devoted to the ancient Greek philosopher Plato and found much in common with him. Ruskin wrote in 1843 that "I ... think myself very wrong if I do not read a little bit of Plato very accurately every day."[92] "In later years he began each morning by translating passages of Plato's Laws in his diary."[93] In the same way that we find many of Plato's thoughts about honor, virtue, courage, truth, and beauty in Ruskin, we also find many of Ruskin's thoughts about the same in Le Corbusier - including Ruskin's later ideas about aesthetics, which diverged from Plato's. Additionally, Le Corbusier was a keen reader in general and the journal he co-edited, *L'Esprit Nouveau,* included regular sections on literature, aesthetics, economics, politics, sociology, and philosophy. Given the topics he engages with, it is hard to imagine that he was not aware of the discourse and the intellectual context in which he was writing, which makes it even more puzzling that he references none of them in *Towards a New Architecture*.

The lessons of Ruskin are clearly visible in this pairing of two column capital studies. Le Corbusier, *Study of column capital* (top); John Ruskin, *Study of the column capital of Torcello Cathedral* (bottom).

88 Ruskin's *Stones of Venice* included beautiful sketches and watercolors of buildings and architectural details which he recorded through intense and precise in-person observation.

89 Le Corbusier, *The Decorative Art of Today.* Translated by James Dunnett (Cambridge, Massachusetts: The MIT Press, 1987),132. Translation cited in: Phaidon Editors, with an introductory essay by Jean-Louis Cohen, *Le Corbusier Le Grand* (London: Phaidon Press, 2014), 67.

90 Le Corbusier and Fondation Le Corbusier, *Le Corbusier Sketchbooks,* Volumes 1–4.

91 Mark Swenarton, "Ruskin and the Moderns," in *Artisans and Architects* (London: Palgrave Macmillan, 1989), 192–194.

92 John Ruskin, *The Works of John Ruskin.* Edited by E. T. Cook and Alexander Wedderburn (London: George Allen, 1903–1912), Volume 1, 494.

93 Sara Atwood, "Imitation and Imagination: John Ruskin, Plato, and Aesthetics," *Carlyle Studies Annual,* 26 (2010): 142.

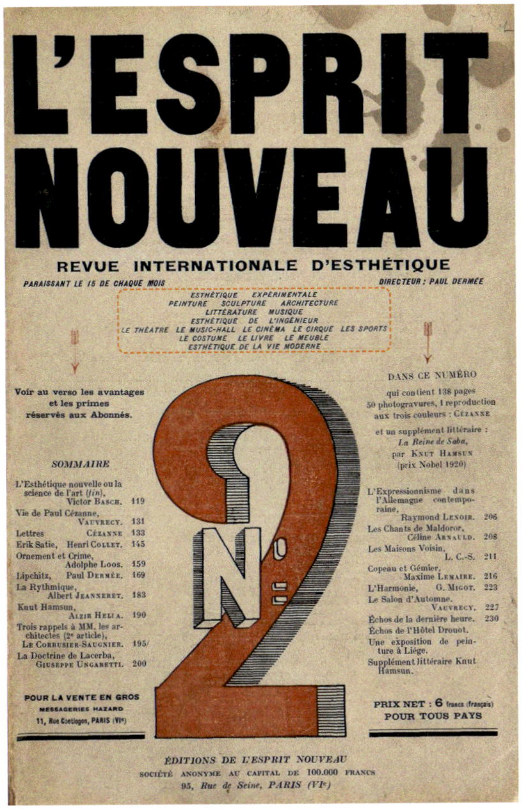
L'ESPRIT NOUVEAU

REVUE INTERNATIONALE D'ESTHÉTIQUE

PARAISSANT LE 15 DE CHAQUE MOIS — DIRECTEUR : PAUL DERMÉE

ESTHÉTIQUE EXPÉRIMENTALE
PEINTURE SCULPTURE ARCHITECTURE
LITTÉRATURE MUSIQUE
ESTHÉTIQUE DE L'INGÉNIEUR
LE THÉATRE LE MUSIC-HALL LE CINÉMA LE CIRQUE LES SPORTS
LE COSTUME LE LIVRE LE MEUBLE
ESTHÉTIQUE DE LA VIE MODERNE

Voir au verso les avantages et les primes réservés aux Abonnés.

N° 2

SOMMAIRE

L'Esthétique nouvelle ou la science de l'art (fin), Victor Basch.	119
Vie de Paul Cézanne, Vauvrecy.	131
Lettres Cézanne	133
Erik Satie, Henri Collet.	145
Ornement et Crime, Adolphe Loos.	159
Lipchitz, Paul Dermée.	169
La Rythmique, Albert Jeanneret.	183
Knut Hamsun, Alzir Hella.	190
Trois rappels à MM. les architectes (2e article), Le Corbusier-Saugnier.	195
La Doctrine de Lacerba, Giuseppe Ungaretti.	200

DANS CE NUMÉRO qui contient 138 pages 50 photogravures, 1 reproduction aux trois couleurs : Cézanne et un supplément littéraire : *La Reine de Saba*, par Knut Hamsun (prix Nobel 1920)

L'Expressionnisme dans l'Allemagne contemporaine, Raymond Lenoir.	206
Les Chants de Maldoror, Céline Arnauld.	208
Les Maisons Voisin, L. C.-S.	211
Copeau et Gémier, Maxime Lemaire.	216
L'Harmonie, G. Migot.	223
Le Salon d'Automne. Vauvrecy.	227
Échos de la dernière heure.	230
Échos de l'Hôtel Drouot.	
Une exposition de peinture à Liége.	
Supplément littéraire Knut Hamsun.	

POUR LA VENTE EN GROS
MESSAGERIES HAZARD
11, Rue Coetlogon, PARIS (VIe)

PRIX NET : 6 francs (français)
POUR TOUS PAYS

ÉDITIONS DE L'ESPRIT NOUVEAU
SOCIÉTÉ ANONYME AU CAPITAL DE 100.000 FRANCS
95, Rue de Seine, PARIS (VIe)

↑↑ Le Corbusier's sketch of the Jura Mountains, 1914.

↑ Cover of *L'Esprit Nouveau 2*. The placement of the table of contents on the front cover emphasizes the vast array of topics by various authors in each issue.

94 Swenarton, "Ruskin and the Moderns," 189.

The intellectual and theoretical kinship between Le Corbusier and Ruskin and, through Ruskin, to Plato will appear far-fetched to readers of modern architecture, as Ruskin has been kept far from the modern movement and instead connected to the Arts and Crafts movement. In his 1989 essay "Ruskin and the Moderns," Mark Swenarton argues that:

> The prevalence of this view can be attributed to the way that the history of modernist thought was presented in two highly influential studies: Nikolaus Pevsner's *Pioneers of the Modern Movement* and Reyner Banham's *Theory and Design in the First Machine Age.* Written respectively in the 1930s and the 1950s … Successive generations of architects and designers, particularly in Britain, have been raised on these books, which are widely regarded as the authoritative studies of modern architectural thought. And while Banham's interpretation differed in several key respects from Pevsner's (and was indeed conceived as a deliberate revision of the Pevsnerian view), in one important respect Pevsner and Banham were at one: both excised Ruskin from modern architectural thought.[94]

Despite these histories of modern architecture that diminish Ruskin's role in modernity, for Le Corbusier, Ruskin was the foundation, not only literally for him as a young man but also figuratively for his career as an architect and thinker. The connection between Le Corbusier and Ruskin is established literally, through reading and his studies at the Municipal Art School, while his route to Plato is indirect, passing through Ruskin. Also, indirectly through Ruskin and emanating from Plato, he is connected to Vitruvius and Alberti. Despite his incredibly inventive formal and spatial built works, his writing is embedded within a long history of architectural theory and abides almost strictly by its canons.

Ruskin distinguishes building from architecture when he argues that:

> … building does not become architecture merely by the stability of what it erects [Vitruvius's *firmitas*]; and it is no more architecture which raises a church, or fits it to receive and contain with comfort a required number of persons occupied in certain religious offices [Vitruvius's *utilitas*] … Let us, therefore at once confine the name [architecture] to that art which, taking up and admitting, as conditions of its working, the necessities and common uses of the building, impresses on its form certain characters venerable or beautiful, but otherwise unnecessary [Vitruvius's *venustas*].[95]

Ruskin is clearly establishing the chronology and staging of the work in this statement. Without the structural and utilitarian "forms" already in place, there is nothing upon which to "impress" the "certain character." In other words, beauty is added to utility. As this "certain character" that brings about delight and beauty is useless, it can simply be removed and we would end up with a building which would work perfectly fine in every possible way, except that it would not provide delight.

Ruskin's statement is controversial in the context of 1800 years of architectural theory. In Vitruvius, firmness *(firmitas)*, commodity *(utilitas)*, and delight *(venustas)* altogether and at once create architecture. They are the necessary conditions, the necessary characteristics of architecture. In Ruskin, delight is what makes architecture. Everything without "delight" is merely a building. It will satisfy firmness: structural integrity and commodity; usefulness, and utility – but until it achieves delight, it is only a building. Ruskin writes, "Architecture concerns itself only with those characters of an edifice which are above and beyond its common use."[96]

Ruskin records an important shift in architectural thought, one that had been in the making since the Renaissance and Alberti's treatise: the primacy of aesthetics over the utilitarian conditions of architecture. We know that Alberti highlighted the importance of "delight" over firmness and commodity, but both Vitruvius and Alberti posed all three as the necessary conditions of architecture. The shift of the architect's role towards aesthetics that was initiated

95 John Ruskin, *The Seven Lamps of Architecture* (New York: Farrar, Straus and Giroux, 1979), 15–16.
96 Ruskin, *The Seven Lamps of Architecture,* 16.

→ John Ruskin, Part of the façade of the destroyed Church of San Michele in Foro, Lucca, Italy, sketched in color, 1846. Partial black-and-white version included in *The Seven Lamps of Architecture*, Plate VI.

during the Renaissance finally shifts architectural theory four hundred years later in Ruskin's *The Seven Lamps of Architecture* to concentrate on "delight" and beauty as the condition of architecture: that which effaces building and transforms it into architecture by adding beauty to it, whether through adornment or the particular disposition of the edifice. We see the influence of Ruskin's theories on Le Corbusier where he insists, in writing, on the separation of the utilitarian conditions of architecture, relegated to the engineer, from the plastic conditions of architecture, related to the architect-as-plastic-artist.

FROM TRIPARTITE TO DUAL

Le Corbusier did indeed adhere to the classical thought that has been the foundation of Western civilization and recorded in every architectural treatise since antiquity. However, he also re-projected the tripartite structure (firmness, commodity, and delight) as a dual, oppositional structure. In this, he belonged to the intellectual foundations of architectural theory, yet also posited new aesthetic proposals that were not governed by those same foundations. Kenneth Frampton, architect and historian, in his book, *Modern Architecture: A Critical History,* devotes three sections to Le Corbusier.[97] Frampton sets out to describe Le Corbusier and his work in the context of a "dual condition," which he calls "dialectical." First, he finds the source of his theory in Le Corbusier's upbringing:

> Above all it seems necessary to remark on the distant Albigensian background of his otherwise Calvinist family, on that half forgotten but latent Manichean view of the world which may well have been the origin of his "dialectical" habit of mind. I am referring to that ever-present play with opposites – with the contrast between solid and void, between light and dark, between Apollo and Medusa – that permeates his architecture and is evident as a habit of mind in most of his theoretical texts.[98]

One of the ways in which Frampton's proposition manifests itself is through Le Corbusier's dual condition of the engineer and the plastic artist. Although both work in and on the material world and their work is in the realm of the sensible, Le Corbusier's conception of their practice – one engaged in universal law and mathematical precision to create harmony and the other engaged in a higher order to create beauty – is a rewriting of the tripartite structure of firmness, commodity, and delight into a dual, oppositional structure.

THE ENGINEER AND THE PLASTIC ARTIST

"Mere engineer," writes Le Corbusier in the opening argument of the *Towards a New Architecture* chapter on "Architecture, Pure Creation of the Mind."[99] In contrast, he writes of the architect, "Profile and contour are the touchstone of the Architect. Here he reveals himself as artist or mere engineer." One above the other: one "mere," the other whole. "Profile and contour are free from all constraint." The "mere" engineer works with constraint and the "artist" architect works free from all constraint. "There is here no longer any question of custom, nor of tradition, nor of construction, nor of adaptation to

97 Frampton, *Modern Architecture: A Critical History,* "Le Corbusier and the Esprit Nouveau 1907–31," "Le Corbusier and the Ville Radieuse 1928–46," and "Le Corbusier and the Monumentalization of the Vernacular 1930–60."
98 Frampton, *Modern Architecture: A Critical History,* 149.
99 Le Corbusier, *Towards a New Architecture,* 186. The essay "Architecture, Pure Creation of the Mind" was originally published in Volume 16 of *L'Esprit Nouveau*. The essay as published in *L'Esprit Nouveau* was credited to Le Corbusier-Saugnier.

→ Le Corbusier's pairing of engineering and architectural artifacts, pointing to their refinement over time towards perfection. *Towards a New Architecture*, pages 134–135.

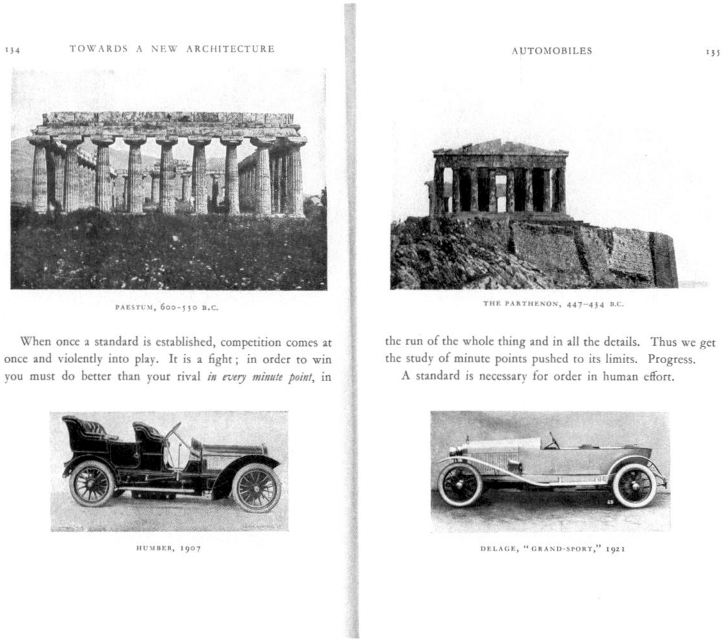
134 TOWARDS A NEW ARCHITECTURE

PAESTUM, 600–550 B.C.

When once a standard is established, competition comes at once and violently into play. It is a fight; in order to win you must do better than your rival *in every minute point*, in

HUMBER, 1907

AUTOMOBILES 135

THE PARTHENON, 447–434 B.C.

the run of the whole thing and in all the details. Thus we get the study of minute points pushed to its limits. Progress.

A standard is necessary for order in human effort.

DELAGE, "GRAND-SPORT," 1921

utilitarian needs. Profile and contour are a pure creation of the mind; they call for the plastic artist."[100] On the one hand, the "mere" engineer works within the bounds of custom and tradition, follows customary and acceptable methods of construction and attends to utilitarian needs. The plastic artist, on the other hand, attends to profile and contour, to form and space, free from all constraint. While this statement privileges one over the other and relinquishes one from utilitarian responsibility and invests it in the other, it concurrently suggests a separation of the two. On the face of it, we are allowed, maybe even encouraged, to consider the two as independent from one another, without any pressure from one to the other, and discouraged from seeing the two as being the same. Although it appears that the "mere" engineer can be *elevated* to the status of plastic artist, if s/he can attend to profile and contour, we are not sure if the two are ever the same. In a moment of judgment of form, profile, and contour, the fate of the individual is decided – whether a "mere" engineer or a plastic artist. Is it within the engineer ever to become a plastic artist? Is one destined to become one and the other to become the other? This brief "argument" provides a glimpse of Le Corbusier's rhetorical and polemical style of writing in *Towards a New Architecture,* in setting up dual conditions while also pointing to the complexity of the issues at work. The roles and spheres of engineers and architects switch, overlap, and collude in search of clarity but remain opaque, at times even becoming more opaque with Le Corbusier's prescriptive statements. In Le Corbusier's search for clarity of ideas and intentions, his absolute proclamations, within their individual clarity, add to the opacity of the overall topic. Walt Whitman's "Do I contradict myself? Very well then, I contradict myself, (I am large, I contain multitudes)"[101] might well have been written for Le Corbusier.

The engineer plays a prominent role in *Towards a New Architecture*. The first essay is titled "The Engineer's Aesthetic and Archi-

100 Le Corbusier, *Towards a New Architecture,* 186.
101 Walt Whitman, "Song of Myself, 51," in *Leaves of Grass* (Brooklyn, New York: Rome Brothers, 1855).

tecture." The three essays that appear under the section "Eyes Which Do Not See" were first published in *L'Esprit Nouveau* under a section titled the "Engineer's Aesthetic,"[102] although that titling was eliminated from the book *Towards a New Architecture.* Even chapters/sections of the book that do not directly refer to engineering or engineers in their titles are full of references to engineering. This prominent role, however, is always fraught with complexities. Which does Le Corbusier privilege – architecture or engineering – and in what context?

"The Engineer's Aesthetic and Architecture,"[103] the first chapter of *Towards a New Architecture,* begins with the following statement: "The Engineer's Aesthetic and Architecture, are two things that march together and follow one from the other: the one being now at its full height, the other in an unhappy state of retrogression."[104] In this case, engineering appears at its full height and architecture in retrogression, while still marching together. Here, we catch a different glimpse. First, that architecture and engineering are parallel as they march together, maybe even holding hands. They follow one from the other, in an interchangeable manner. Either could take the lead and the other would progress from there. But engineering is at its full height, and architecture is in retrogression. We could see this as, simply, an analysis of the contemporary states of engineering and architecture, and not an evaluation of the disciplines. Le Corbusier could be arguing that, at this time, architecture was not progressive, following neoclassical traditions promulgated by the École des Beaux-Arts; and engineering, as far as he saw it, had assumed leadership in the Industrial Revolution and was producing remarkable products – from everyday household objects to automobiles, aircraft, oceanliners, and buildings. But there may be more to it.

We know that Le Corbusier did not have a formal education in architecture. After his high-school training at the Municipal Art School of La Chaux-de-Fonds, he worked in the offices of the Perret brothers, pioneers of reinforced concrete, and Peter Behrens, an industrial designer and architect who served as the chief architect for AEG,[105] designing factory buildings and a mass-producible house for the German electrical engineering company. His fondness for engineering was clearly at the inception of his attraction to architecture. In addition, from these choices, we can surmise that he believed that engineering was foundational to architecture. The question that arises is why, then, is the engineer a "mere engineer," if "inspired by the law of Economy and governed by mathematical calculation, [the engineer] puts us in accord with universal law. He achieves harmony."[106] How can anyone that aligns his creations with universal law be a "mere" engineer? Why do universal law and harmony not achieve what the plastic artist/architect achieves, and what is it that the plastic artist achieves that the engineer does not? What can be beyond universal law and harmony? On a different plateau? Not achievable through universal law and harmony?

102 The three essays appeared in issues 8, 9, and 10 of *L'Esprit Nouveau*. Each of the three essays was titled "Eyes Which Do Not See" and subtitled "I. Liners," "II. Airplanes," and "III. Automobiles" – all engineered products.

103 Le Corbusier, *Towards a New Architecture,* 16. This essay, "The Engineer's Aesthetic and Architecture," was originally published in the double issue 11/12 of *L'Esprit Nouveau* and credited to Le Corbusier-Saugnier (132–135).

104 Le Corbusier, *Towards a New Architecture,* 16.

105 Stanislaus von Moos and Arthur Rüegg, eds., *Le Corbusier Before Le Corbusier* (New Haven, Connecticut, and London: Yale University Press, 2002), 19–21.

106 Le Corbusier, *Towards a New Architecture,* 16.

Peter Behrens, Sketch of AEG Hochspannungsfabrik-Berlin, 1909 (top); Peter Behrens, AEG Turbinenfabrik, Berlin, interior, 1910–1912 (bottom).

HARMONY

Despite all the inconsistencies in Le Corbusier's language relating to harmony, we surmise that he is totally wedded to the universal laws of nature and geometric precision, which he believed to belong to universal law, as the sources of harmony in nature and in architecture. Like Plato, for Le Corbusier, harmony is achieved through alignment with universal order and the precision of geometry and mathematical calculations. Beyond harmony lies beauty for Le Corbusier, as it did for Plato: a higher order, on a different plane, one that cannot be occupied by the "mere" engineer and, according to Plato,[107] cannot be achieved by "mere" mortals. Le Corbusier expresses this notion as follows:

> The Architect, by his arrangement of forms, realizes an order, which is a pure creation of his spirit; by forms and shapes he affects our senses to an acute degree and provokes plastic emotions; by the relationships which he creates he wakes profound echoes in us, he gives us the measure of an order which we feel to be in accordance with that of our world, he determines the various movements of our heart and of our understanding; it is then that we experience the sense of beauty.[108]

The architect realizes an order – an order that is not the universal order derived from universal law and mathematical calculation (the territory of the engineer) but one that is a pure creation of his spirit, unbound by custom, traditions, and utilitarian needs, and whose measure is in accord with our world, the world that Le Corbusier considers to be beyond the universal, on a different plateau. However, on this plateau, forms and spaces affect our senses. This belongs to the *sensible* world. This order of beauty is awakened when architecture reverberates in accord with our *heart* and *understanding*. It puts our innermost depths in accord with the world. We *sense* the beauty of architecture because it reverberates with our heart and understanding in unison. It awakens something deep within us that is the foundation of our order, with which it is synchronous. In achieving harmony, the engineer puts us in accord with universal law. In achieving beauty, the architect puts us in accord with our world. They each move us in alignment with, and with echoes of, "universal order" and "our world," a world which is beyond the sensible but is taken in through the senses. Beauty, however, communicates with our intelligence, our heart, and understanding; not simply through our senses.

In "The Engineer's Aesthetic and Architecture," Le Corbusier makes a definitive and hierarchical division between architecture and engineering. One stems from universal order and leads to harmony, the other stems from the spirit of the plastic artist and leads to

107 Plato, "Phaedrus," in *Selected Dialogues of Plato*, the Benjamin Jowett translation, revised, and with an introduction by Hayden Pelliccia (New York: The Modern Library, 2001), 144–147. Plato describes fluctuations between the mortal and the immortal and their territory from the earth to the multilayered heavens.

108 Le Corbusier, *Towards a New Architecture*, 7.

beauty. This is in line with Platonic harmony, related to geometric order and mathematical precision, and beauty in relation to the work of the "Craftsman." In "Architecture, Pure Creation of the Mind," an essay originally published in *L'Esprit Nouveau* Issue 16, four issues after "The Engineer's Aesthetic," this delineation and hierarchy is not so evident. The relationships are much more circular and ambiguous. There, Le Corbusier writes "that a face is handsome when the precision of the modelling and the disposition of the features reveal proportions which we *feel to be harmonious* because they arouse, deep within us and beyond our senses, a resonance, a sort of soundingboard, which begins to vibrate. An indefinable trace of the Absolute which lies in the depths of our being."[109] Here, harmony arouses a resonance deep within us, beyond our senses. In the "Engineer's Aesthetic and Architecture," the engineer would deliver harmony through mathematical calculation and universal law – the law of physics, gravity, loads, material strength, beam deflection – all within the realm of the senses, and create harmony that is to be sensed visually. Here, in "Pure Creation," harmony is beyond the senses. It is "felt" deep within us, through a resonance with the ABsolute. Not simply the absolute of harmonic orders, nor of mathematical calculations, nor of geometric perfection, but the absolute ABsolute that lies both beyond the senses and at the depths of our being. And not one that may be seen, as one would geometric harmony, but would rather be *felt* as vibration, as resonance with something beyond. Something at our core finds alignment and resonates with the ABsolute. We find harmony with the ABsolute.

Le Corbusier continues, "This sounding-board which vibrates in us is our criterion of harmony. This is indeed the axis on which man is organized in perfect accord with nature and probably with the universe, this axis of organization … ."[110] Our organization is founded on harmony, the same harmony that organizes nature and the whole Platonic universe. It is the alignment of these organizations that propels our synchronized vibration with universal law, our resonance with the ABsolute. The foundation of our organization, each of us being a part of nature, is nature; and nature is the paradigm of the absolute, of universal law. And that is precisely where harmony resides: in nature, as universal law that is absolute.

Le Corbusier does not stop with the declaration that harmony is a component of universal law. He further declares that "this axis of organization, which must indeed be that on which all phenomena and all objects of nature are based … leads us to assume a unity of conduct in the universe and to admit a single will behind it."[111] Not only is nature organized based on harmony and universal laws, but, additionally, all is governed by a single will, which describes why nature operates in such unison, with such unity of conduct. We feel harmony because somewhere deep within us, at our core, we are created based on the harmonious and absolute laws of nature, which are awakened when we feel harmony that aligns with our core. Be-

109 Le Corbusier, *Towards a New Architecture*, 187 [emphasis in original].
110 Le Corbusier, *Towards a New Architecture*, 192.
111 Le Corbusier, *Towards a New Architecture*, 192–193.

cause we are created in the image of the single "will," we, as a part of nature, and all of nature, operate in accord with the "will" of the craftsman.[112]

So far, Le Corbusier has declared universal law, the law of nature, as the source of harmony and harmony as absolute, not debatable; harmony as absolute as a mathematical calculation, and gravity. He goes further and reinforces the theological idea of the primal will, the will of the original architect of the universe. "The laws of physics are thus a corollary to this axis, and if we recognize (and love) science and its works, it is because both one and the other force us to admit that they are prescribed by this primal will. If the results of mathematical calculation appear satisfying and harmonious to us, it is because they proceed from the axis."[113] Harmony is as absolute as the primal will, because it is in the image of the primal will – in the image of the craftsman, and of nature. The "mere" engineer organizes buildings in the image of the absolute laws of the universe, with precise mathematical calculations and in harmony with nature, awakening in our core the feeling of being in accord with the universe: Plato's material universe.

THE PLASTIC ARTIST

The "mere" engineer also organizes construction bound by utilitarian, structural, and constructive necessities, while the architect works on the poetics of form and space. "This is everywhere allowed in the case of painting and music; but architecture is lowered to the level of its utilitarian purposes: boudoirs, W.C.'s, radiators, ferro-concrete, vaults or pointed arches, etc., etc. This is construction, this is not architecture. Architecture only exists when there is a poetic emotion. Architecture is a plastic thing. I mean by 'plastic' what is seen and measured by the eyes."[114] The work of the "mere" engineer is elevated to architecture when its plasticity – its spatial and formal configuration, its profile and contour – conjures poetic emotions in us upon sight, upon sensing it. Here, the senses are back and elevated above the absolute of harmony, which, Le Corbusier previously argued, is felt. We take in the "plastic" through the senses, we see and measure it with our eyes. And the sight conjures poetic emotions in us. That is how we know the difference between the architect and the engineer.

Thus, Le Corbusier presents the architect and the engineer as two possibilities within the same spectrum, chronologically engaged in the process of building. The engineer part of the architect is responsible for the utilitarian, structural, and constructive parts of the process, followed by the plastic artist, the sculptor, who will carve to shape what s/he has been given by the engineer: "... the engineer is effaced and the sculptor comes to life."[115] In a transformative moment, the engineer is erased and the sculptor is brought to life in order to install the "plastic" within the utilitarian, in order to trans-

112 This, "the craftsman," is the term that Plato uses to describe the creator, the divine. For an expanded description, see: Plato, "Timaeus," in *Plato: Complete Works.* Edited by John M. Cooper (Indianapolis, Indiana, and Cambridge, Massachusetts: Hackett Publishing Company, 1997), 1253–1254. 50c–51a.

113 Le Corbusier, *Towards a New Architecture,* 193.

114 Le Corbusier, *Towards a New Architecture,* 198–199.

115 Le Corbusier, *Towards a New Architecture,* 202.

form the process from one that brings utilitarian resolution to another that brings plastic emotion. Moreover, this installation is free from any constraint that, by necessity, was in place for the utilitarian to come to resolution. "Then comes the moment when he must carve the *lineaments* of *the outward aspect.* He has brought the play of light and shade to the support of what he wanted to say. Profile and contour have entered in, and they are free of all constraint."[116] The transformative moment is when the engineer becomes a sculptor and when the mere construction becomes architecture. This transformation can only be brought about with the unconstrained sculpting of the outward appearance of forms, independent of all their structural, constructive, and utilitarian attributes. Here, Le Corbusier follows in the exact footsteps of Ruskin and his proposal for the transformation of building into architecture.

Profile and contour "are a pure invention which makes the outward aspect radiant or dulls it. It is in his contours that we can trace the plastic artist; the engineer is effaced, and the sculptor comes to life. Contours are the touchstone of the architect; in dealing with them he is forced to decide whether he will be a plastic artist or not."[117] Here, we receive assurance that the engineer and the architect are the same person, albeit at different stages and with different roles and capacities, yet they are never equal. Not only does the transformative moment erase the engineer and bring the sculptor to life, but, most importantly, this transformative moment is a decisive one. The architect is forced to decide whether s/he will remain a "mere" engineer or take on plastic artistry and thus be elevated to an architect. "Architecture is the skillful, accurate and magnificent play of masses seen in light; and contours are also and exclusively the skillful, accurate and magnificent play of volumes seen in light. Contours go beyond the scope of the practical man, the daring man, the ingenious man; they call for the plastic artist."[118]

As an example of the play of volumes in light, Le Corbusier cites the Parthenon of the Acropolis of Athens. He goes so far as to declare that "Phidias, Phidias the great sculptor, made the Parthenon."[119] And Ictinus and Callicrates, the official architects of the Parthenon, did not elevate the building to architecture, as they had designed other Doric temples that seemed "cold and not over-interesting."[120] About the Parthenon, he writes further, "Here, the purest witness to the physiology of sensation, and to the mathematical speculation attached to it, is fixed and determined: we are riveted by our senses; we are ravished in our minds; we touch the axis of harmony."[121] The Parthenon has inspired the senses and, in turn, our senses have ravished our minds. Even the axis of harmony is "touched," rather than brought into accord with our feelings. Every time we come near beauty, we are involved in ambiguous language that shifts from feeling to seeing to sensing. From vibrating to coming to accord:

Le Corbusier, *Towards a New Architecture,* page 194. The caption reads "The Parthenon, The Plastic System, articulating the play of volumes in light and shadow."

116 Le Corbusier, *Towards a New Architecture,* 202 [emphasis in original].
117 Le Corbusier, *Towards a New Architecture,* 202.
118 Le Corbusier, *Towards a New Architecture,* 202.
119 Le Corbusier, *Towards a New Architecture,* 203.
120 Le Corbusier, *Towards a New Architecture,* 203.
121 Le Corbusier, *Towards a New Architecture,* 204.

> ... the Parthenon gives us sure truths and emotion of a superior, mathematical order. Art is poetry: the emotion of the senses, the joy of the mind as it measures and appreciates, the recognition of an axial principle which touches the depth of our being.[122]

TRUTH

Even the Parthenon cannot escape this ambiguity. Le Corbusier posits that it gives us sure truths and indeed it does by many accounts. But the same stone detailing of the Parthenon frieze that ravished Le Corbusier's mind is the one that Vitruvius attributed to an imitation of an "original" wooden structural element: a petrification of timber construction, far from its structural truth. And this "superior mathematical order" is the same one that had to be "adjusted" through the introduction of entasis and the curving of the steps and the plinth in order to account for the distortion of human vision.[123] Elsewhere in *Towards a New Architecture,* Le Corbusier attributed mathematical order to the engineer and placed it at the service of producing harmony, rather than beauty. Here, the two are mixed. Art and poetry causes the senses to emote and provide pleasure to the mind as it assesses the size, scale, and proportion of the artifact and recognizes its beauty – all through measurement. This recognition then awakens an "axial principle" that touches us in our depths. We are once again back to universal law and the language that Le Corbusier emphatically engaged with the work of the engineer and the production of harmony: mathematical precision and order. Every time we are near beauty, we face ambiguities – and to remain emphatic, the only emphatic language to which we have access, that of mathematical order and geometric precision, is resurrected.

BEAUTY

We see Le Corbusier following in the footsteps of Ruskin when he calls architecture a plastic art and holds it and the activity of the architect-as-plastic-artist in the highest rank, that which is solely responsible for effacing the engineer and bringing forth the architect. The role of the architect, then, is to arouse deep emotions. He writes, "but suddenly you touch my heart, you do me good, I am happy and I say: 'This is beautiful.' That is Architecture. Art enters in."[124]

Le Corbusier did indeed adhere to the classical thought that has been the foundation of Western civilization and recorded in every architectural treatise since antiquity, both in his writings and buildings. As much as he maintained strict ties with the canon of architectural theory, he also made a break with the two-thousand-year-old discourse of architecture that had concentrated on the

122 Le Corbusier, *Towards a New Architecture,* 205.
123 There are other theories on the logic of the curvatures, but none as convincing as the visual logic. Richard Etlin's essay provides a succinct history of the arguments. Etlin, "Le Corbusier, Choisy, and French Hellenism," 268.
124 Le Corbusier, *Towards a New Architecture,* 187.

simultaneous coexistence of firmness, commodity, and delight: the tripartite structure that has defined architectural theory since Vitruvius. In its stead, he proposed the dual structure of engineer and plastic artist, favoring delight (beauty) achieved by the plastic artist/architect over firmness and commodity achieved by the engineer. He is, however, unable to provide us with a sense of what precisely constitutes this beauty, beyond mathematical precision, following precisely in the footsteps of Vitruvius.

In this study, I have argued that Le Corbusier was wedded to the ideal of rational building systems and geometric order. He, however, had a more complex agenda in his work, which was to create singular plastic experiences through a systemically conceived architecture. His built work, when analyzed carefully through close reading, speaks of the architect's struggle made visible through the manipulation of rationalized building systems to reach a plastic experience that cannot be projected by those same systems. His work was created through a constant tension between these two realms: the systematicity and rationality of building systems such as structural, plumbing, sun-shading, and circulation ones, tethered to the engineer; and the plasticity and malleability of space and form in light, shadow, color, and texture, associated with the architect. In Le Corbusier's context, the engineer's realm is the realm of universal laws of nature, geometric harmony, and the organization of the building's technical systems. On the contrary, the realm of the architect is to acutely affect the senses through space, light, and texture, reaching heightened emotion that moves us. In *Towards a New Architecture,* he is very precise and specific in relation to harmony, geometric order, and organization – all in the engineer's realm. However, when it comes to beauty and delight – in the realm of the architect – he is generally unable to maintain that precision. He refers to it as the ineffable quality; as the indescribable, plastic emotion; or as affecting our senses to an acute degree. These all refer to something that lies outside the bounds of codified prescriptions, yet all are achieved along with those prescriptions and through them. Le Corbusier follows in the footsteps of architectural theorists so long as he is in the realm of prescriptions, geometric precision, and harmony. However, the moment he ventures away from that definable, finite, and static realm, he is in a territory that is, at best, at the margins of architectural theory. His capacity as an architect allows him to formulate these indescribable spaces and forms in material, but as a writer and a theorist he remains trapped in vague and contradictory language as soon as he leaves geometry and harmony.

THE SUBLIME

He comes closest to clarity in *Towards a New Architecture,* where, describing the intensity of this dual condition between the two realms of the engineer and the architect, he writes:

> Architecture has graver ends; capable of the sublime, it impresses the most brutal instincts by its objectivity; it calls into play the highest faculties by its very abstraction. Architectural abstraction has this about it which is magnificently peculiar to itself, that while it is rooted in hard fact, it spiritualizes it, because the naked fact is nothing more than the materialization of a possible idea.[125]

Here, he reiterates the Platonic divide between the sensible and the intelligible: between sensible objecthood and intelligible abstraction, understood only by the highest faculties. Then, there is the Platonic turn, architecture spiritualizes hard facts: it turns object into spirit, material into idea, sensible into intelligible. There is yet another thing at work here: the sublime. Up until the eighteenth century, our only conception of aesthetics was limited to beauty – and that achieved only through the harmony of geometric orders. In the eighteenth century, Edmund Burke's *A Philosophical Inquiry into the Origin of our Ideas of the Sublime and Beautiful* theorized a different aesthetic experience, the sublime, which worked on our emotions, creating intense feelings. Burke theorized a different version of nature: not an organized, controlled, harmonious, and unified whole but one capable of overwhelming our senses through force, terror, and exhilaration.[126] Le Corbusier's inclusion of the sublime confirms his keen awareness of contemporary theoretical proposals and, most importantly, introduces a break with the four-thousand-year-old history of architecture, the same "old architectural code, with its mass of rules and regulations evolved during four thousand years, [that] is no longer of any interest … ."[127] Le Corbusier, in *Towards a New Architecture,* has put forth a theory that has at its core the classical ideas put forward by Plato, Vitruvius, Alberti, and Ruskin.[128] His theory, however, includes the sublime – all that could not be included in classical thought. Le Corbusier created yet another oppositional structure in which the two sides, in this case the beautiful and the sublime, are held together in tension. Rather than proposing them as opposites that could not share in one another's arena, he poses them as simultaneous: architecture must achieve beauty through the rules of geometry and harmony, governed by universal law, and achieve the sublime by plastic artistry, delineating forms and spaces that acutely affect us emotionally.

125 Le Corbusier, *Towards a New Architecture,* 27–28.
126 Edmund Burke, *A Philosophical Inquiry into the Origin of our Ideas of the Sublime and Beautiful* (New York: Garland, 1971).
127 Le Corbusier, *Towards a New Architecture,* 268.
128 Ruskin was critical of Greek classical architecture as he believed it promoted imitation of the orders. Nonetheless, he followed Plato, the Greek philosopher of the same era.

CONCLUSION

Le Corbusier did indeed adhere to classical thought both in his writings and buildings. He has, however, also projected the oppositional structure of the dual condition into a "tense space" where the two conditions are made to conspire together to deliver conceptual material and realized ideations. In this, he not only belonged to the intellectual foundations of classical architectural theory but also posited new aesthetic proposals that could not be governed by those same principles. Where his writings were unable to bring clarity, his buildings were able to project the new aesthetic proposals in built form.

In the next chapter, through an analysis of Le Corbusier's Ahmedabad Millowners' Association Building, the dual condition between the pragmatics of the building's technical requirements satisfied through geometric solutions and the plasticity of space and form acutely affecting our senses will be examined. The chapter will explore the tension between systematicity, geometric determination, and the organization of a structure bound by the regularity of the building systems, and the formation of plastic experience by molding space, form, movement, and texture within the building. My contention is that Le Corbusier created this work through a constant tension between these two realms: the systematicity and geometric order of building systems, and the plasticity and malleability of space and form in light, shadow, color, and texture, experienced through movement – what he called the "architectural promenade." Le Corbusier's manifestation of the dual condition is visible through the manipulation of rationalized building systems in order to reach a plastic experience which cannot immediately be projected by those same systems. This struggle is intensified by the social, climatic, and cultural forces in India, with which he was not familiar prior to his Indian commissions.

III
AHMEDABAD MILLOWNERS' ASSOCIATION BUILDING: SOLIDS AND VOIDS

← Partial west façade from the access ramp.

British rule in India existed in multiple forms from 1612. Initially in competition with the Portuguese, Danish, and the Dutch, the British held trading posts in the subcontinent till the mid-eighteenth century. These trading posts ruled over large parts of India which were later shared with the British Crown. The Indian Rebellion of 1857 helped focus all rule under the Crown, but also initiated the seeds of self-rule in India. After almost ninety years of the independence movement, in 1946, just after the Second World War, the British government was finally convinced that the Indian subcontinent was to be independent, and, in August 1947, the Indian independence movement succeeded in gaining freedom from British rule under the guidance and leadership of Mahatma Gandhi. The British government announced its agreement with the principle of independence and with the division of "British India" into two self-governing states, those of India and Pakistan – the latter included East Bengal, also called East Pakistan, which later declared independence as the People's Republic of Bangladesh in 1971.

Gandhi hailed from Gujarat in western India and began his famous "salt march" of 1930 from the Gandhi Ashram in Ahmedabad, where he had resided for fifteen years. The city is named after Ahmed Shah, who established it as the capital of Gujarat on the banks of the Sabarmati River in 1411. One of the largest cities in India, it is also one of the largest producers of cotton and has been the hub of the Indian textile industry. Due to its central role in the independence movement, it holds a special place in the contempo-

↑ East façade of Le Corbusier's Ahmedabad Millowners' Association Building, photographed from the opposite bank of the Sabarmati River, 1975.

rary Indian psyche while also remaining one of the country's main economic and cultural centers.

During the partition of 1947, India not only lost what we now know as Pakistan and Bangladesh but, in the process, it also lost Lahore, the capital of Punjab. Hindus of the West Punjab and East Bengal had overnight become residents of a primarily Muslim country, Pakistan. Many left their ancestral homes, which had suddenly been assigned to a new Muslim country and relocated to the "new" India. This division and the shifting of cultural and ethnic boundaries created a great deal of uncertainty and scarred the Indian psyche. Healing these scars and reuniting the people became the new India's largest endeavor.

Jawaharlal Nehru was an instrumental leader in the Indian independence movement and was arguably Gandhi's political heir. He became the nation's first prime minister in 1947. Given the partition, which on its own had created severe turmoil, along with dislocated and disenfranchised populations who may have fled religious persecution, he faced serious challenges and wanted to find a way to unite a freshly divided country and populace. India's population was and remains diverse in culture, language, and religion. Nehru managed successfully to establish reforms that brought the country together on economic, social, and educational fronts. One of his visionary statements focused on "the nation's faith in the future," which he put into action in imagining a new planned city, a new capital for the Punjab province. The new capital was not only a necessity as a replacement for Lahore, but also as an important instrument of social and class unification and future-centric thinking that embraced modernity and innovation.

LE CORBUSIER IN INDIA

Nehru made his commitment to this project public by commissioning the American planner Albert Mayer to design the master plan for the new city, called Chandigarh in reference to Chandi, the Hindu goddess of power. The planning was followed by selecting a short list of international architects whom Nehru believed had the innovation and imagination to conceive of a new city – one that could both heal the scars of Partition and propel the country forward, unified, into the age of modernity. Le Corbusier was on that short list: he was not an obvious candidate for the new city, but his modernist vision appealed to Nehru as being able to deliver what the prime minister called "the nation's faith in the future." Nehru's officials P. N. Thapar and P. L. Varma visited Le Corbusier's office at 35 rue de Sèvres in Paris in 1950 to invite him to work as the consulting architect to the government of Punjab on the new capital, Chandigarh.[129] He was initially skeptical, but the chance to give form to a lifetime of urban ideas, which up to that point had remained on paper, was tempting. Chan-

129 For further detail on how Le Corbusier came to be the architect of choice, see Sarbjit Bahga and Surinder Bahga, *Le Corbusier and Pierre Jeanneret: Footprints on the Sands of Indian Architecture* (New Delhi: Galgotia Publishing Company, 2000), 12–23.

digarh gave Le Corbusier an opportunity to design a modern city around his ideas about planning cities centered on modern transportation, a concept that he had carried with him since the 1920s. His first trip to India began on February 18, 1951, to meet Nehru and study the culture of the country, its climate, architecture, traditions, and the site of the commissioned project. His contract with the Punjab government mandated a minimum of two trips annually to India, totaling sixty days. Le Corbusier's sketchbooks E18 and E19 record the first trip, between February and April 1951.[130] Sketchbook E18 is dated February 1951 and "INDIA" is indicated on the cover in capital letters, along with "AHMEDABAD" and "RONCHAMP." Sketchbook E19 is marked March–April 1951 and "INDIA" is written on the cover as well.

The trip of roughly six weeks was spent mostly in Chandigarh and at governmental functions in New Delhi. The very first note about India in E18 records Le Corbusier's thoughts about the Jantar Mantar, the eighteenth-century astronomical observatory in New Delhi, where he writes "They point the way: bind men to the cosmos"[131] and also that it definitely "beats out the best qualities of the Englishman Lutyens."[132] Peter Serenyi has argued that this single page in the sketchbook defines both the interest visible in the symbolism of the cosmos from Jantar Mantar and the broad boulevards that eventually appear in Chandigarh, which Lutyens had planned for New Delhi.[133] After four weeks, Le Corbusier traveled to Ahmedabad. Why Ahmedabad? Jawaharlal Nehru's sister, Krishna Nehru, had married into the Hutheesing family, one of the industrialist dynasties of Ahmedabad involved in the cotton trade and textile manufacturing. Word of Le Corbusier's commission in India had quickly reached the ears of the leading families of Ahmedabad, who commissioned several projects to him. This was a group of very tightly knit Jain industrialists with grand visions of industry and cultural philanthropy. Chinubhai Chimanbhai, the mayor of Ahmedabad, commissioned Le Corbusier to design a house for him and his family, which was never built. He also commissioned Le Corbusier to design a cultural center at the hub of which was a museum. The museum was built, but the remaining buildings were not. Surottam Hutheesing, Krishna Nehru's brother-in-law, then also the president of the powerful Millowners' Association, commissioned Le Corbusier to design a headquarters for the Association and later, a private residence for himself, a bachelor at the time. The Ahmedabad Millowners' Association Building, the subject of this study was completed, and the design of the Hutheesing house was passed on to a fellow millowner, Shyamubhai Shodhan, and built on a different site. The residence is now known as the Shodhan House. The last of the Ahmedabad commissions was for the Sarabhai House, designed for Manorama Sarabhai and completed in 1955.

Le Corbusier Sketchbooks E18 and E19, in which he recorded his first trip to India in 1951.

130 Le Corbusier used sketchbooks to write notes and sketch ideas and impressions. He established a cataloging system for these sketchbooks, which are in series from "A" through "T." Within each series, there are numbered volumes, A1, A2, A3...; B1, B2...; to T1, T2. The numbers were stenciled on the cover, along with a date.

131 Le Corbusier and Fondation Le Corbusier, *Le Corbusier Sketchbooks,* Volume 2, 329.

132 Le Corbusier and Fondation Le Corbusier, *Le Corbusier Sketchbooks,* Volume 2, 329.

133 Peter Serenyi, "Timeless, but of its Time: Le Corbusier's Architecture in India," *Perspecta* 20 (1983): 92–93.

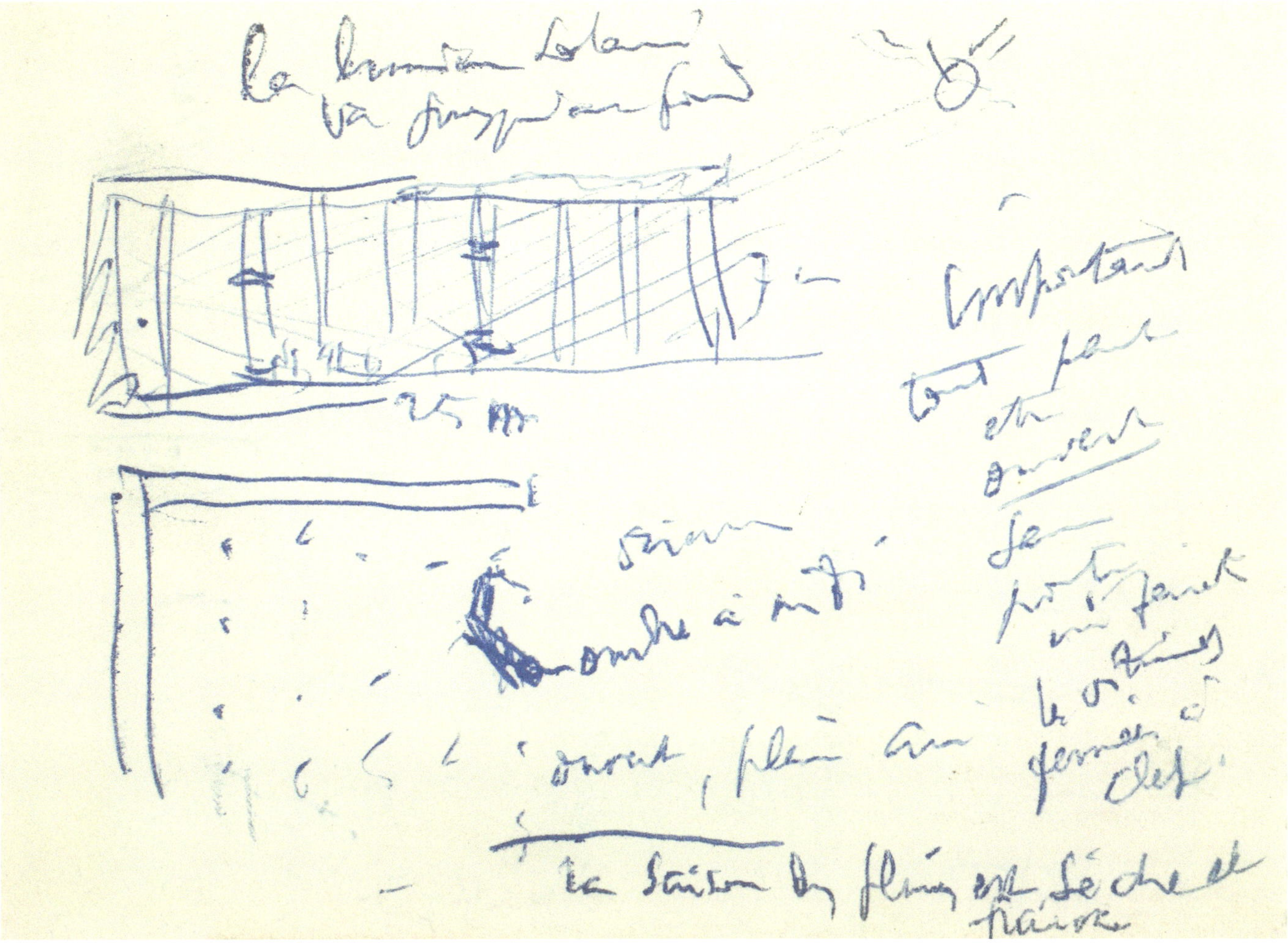

Le Corbusier and Fondation Le Corbusier, *Le Corbusier Sketchbooks*, Volume 2, 358, with notes on sun and shade.

INDIA IN SKETCHBOOKS

In addition to meeting many influential clients during this first trip, Le Corbusier also carefully observed the Indian context and recorded thoughts and ideas in his sketchbook. The second page recording India documents "the precise adaptation of forms and organisms to the sun, rain, air, etc.,"[134] recognizing the incredible effect of climate on architecture in India. Later in the same sketchbook, he records more specific thoughts about the sun and shade, and almost predicts the open-air environments he later created in Ahmedabad and Chandigarh. His description in the sketchbook reads:

> sunlight reaches all the way in // 25 m.
> orient // shadow at noon // open, open air
> important everything can be open without doors or
> windows display cases locked.
> the rainy season is dry and cool[135]

Françoise de Franclieu, in her introduction to the E19 sketchbook, paraphrases Le Corbusier's written notes and writes, "in Chandigarh, there must be no hesitation to create large empty naves in deep shadow, generators of air currents (403); and one must also take into

134 Le Corbusier and Fondation Le Corbusier, *Le Corbusier Sketchbooks,* Volume 2, 330.

135 Le Corbusier recorded ideas and information about the climate of Ahmedabad in his sketchbook. Translation of sketch 358 provided in: Le Corbusier and Fondation Le Corbusier, *Le Corbusier Sketchbooks,* Volume 2, 358.

account the climatic conditions (alternating periods of sun and rain) in the design of the roof structures (397) and in the conception of the *brise-soleil,* which should be integrated into the very structure of the building."[136] The sketchbooks document the very fluid and spontaneous intake of the environment, their analysis and synthesis, and at times even formal proposals. Already here, at this very early stage, we begin to see all the components of a future building. However, the way in which they appear in different projects differs greatly. Franclieu, in her introduction to E18, the first of the Indian sketchbooks, notes, "this sketchbook is also a rich source of information on the genesis of the chapel at Ronchamp. Before his departure for India on February 18, 1951, Le Corbusier went again to Ronchamp where he made various sketches (312–322, 325–328). Some of the sketches here date from June 1950 (313), the time of his first trip there, others from February 12 (320, 324) and February 15, 1951 (325) (the latter was re-dated 'February 20, 1951,' while the architect was flying over Crete). These pages illustrate the architect's creative method, ..."[137] which I have cited elsewhere.[138] When working on a project, Le Corbusier noted that he does not try to solve the problem immediately, rather he waits for months without making a sketch, and instead accumulates all the concerns and provocations of the project in his mind. "Then one day, a spontaneous initiative of the inner being takes place, everything falls into place; one takes a pencil, a bit of charcoal, some colored pencils (color is the key to the process) and one gives birth right there on the paper: the idea comes forth, the child comes forth, it has come into the world, it is born."[139] Although Le Corbusier wrote this particular note about Ronchamp, both Franclieu and Pauly have argued that the method is not unique to that building but is rather a general design method which may be applied to Le Corbusier as a rule.[140] Franclieu cites Chandigarh as an example of this creative method which may be viewed on the pages of the sketchbooks. This is generally true, but the same sketchbooks may be used to note differences in approach between different projects. For example, sketchbook E18, 313 records a sketch of Ronchamp from the first visit, already delineating building form and situating the chapel on top of the hill. Subsequent sketches record developments of the chapel's formal characteristics, with multiple plan developments and details. A similar, yet less form-based, approach may be found in the case of Chandigarh. Apparent throughout these sketches is a genuine sense of learning and discovery. They record elements from the Indian context that relate to climate, architectural details and culture, the landscape, and patterns of urban and rural development. The sketches gradually turn to explorations of form and formal developments over time. The Ahmedabad Millowners' Association Building follows a different path, closer to Le Corbusier's explanation. Between March 1951, his first visit to Ahmedabad, and November 25, 1951, eight months later, when the first sketch of "AMOA"[141] is recorded, there are no other building-specific sketches or notes. However,

136 Françoise de Franclieu, notes in Le Corbusier and Fondation Le Corbusier, *Le Corbusier Sketchbooks,* Volume 2, page 31.
137 Franclieu, notes in Le Corbusier and Fondation Le Corbusier, *Le Corbusier Sketchbooks,* Volume 2, page 27.
138 For further details, see Chapter I, Section "Seven Buildings," page 35 in this book.
139 Le Corbusier, *Textes et dessins pour Ronchamp,* cited in Franclieu, notes in Le Corbusier and Fondation Le Corbusier, *Le Corbusier Sketchbooks,* Volume 2, page 27.
140 Cited and analyzed in Chapter I, Section "Seven Buildings," page 35 in this book.
141 Le Corbusier and Fondation Le Corbusier, *Le Corbusier Sketchbooks,* Volume 2, 675, page 71 of this book.

Le Corbusier's sketch of the Hutheesing temple and its courtyard, resembling the plan of the second floor of the Millowners' Association Building. *Le Corbusier Sketchbooks,* Volume 2, 350.

there are numerous sketches and notes related to climate and culturally specific architectural details, for instance:

> attention // No glass windows in Ahmedabad (Chandigarh??) but solid wood panels (against burglar etc. // open during the day // closed at night // or can be left open // provide air holes around panels[142]

Here, he notes a new discovery: something between open and closed. It operates like a window, but it is not transparent. It is made of wood, like a door that opens and allows air to circulate but can be closed and appear opaque – in this case, "against burglars." This is something that was rarely possible or useful in climates in which Le Corbusier worked: France and Switzerland. We can see that he is very much attuned to solutions that have arisen from climatic concerns and we will see later that he adapts these very solutions in the Millowners' Association Building and other buildings in India.

In his sketchbooks we see Le Corbusier taking note of the climate and comparing it with standards he knew well.[143] The temperature 37 degrees Celsius is that of the human body, which is also the average temperature in Chandigarh. On sketch 350, he writes: "Ahmedabad // this is an enclosed courtyard of a temple"[144] referring to what appears to be the Hutheesing Temple (one of the philan-

142 Le Corbusier recorded climate-related impressions and ideas from Ahmedabad in his sketchbook: Le Corbusier and Fondation Le Corbusier, *Le Corbusier Sketchbooks,* Volume 2, 683.

143 Le Corbusier took note of temperatures in Ahmedabad in his sketchbook: Le Corbusier and Fondation Le Corbusier, *Le Corbusier Sketchbooks,* Volume 2, 333, as follows:

100°	212
37°	100 average in Chandigarh
0°	32
(Centigrade)	(Fahrenheit)

144 Le Corbusier and Fondation Le Corbusier, *Le Corbusier Sketchbooks,* Volume 2, 350.

thropic cultural efforts of one of Le Corbusier's Ahmedabad clients). This statement is followed on the next page by naming a set of architectural elements in the courtyard and multiple pages of sketches recording the situation of the temple, each with dimensional specificity, almost as if they were exact and independent elements in a cubist collage, unrelated until they arrive on the canvas - or, in this case, the courtyard of the temple. On the next sketch that appears in the *Sketchbooks,* 351, he writes: "yellow stone a = 4m. wall // b c = kiosk // d = ramp // e = temple."[145] The walls of the courtyard serve as the frame of a canvas that would support a set of unrelated architectural elements in a collaged composition, a superimposition of unrelated architectural elements that have been placed in compositional proximity to one another.

EARLY SKETCHES

This collection of architectural elements and climatic notes is the mode of recording thoughts and ideas about Ahmedabad and the many projects that Le Corbusier had there. The first sketch specifically related to the Millowners' Association Building is 675,[146] dated November 25, 1951, which depicts a site plan, a sketch outlining the general location on the truncated rectangular site fronting Ashram Road to the west and the Sabarmati River to the east. The north and south sides of the long, rectangular site are bordered by other building lots. The sketch also includes a corresponding site section through the river, the site, and the street with mature trees.[147] Already here, there is strong recognition of the role and value of the Sabarmati River, both as a view and as a structural threat. The notes alongside the sketch mention a stone-faced retaining wall both to keep the river contained and to provide a level garden plateau with river views for parties.[148]

The site plan and section sketch locates a three-story building, the garden facing the river to the east, and the street entrance and parking to the west. Beyond the site plan, the sketches record anecdotes, mostly related to Chandigarh but later also applied to the Millowners' Association Building. Next in the timeline, we encounter a set of drafted drawings produced by Atelier Le Corbusier at 35 rue de Sèvres in Paris,[149] drawn by Balkrishna Doshi,[150] dated March 7, 1952: a site plan, three floor plans, and an elevation, a year after the visit to Ahmedabad. Also from the same timeframe is a detailed plan with furnishings of the main floor and an exterior perspective *(ill. p. 72)* outlining the main components of the building. Although this view does not exactly resemble the final project, most of the components of the final project are present in these drawings, drafted soon after the gestation period that Le Corbusier made famous and resulting in the synthesis of the notes and ideas, long before the start of construction.

145 Le Corbusier and Fondation Le Corbusier, *Le Corbusier Sketchbooks,* Volume 2, 351.

146 Le Corbusier and Fondation Le Corbusier, *Le Corbusier Sketchbooks,* Volume 2, 675.

147 The *Le Corbusier Sketchbooks* include an English translation along with each sketch. Le Corbusier's hand-written comment on the site plan and section sketch reads: "Cotton Mill Owners' Association / November 25, 1951 river // make a ... wall with stone facing // garden parties // 3 floors // low construction not too visible // parking [for] 60 automobiles 20 as a rule // road // small valley fill it in or not?"

148 Le Corbusier and Fondation Le Corbusier, *Le Corbusier Sketchbooks,* Volume 2, 675.

149 Atelier Le Corbusier drawing number 4389. Fondation Le Corbusier cataloging number 6761.

150 Balkrishna V. Doshi, Indian architect who won the 2018 Pritzker Architecture Prize, worked in Atelier Le Corbusier and was the on-site architect for Le Corbusier's Ahmedabad projects.

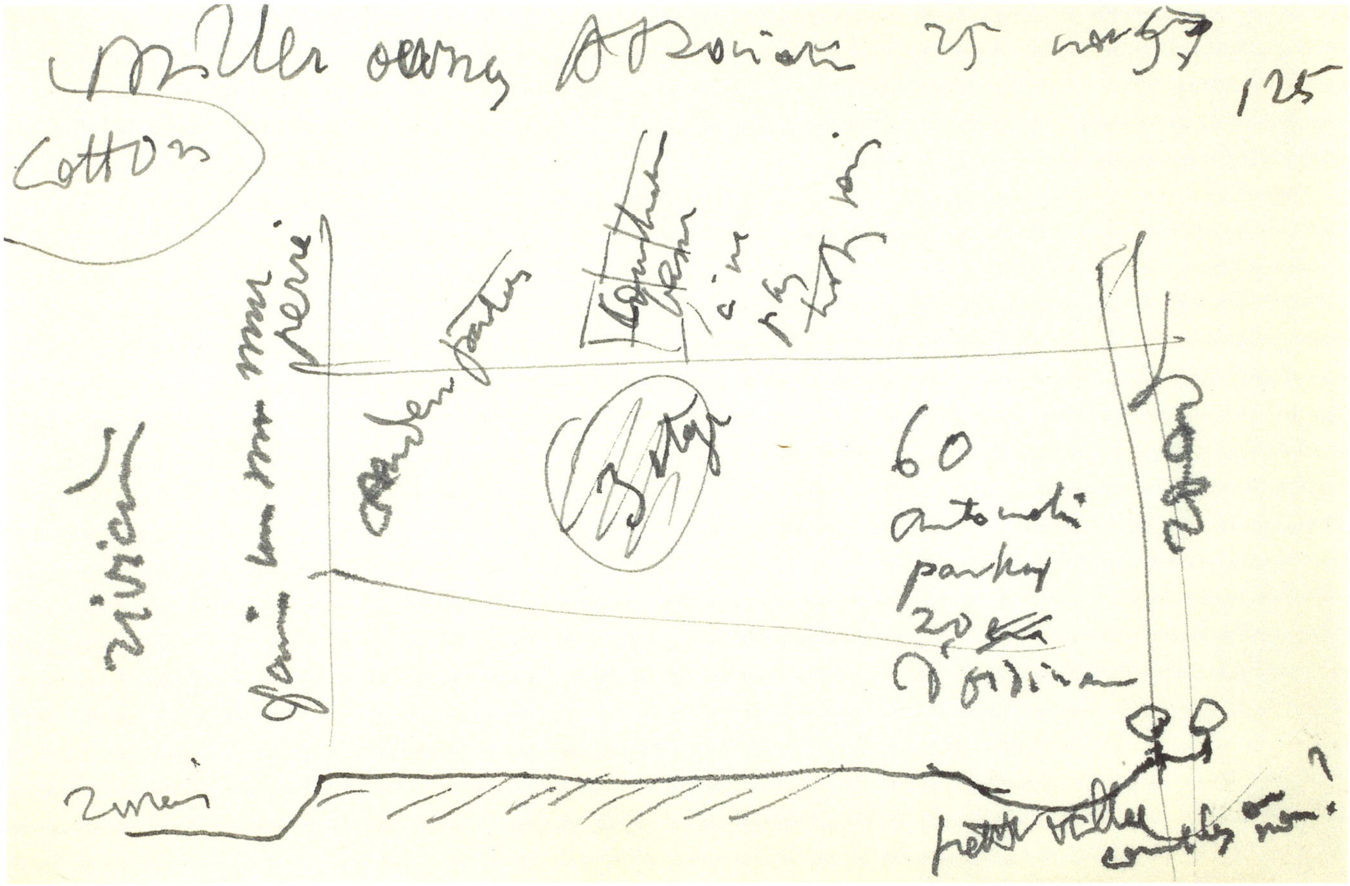

Site plan and section sketch, Le Corbusier sketchbook E25, 675. The Sabarmati River is to the left and Ashram Road with its trees to the right.

EARLY DRAWINGS AND DUAL CONDITIONS

Already here, in the March 7, 1952 drawings, a series of dual conditions are manifested: conditions between utilitarian elements, their placement and formation; and sculptural transformations with spatial and formal desires that acutely affect the senses. In the only "book-like" document on the Millowners' Association Building,[151] a brief duograph on two of Le Corbusier's late buildings, Kenneth Frampton hints at the "dialectical imagination" in the title of his essay. The duograph also includes thirteen beautiful images of the building, taken by Yukio Futagawa. Frampton attributes the "parasol" roof and the outdoor life of the Indian buildings to an earlier villa from 1928, "Villa at Carthage." He frames the two building subjects of the book in a dialectical relationship with one another in the context of a "figure-ground" reading. He notes that the "play of this form [meeting hall on the second floor] as an elliptical 'figure' against a rectilinear 'ground' suggests that we may think of the Millowners' Building as being the introverted classical model, for which the Carpenter Center was eventually destined to become the extroverted anti-thesis."[152] Frampton continues this line of inquiry and delineates a number of elements in the Ahmedabad Millowners' Association Building that fall into this "dialectical" reading: the plan of the meeting hall vs. its section; the dog-leg stair vs. the ramp; the

151 It is a brief book, a duograph on the Ahmedabad Millowners' Association Building and Le Corbusier's Carpenter Center, which includes a short essay by Kenneth Frampton and thirteen images of the former building: Kenneth Frampton, "Le Corbusier and the Dialectical Imagination," in *GA 37: Le Corbusier Millowners Association Building Ahmedabad, India. 1954. Carpenter Center for Visual Arts, Harvard University, Cambridge, Massachusetts, USA, 1961–1964* (Tokyo: A.D.A. Edita, 1975).

152 Frampton, "Le Corbusier and the Dialectical Imagination," *GA 37*, page 3 of the essay (the book is unpaginated).

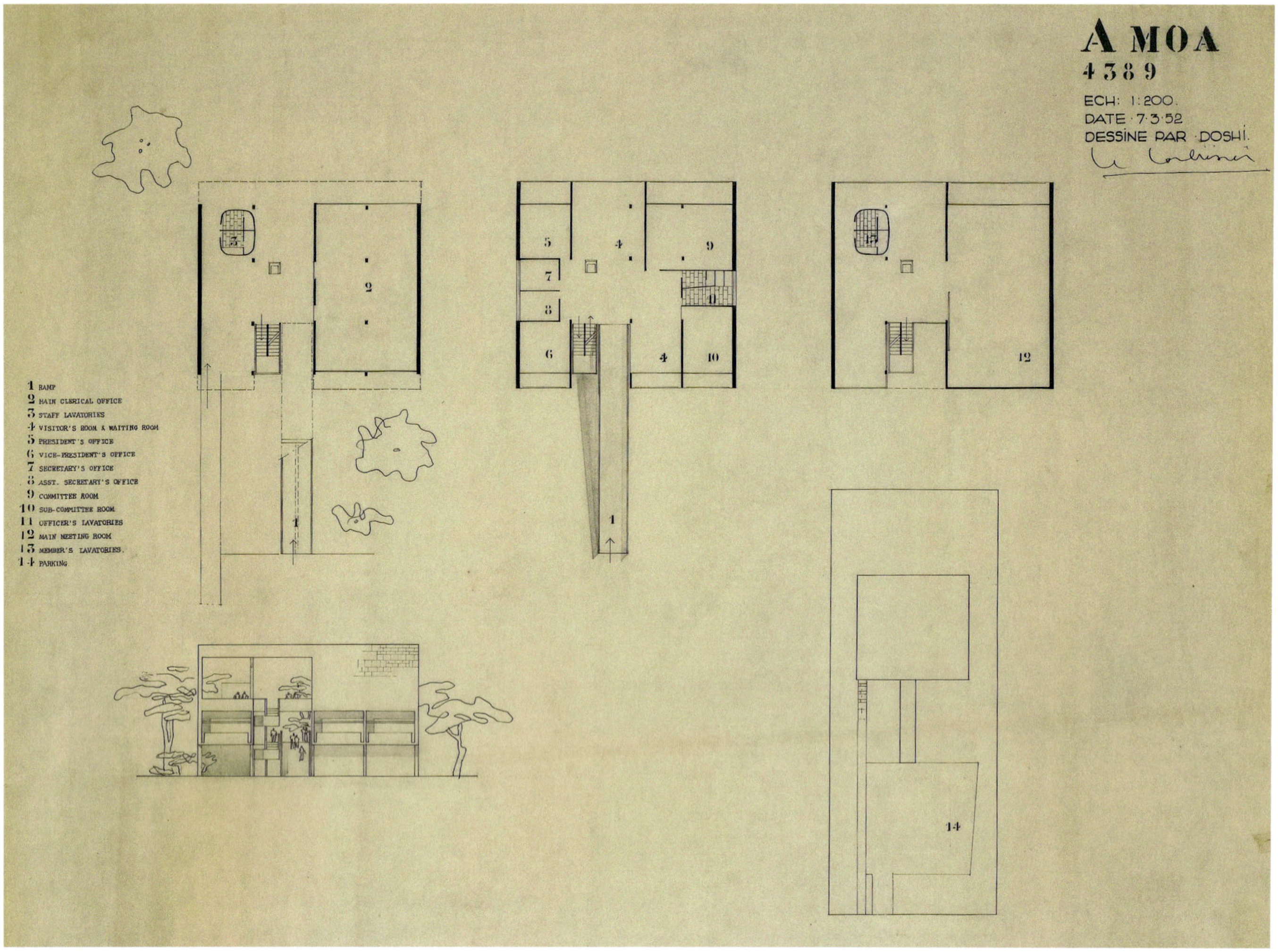

"crustacean form of the meeting hall" vs. the "orthogonal framing of the adjacent 'minstrels'"; the concrete of the exterior vs. the stone-faced interior; the diagonal brise-soleil vs. the orthogonal; the cloakroom vs. the boomerang stair; and finally, the male/female toilets with their symbolic and "erotic" overtones. Frampton's observations are astute and confirm Le Corbusier's interest in dual conditions. Their sources and intentions, however, arise from different origins and not always in the context of a strategic oppositional structure, the subject of this study.

For example, the plan vs. the section of the meeting hall: "Not only is the meeting hall set against its container, but also the elliptical outline of its plan is brought into conflict with the inverted parabolic section of the parasol."[153] The relationship between the meeting hall and its container is defined by the tension between the utility of the container and the sculptural form of the hall. The relationship between the plan and the section of the hall is, however, not defined by their opposition to one another; rather, they both belong to the same side of an oppositional structure that sets them against the "container," the same structural grid in both plan and section. The plan shape and the section shape are certainly in dialogue with one another and the two together create increasingly interesting spatial, material, and lighting conditions. In my view, however, they do

↑ First set of drawings of the Ahmedabad Millowners' Association Building, Atelier Le Corbusier, March 7, 1952.

↗ Study of the second floor meeting hall, plan and partial section.

↘ Second floor plan showing the free-form of the meeting hall against the square building shape.

153 Frampton, "Le Corbusier and the Dialectical Imagination," *GA 37*, page 3 of the essay.

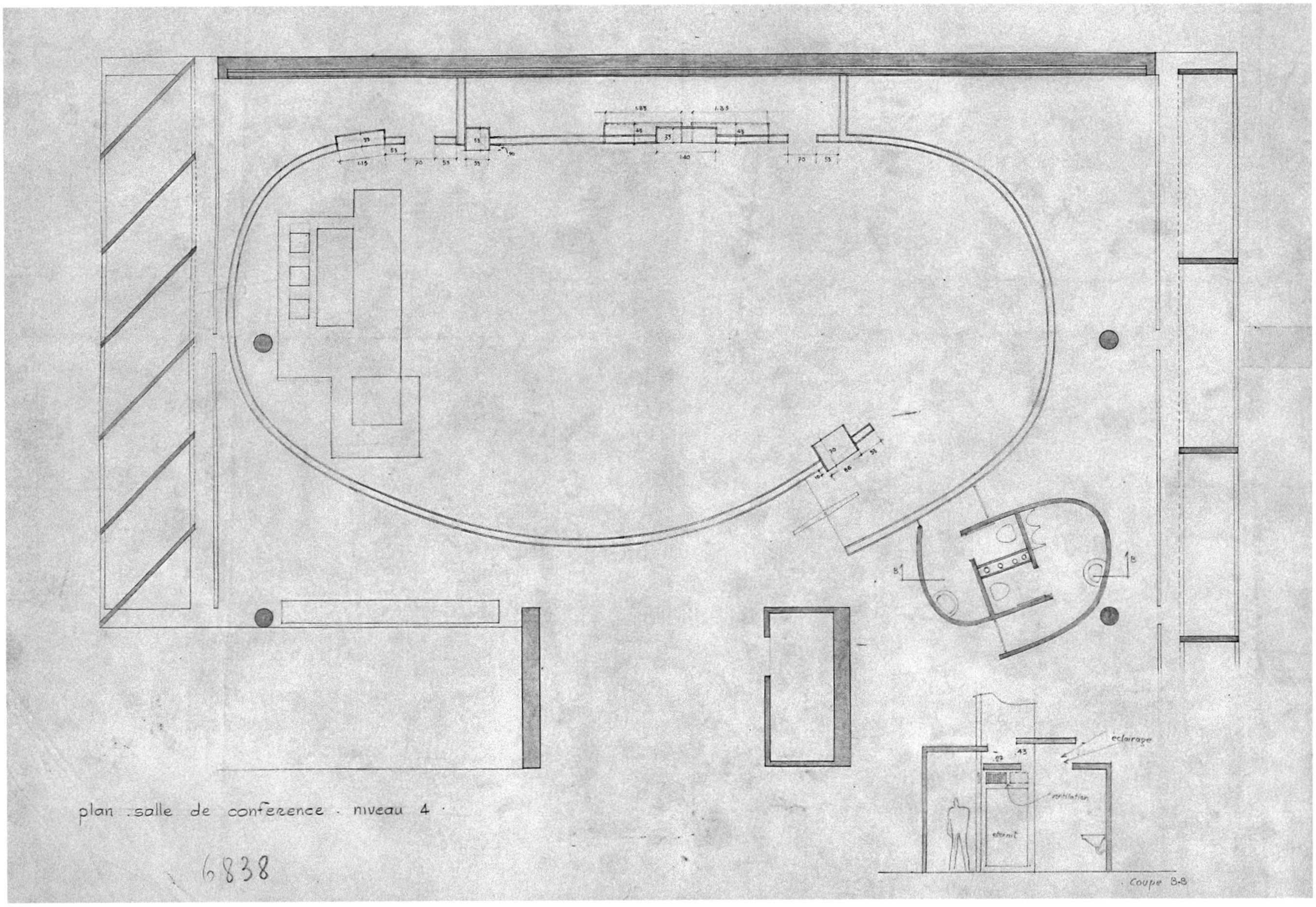

plan salle de conference niveau 4
6838
eclairage
ventilation
eternit
Coupe B-B

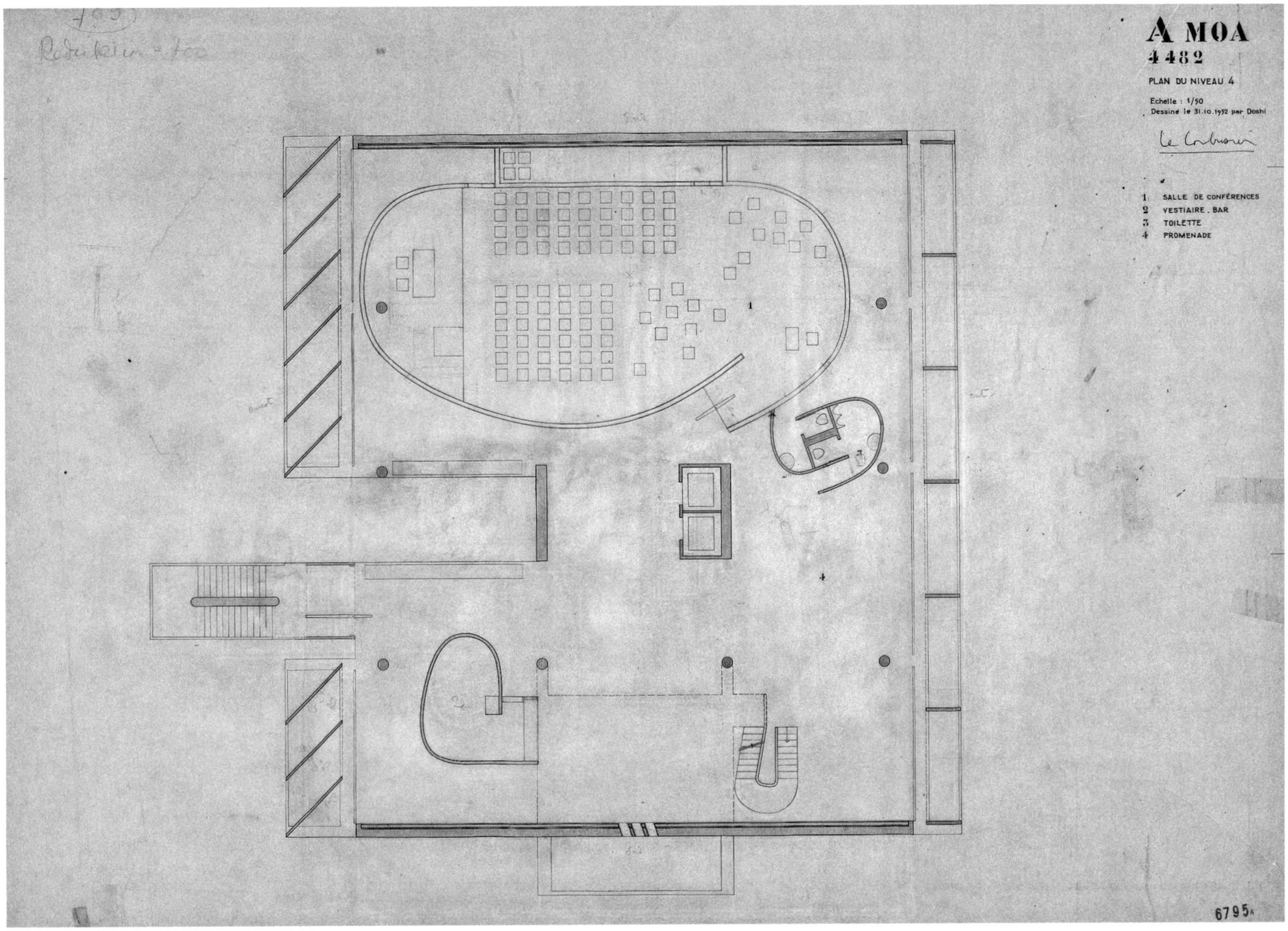

A MOA
4482
PLAN DU NIVEAU 4
Echelle : 1/50
Dessiné le 31.10.1952 par Doshi
Le Corbusier
1 SALLE DE CONFÉRENCES
2 VESTIAIRE . BAR
3 TOILETTE
4 PROMENADE
6795

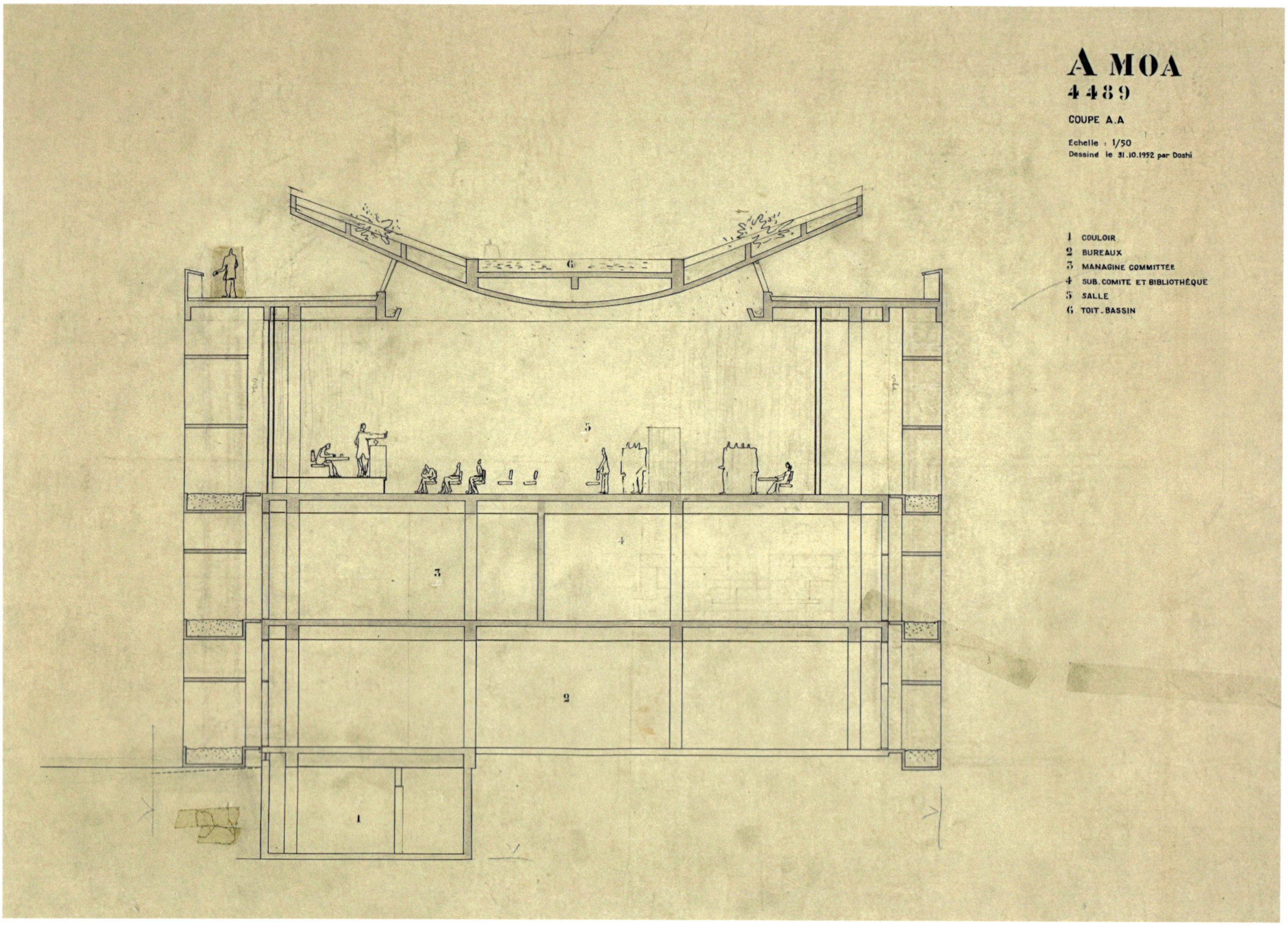

West–east section through the second floor meeting hall.

not belong to contrasting sides of an oppositional structure; they are on the same side and face the utility of the building's structure on the other side. One defines space and form in the horizontal; the other, in the vertical.

The same may be said about the way "the concrete exterior stands in strong contrast to the stone-faced interior."[154] There is clearly a contrast between the two materials. The question remains whether this contrast constitutes a decisive dialectical structure. The exterior brise-soleil, ramp, stair, and floor slabs are concrete, but the north and south walls of the building are brick and so are the cafeteria walls. In the interior, the north and south walls are faced with stone, as Frampton notes, but other walls are concrete; some contain wood cabinetry; others are plastered, painted, and so on. So, in my view, the contrast is simply that: a contrast. It does not contribute to a decisive dialectical structure set up by Le Corbusier to place the utilitarian world of the engineer and the plastic artistry of the architect in tension. Frampton's essay is a short study of the building and is not meant to be exhaustive and detailed. Considering the dialectical structure that Frampton foregrounds, I will explore the main architectural themes in the Ahmedabad Millowners' Association Building in the context of eleven dual conditions decisively and strategically set up by Le Corbusier.

154 Frampton, "Le Corbusier and the Dialectical Imagination," *GA 37*, page 4 of the essay.

↘ Party-wall diagram emphasizing west-east flows from Ashram Road to the Sabarmati River. The building presents two open sides and two closed sides.

ELEVEN DUAL CONDITIONS

1 OPEN-CLOSED (PARTY WALL)

Although the Ahmedabad Millowners' Association Building does not share a wall with its neighbors and is separated from both the north and south lot lines by almost 6 meters, it was treated as a party-wall building from its inception.[155] Other commentators have compared it with Villa Cook from 1926,[156] a true party-wall building of Le Corbusier's in Boulogne. However, in Ahmedabad, we are dealing with a free-standing building with lot lines in proximity but not in an urban, party-wall condition. Both the Ahmedabad Millowners' Association Building's northern and southern faces are solid and opaque except for a single, large, protruding volume on the south side in the building's final form, which is almost entirely glazed. In the earliest drafted proposal from March 1952, *(ill. p. 72)* there are two large windows shown, one each, on the northern and southern faces on the main floor. Although there are many manifestations of this scheme throughout the development of the building, the north and south faces remain essentially opaque while, continuously, the east and west faces are primarily open. Although there is a large opening on the south side, and also volumes that are closed to the east and west, the building essentially remained in this dual condition from its inception: a square-shaped plan with two open and two closed faces.

155 A party wall is one that separates two adjacent buildings that share the wall, the wall being owned by two parties. This is a common condition in urban buildings – for example, typical town-houses share a party wall.

156 Villa Cook is a small, single-family residence in Boulogne built in 1926. It incorporates all five of Le Corbusier's "five points": pilotis; free plan; free façade; roof garden; and the continuous, horizontal window.

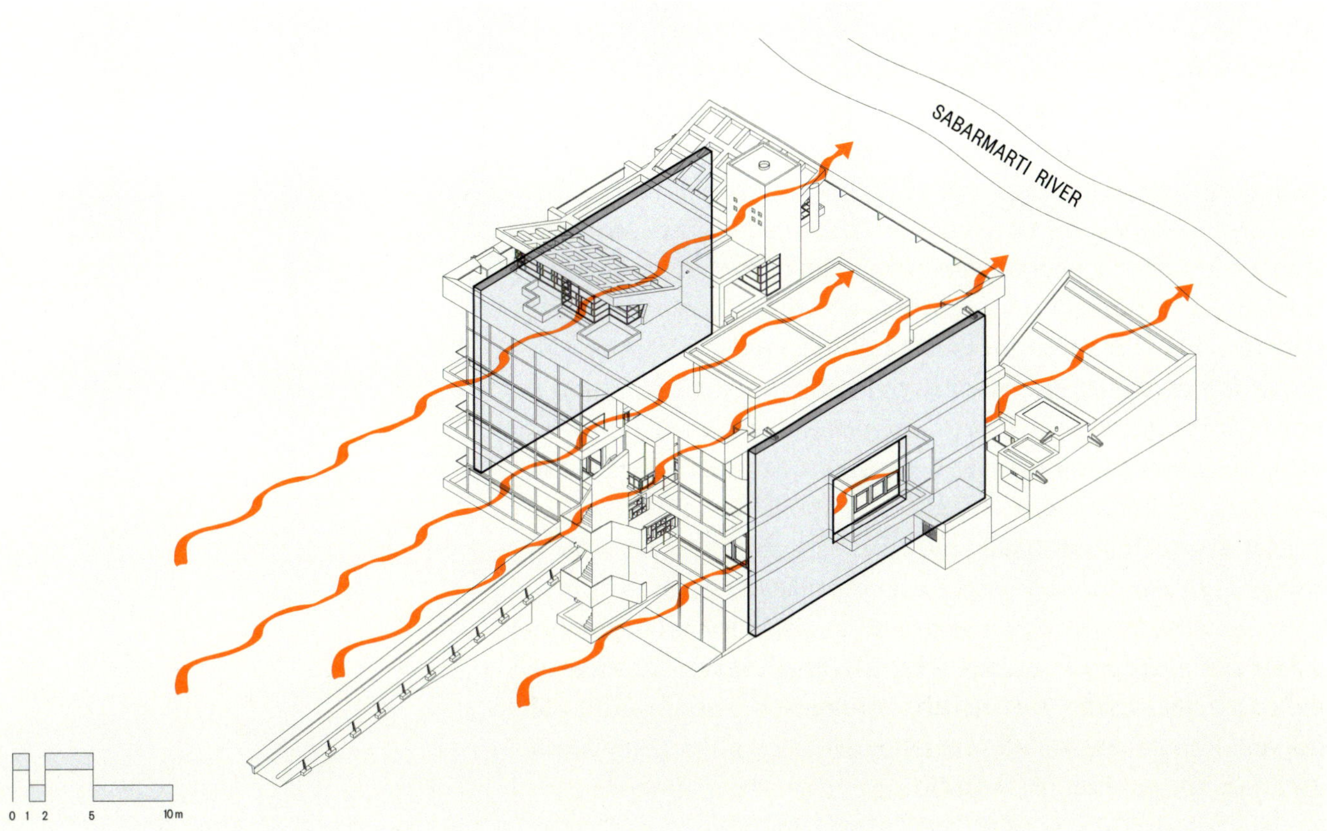

↖ View from the southeast, highlighting the role of the east-west brick party wall in dissolving the corner condition. The brick wall does not meet a north-south wall to define a corner.

↑ Northwest view, showing the dissolved corner. The space of the interior continues un-interrupted to the exterior, along the brick party wall.

The dual condition set up by Le Corbusier remains a defining characteristic of the building from the beginning. The party-wall condition may be understood as a way of maintaining privacy from neighbors in an urban location. This, certainly, has come to be prudent as the area has developed immensely over the past almost seventy years and there are tall, neighboring buildings all around in what is now a densely populated city. However, there is a more formal and sculptural reason for this seemingly pragmatic, utilitarian approach. The building's organizational logic is pushed to extremes by making two of its sides essentially closed and two open. The building is conceptually open west to east. Its open-to-air spaces are all open in a west-east direction. The second floor has no walls in the north-south direction (except the two lateral, structural concrete walls described below in Section 5: Column-Wall.) In general, the "party-wall condition" defines a direction for the building, which is west-east: entrance, ramp, circulation, views, movement, breezes, light. Perhaps most importantly, in terms of architectural vocabulary, the "party-wall condition" avoids corners: there is either wall or glazing/open. There are a few exceptions but, in general, spaces flow along a wall and are not captured or contained by a perpendicular wall; rather, they continue along and beyond the surface of the wall - sometimes far beyond the end of the wall, to the Sabarmati River or to Ashram Road. This continuity of space and the impossibility of its containment defines the Ahmedabad Millowners' Association Building. The space of the building starts at the street, flows through the building in a west-east direction, and continues beyond to the

↓ Early perspective sketch, March 10, 1952, showing the main floor elevated from the ground.

river and the opposite bank of the Sabarmati. What may initially appear as a solely pragmatic and utilitarian decision is not only that but also a formal/sculptural one.

2 UPPER-LOWER (URBAN PALACE)

Although the building has consistently been documented in all Atelier Le Corbusier drawings as Ahmedabad Millowners' Association Building (AMOA), it appears in all French-language documents, including the *Œuvre Complète,* as Palais de l'Association des Filateurs d'Ahmedabad. The French title identifies it as a palace, while the English labels it as a building. As enumerated in his *Une Maison – Un Palais,*[157] Le Corbusier extended his architectural ideas, which he had tested in private houses, to the palace, a building of public stature, and eventually to large public buildings and the city. The Ahmedabad Millowners' Association Building, for Le Corbusier, was indeed an urban palace. Its ownership was private, but its program included the public. In this sense, we must understand the building in relationship to the public moving about and through it: the building as a milling space![158]

As an urban palace, the "noble floor" – *piano nobile* from the Italian palazzos and its equivalent in French architecture, *bel étage* – appears in the building from the first sketch. The main floor of the building is lifted from the ground and a long entrance ramp elevates the visitor to the first floor (in US parlance this would be the "second floor"). The same "class" division that separated the noble from the damp and dark earth and street life and lifted it to the "noble floor" in Italian palaces is at work here. The ground floor in these initial studies is labeled for "clerical offices" with their own separate "staff lavatories."[159] This division of classes is less overtly present in the

157 Le Corbusier, *Une Maison – Un Palais* (Paris: Éditions G. Crès, Collection de "L'Esprit Nouveau," 1928).
158 I am indebted to Kenneth Frampton for this reading of the building.
159 All of the building drawings document "caretakers' residences" near the street on the west side of the building, north of the ramp on the ground floor. Despite multiple studies, the residences were not constructed.

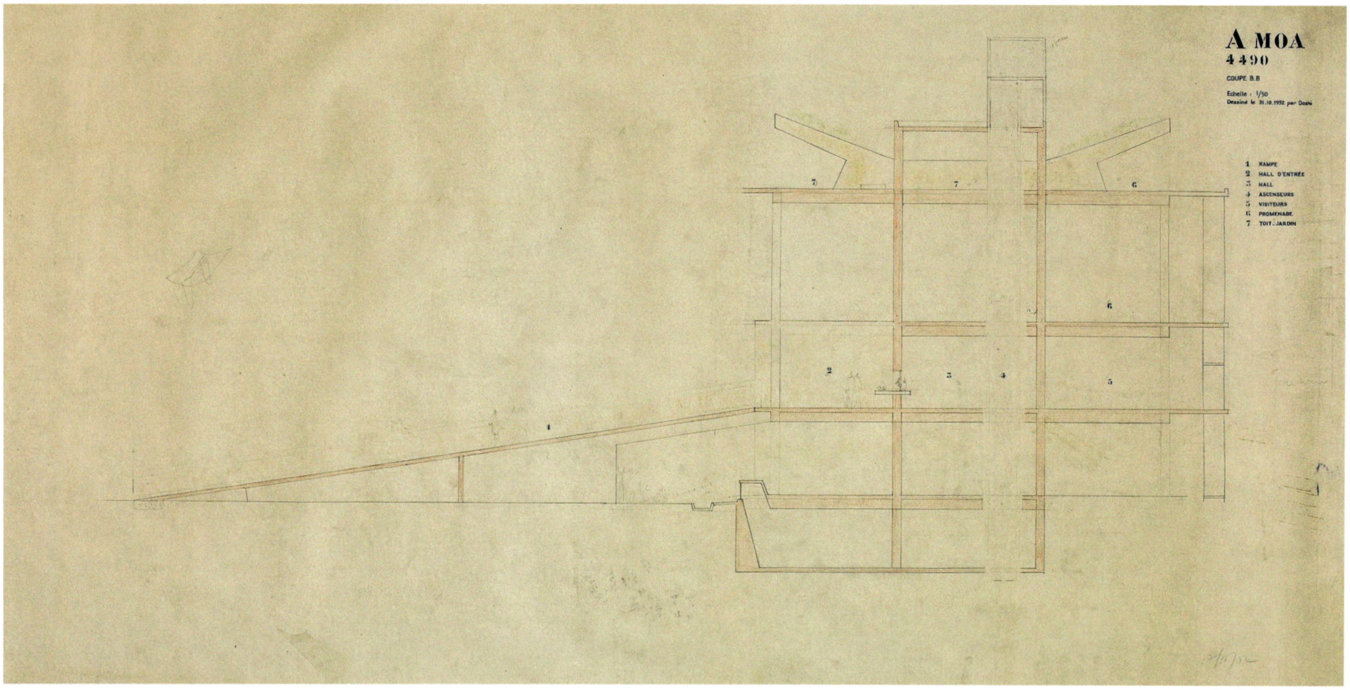

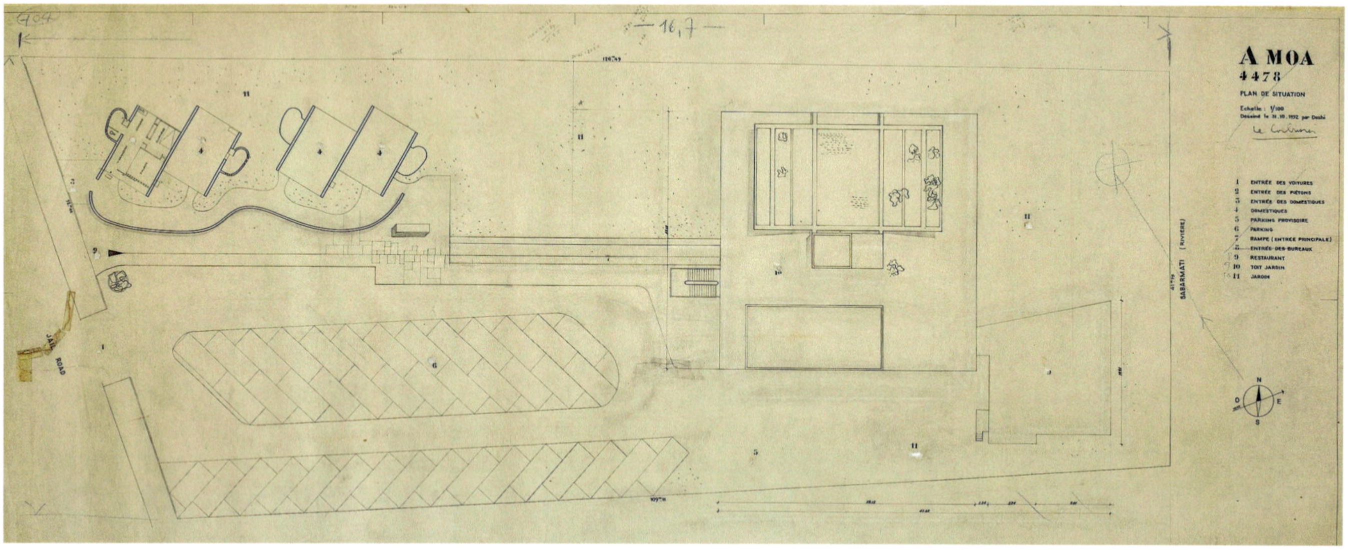

current building program, with its modifications made in the 1970s, but nonetheless, the "noble floor" remains with the distinctive ramp that elevates the visitor to the main entrance "lobby" of the building.

This architectural move is at the same time traditional and, as described above, utilitarian; yet, given the architectural element of the ramp, it is formally novel in its execution. Avoiding street life and its "classes" has a long history in architecture and can be categorized as utilitarian if one believes in separating socio-economic classes. On the other hand, this ascent from the street and entry on to the first floor is generally contained within the volume of the building in palazzos and other urban structures. One enters the building from the street and then ascends a set of ornamental and palatial stairs to the "noble floor." At the Ahmedabad Millowners' Association Building, one steps onto a concrete ramp well outside of the building volume, an elongated extension of what would have been the building's vertical circulation core, ascending to the first floor in the exterior space

↑↑ West-east section through the entrance ramp and the arrival platform on the first floor, showing how visitors may go from the street, up the ramp, through the breezeway towards the Sabarmati views, without ever entering an enclosed space in the building, 1952 study.

↑ Site plan. October 31, 1952. (The caretaker apartments at the northwestern corner of the site were never constructed.)

before ever entering the building. Although ramps were not novel and were used in industrial complexes to move goods, they were novel to the architecture of buildings with cultural aspirations. Borrowing from the methodologies in his Purist paintings, Le Corbusier juxtaposes a "found" industrial element with the architecture of the building. In this case, the dual condition is in the tradition of the "noble floor" accessed via a ceremonial stair within the volume of the building vs. the industrial ramp outside the building. The compositional tactic, the organizational and utilitarian decision to move the main floor one flight up is juxtaposed with the compositional tactic of superimposing several industrial building components, each as an independent element, on a site plan conceived as a canvas that would permit this formal play.

3 SUN-SHADE (SOLAR ORIENTATION)

Despite the persistent set of notes about climatic conditions in India and their effects on architecture – intense midday heat, late-afternoon summer sun penetration, and the solar-orientation markings on every drawing – the building privileges its urban context over its climatic conditions. As argued in previous sections, the building's deportment is that of an urban palace. Its site is a long rectangle with its short sides facing Ashram Road (west side) and the Sabarmati River (east side). A building on an open site respecting solar orientation would have taken advantage of the north side, the side most protected from the sun, and also would have avoided the west side with the low summer sun heating up the depth of the interior in the late afternoons. In this case, however, despite all the notes and conversations about privileging the climate, Le Corbusier favored the "urban palace" condition. The party-wall condition mentioned above is an urban move, ostensibly to protect the privacy of the building from close neighbors (I have presented an additional argument regarding its use in Section 1, p. 75). As a result, the building is exposed to the east and the west. From the earliest drafted drawings from March 1952, Le Corbusier introduces brise-soleil: sun-shading elements. In these early drawings, the brise-soleil are horizontal and mimic the ones he was designing for Chandigarh. *(ill. p. 77)* Horizontal brise-soleil are efficient in mitigating midday southern sun, shining from above. But the real mitigating agent for morning (eastern) and evening (western) sun needs to be vertical, in order to provide shade from the almost horizontal sun shining directly from east and west. This building, from its inception, was organized to have two open sides, east and west, and two closed sides, north and south – essentially admitting morning and evening sun into the depths of its interior. This of course had to be mitigated through the architectural design and the brise-soleil. The building organization worked against the fundamentals of solar orientation and this had to be accommodated otherwise. What appears, in Le Corbusier's proclamations, to

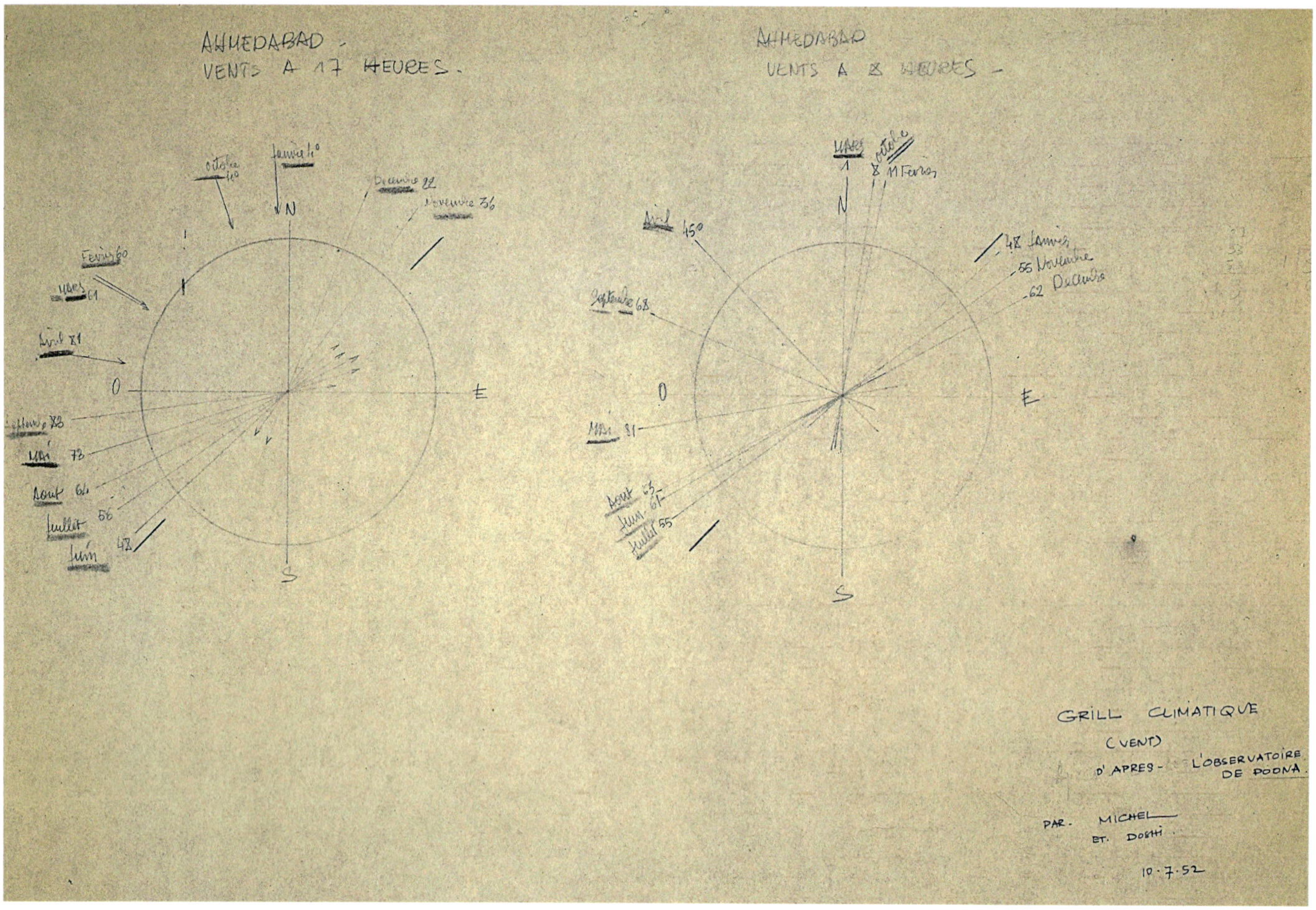

Le Corbusier's recording of sun angles in Ahmedabad, based on information from Poona observatory.

be an adherence to climatic conditions is only engaged for as long as it serves the architectural concerns of the building. When it doesn't, it is addressed as a secondary concern – as is the case here, with the Ahmedabad Millowners' Association Building.

Moreover, the river, the street, and the urban condition of the site play a major role in the building's organization. The first floor ("noble floor"/*piano nobile*/*bel étage*) is a crucial element in the entrance and circulation system within the building. Entering from the street (west side), one ascends a single-run ramp starting from the ground up into the building, arriving on the first floor with an open breezeway continuing straight through to the east side of the building, providing expansive views of the Sabarmati River – all protected by the upper floor and the roof.[160] *(ill. p. 161 bottom)* This breezeway space is also visually connected to the riverfront garden on the east side, the same one that is noted for "garden parties" in the first sketch in sketchbook E25. *(ill. p. 71)* Despite the stated climatic concerns and proclamations, the Ahmedabad Millowners' Association Building's foundational organization is urban, programmatic, and circulation based. One could even go as far so to say it is historically based in organizations that were much more about societal class divisions than climatically driven. Yet, this is not to say that climate and climatic considerations did not play a role in the building; they simply played a more minor one than was proclaimed. Despite the early versions that contained horizontal brise-soleil, the

160 We know from photographs from the 1950s that the building was very close to the river, with the retaining walls on its east side at the riverfront. Currently, with Prime Minister Narendra Modi's economic liberalization and Western-style urban renewal, there are lanes of roadways, a median, and a vast zone between the Millowners' Association Building and the river – including, during my visit in 2019, an entertainment complex with bouncy castles and trampoline parks. The river boundaries have been relocated and controlled by constructed concrete banks.

↑ Partial east façade, with mid-morning sun casting shadows on columns and the meeting hall enclosure.

↓ View from the second floor mezzanine interior through the brise-soleil towards the Sabarmati River.

↑ Interior view from second floor mezzanine with mid-morning sun. Here, the depth of space is emphasized through the cast shadows of building elements onto interior volumes.

↓ Interior view from second floor, showing the play of light and shadow on the architectural volumes.

↑ West façade detail, with afternoon sun making the brise-soleil appear like a volume. The same element appears completely see-through in the morning without sun and shade.

↓ Façade close-up, with afternoon winter sun casting shadows on brise-soleil.

final version has vertical, steeply angled shading devices that mitigate the afternoon western sun. The horizontal eastern brise-soleil, however, remain ineffective and are used primarily for aesthetic reasons: what Frampton calls "appliqué."[161] The building is designed around a set of climatic and formal/sculptural concerns which constantly struggle for primacy. The tension created in this struggle is what holds the building together. There are no formal/sculptural decisions that do not also affect climatic/utilitarian forces, and no climatic/utilitarian decisions that do not affect sculptural ones. The brise-soleil on both the east and west sides create depth of space through the cast shadows of multiple objects in multiple layers onto multiple surfaces.

4 OPEN-CLOSED (WIND ORIENTATION)

From the very early drafted drawings, every directional symbol (north arrow) also includes a prevailing wind direction. This is drawn with a sinuous line crossing the center of the intersecting lines defining north-south and east-west directions. In the Ahmedabad Millowners' Association Building, the sinuous line has a southwest to northeast direction with an arrow at its northeastern end. Air movement as much as solar orientation, informs the building in this hot climate. It is the source of cooling for most buildings of the period in Ahmedabad. Hardly any structures of the Ahmedabad Millowners' Association Building's size in that climatic part of the world were hermetically sealed or utilized a mechanical cooling system. Almost all of them relied on temperature control through sun-shading and breezes.

Although Le Corbusier's early career was invested with an "enthusiasm for 'international scientific techniques' as premises of a truly international architecture, he seems to have quickly returned to the more elementary techniques of environmental control."[162] His concept of "air exact" from the early 1930s, which Le Corbusier tried to implement in the "Cité de Refuge" building in Paris, relied entirely on mechanical techniques of temperature and humidity control. After that period, he relied more on passive environmental systems. The Ahmedabad Millowners' Association Building presents an interesting case where two systems are utilized and mixed. Some of the building's enclosed interior spaces are mechanically conditioned with a passive, indirect, evaporative cooling system, with cooling/spray ponds in the eastern end of the garden at the river's edge.[163] *(ill. p. 153 top)* At the same time, the entire building is considered in relation to shading, air movements, and passive cooling.

Although in the drawings from March 1952 *(ill. p. 72)* we see absolutely no formal response to the wind direction, in later iterations we see brise-soleil on the west façade that orient towards the breeze, almost guiding the wind into the building volume from the southwest. The same brise-soleil orientation is also the result of

161 Frampton, "Le Corbusier and the Dialectical Imagination," page 4 of the essay.

162 Von Moos, *Le Corbusier: Elements of a Synthesis,* 93.

163 The spray-cooling ponds are currently in the yard to the east of the building but are not present on any of the original drawings, nor are the related well and pump stations. Three air conditioning systems were noted on drawing #AMOA 4594 from November 30, 1953: two on the south side for the president's, vice-president's, and secretaries' offices; and one located in the middle of the first floor to accommodate the offices, and managing committee room, and the sub-committee room (currently used as a gallery). These three systems utilized an evaporative-cooling system from their inception but were piped to a cooling pond in the 1970s under the direction of B. V. Doshi's office, which managed the conversion of the ground floor clerical offices into the current auditorium. There is also a fourth system present in the auditorium on the ground floor, installed as a part of the same alteration in the 1970s by B. V. Doshi's office. Even though all the air conditioning systems were operational until recently, none are currently serviceable and have been replaced by contemporary "split" units, thus rendering the evaporative-cooling ponds no longer useful.

→ Sun studies documenting angles and sun penetration at 4pm on the equinox and the summer (presumably solstice) at the Ahmedabad Millowners' Association Building.

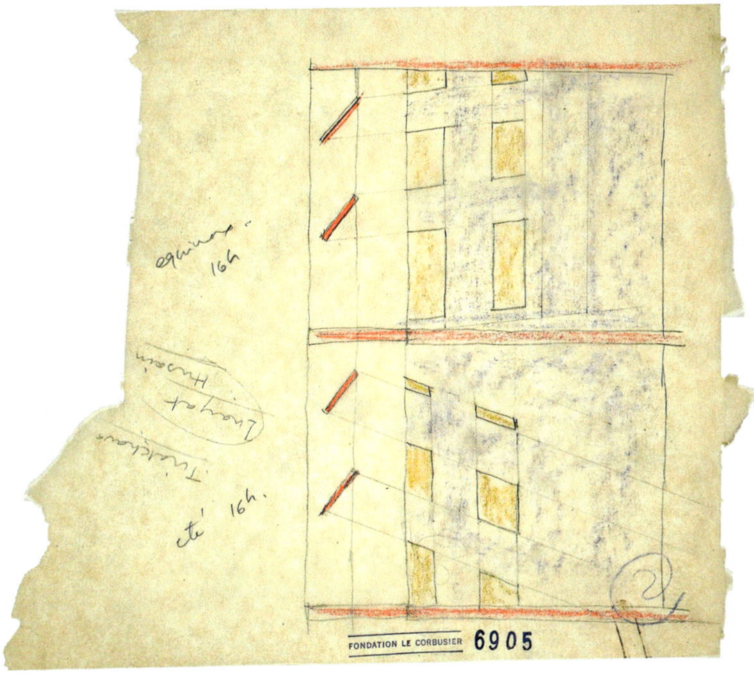

many recorded sun studies that carefully gauge the size, repetition, and angle of the concrete brise-soleil.

Although brise-soleil are typically used to create shade, it is clear that in this case, the angle, repetition, and length of the elements reflects not only shading concerns but also wind direction. Without the breezes, the direction of the brise-soleil would have been perpendicular to their actual orientation. The party-wall conception that left the east and west sides open and the north and south sides closed also works to channel breezes into the building. There are studies from July 1952 that show the south side with several openings, each protected by vertical brise-soleil. These are anomalous in that southern building faces require horizontal rather than vertical shading devices, and also that the direction of brise-soleil as drawn on the south side actually block rather than permit breezes. The openings to the south and the corresponding brise-soleil do not reappear in later drawings. The first drafted drawings of March 7, 1952, describe approximately one half of each of the floors of the three-story building as open – in essence, dividing the building into two parts: open and enclosed. The two parts jog back and forth as they negotiate the building vertically. On the ground and second floors, the southern half is enclosed and the north half is open. On the first floor, the two middle bays are open and the two outer ones enclosed.

Although there are many iterations of the building organization between this early set and the final drawings of October 1954, half of each floor remained open to weather and air movement yet was sheltered from the sun and rain. Here, we see a very direct interplay between the two conditions of open and enclosed throughout the recorded history of the building's development. The utility of the brise-soleil, with their direction defined by solar orientation and

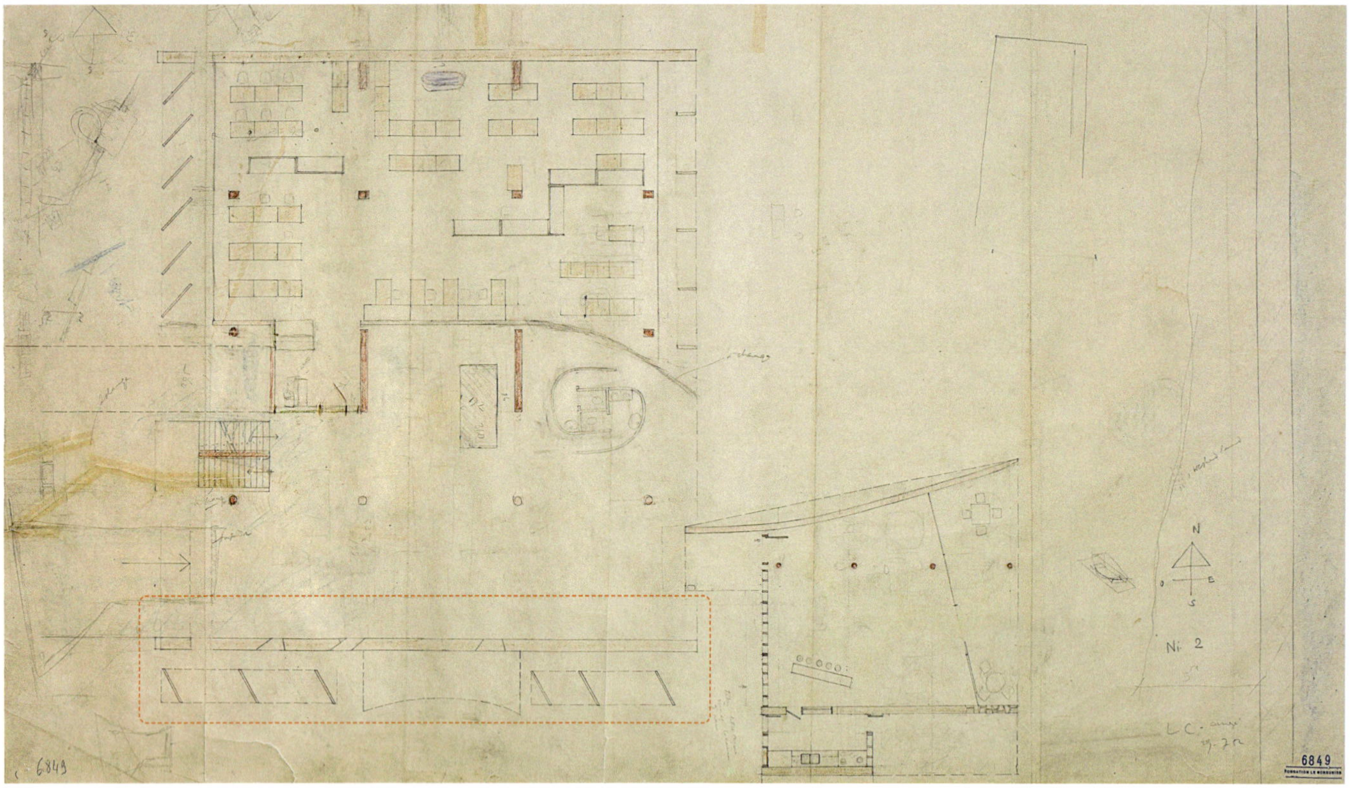

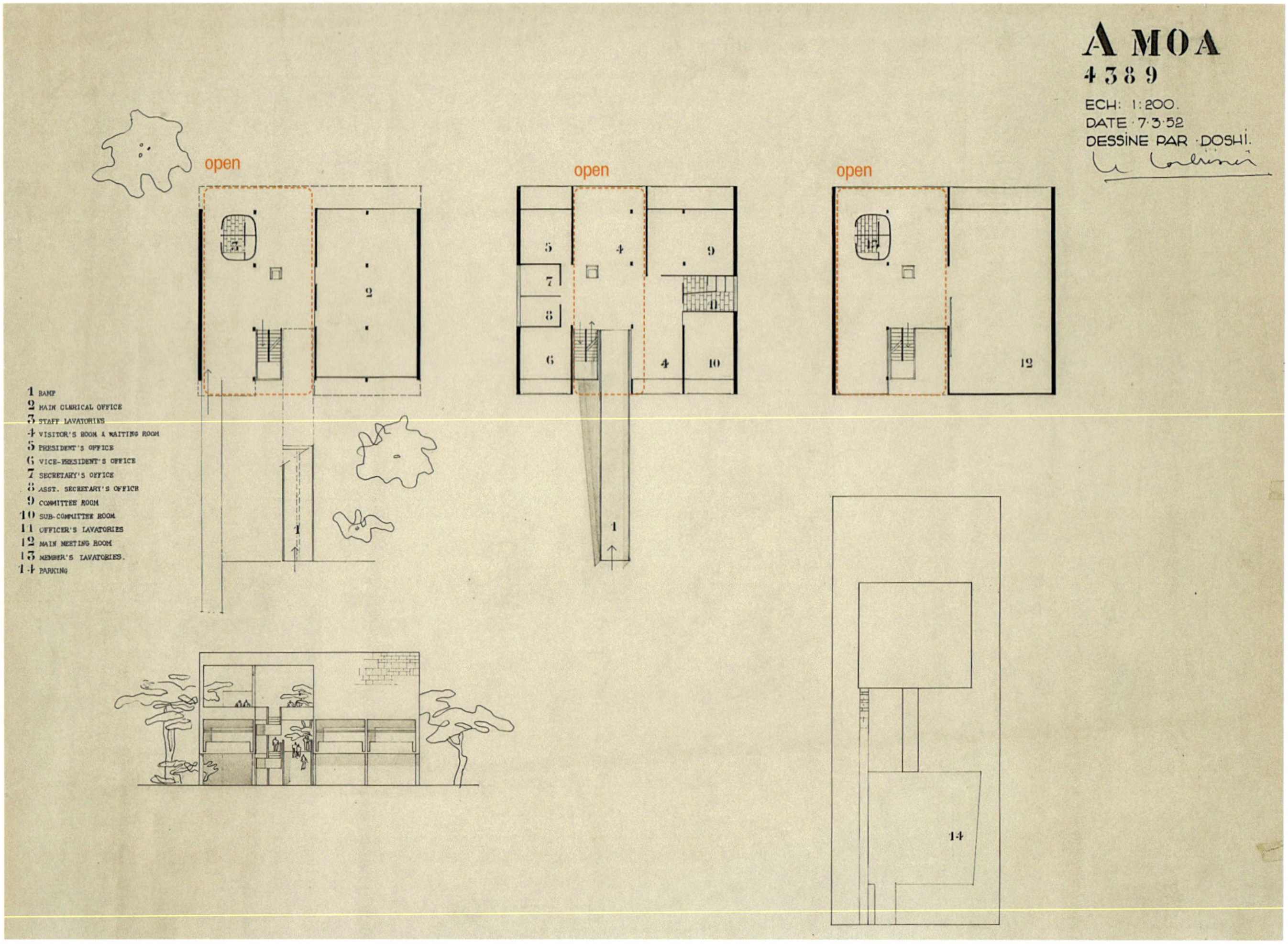

↑ Brise-soleil on south façade with randomized openings (highlights by author).

↓ Partial view of the first set of drafted drawings, March 7, 1952. The open areas on each of the three floors are highlighted by the author.

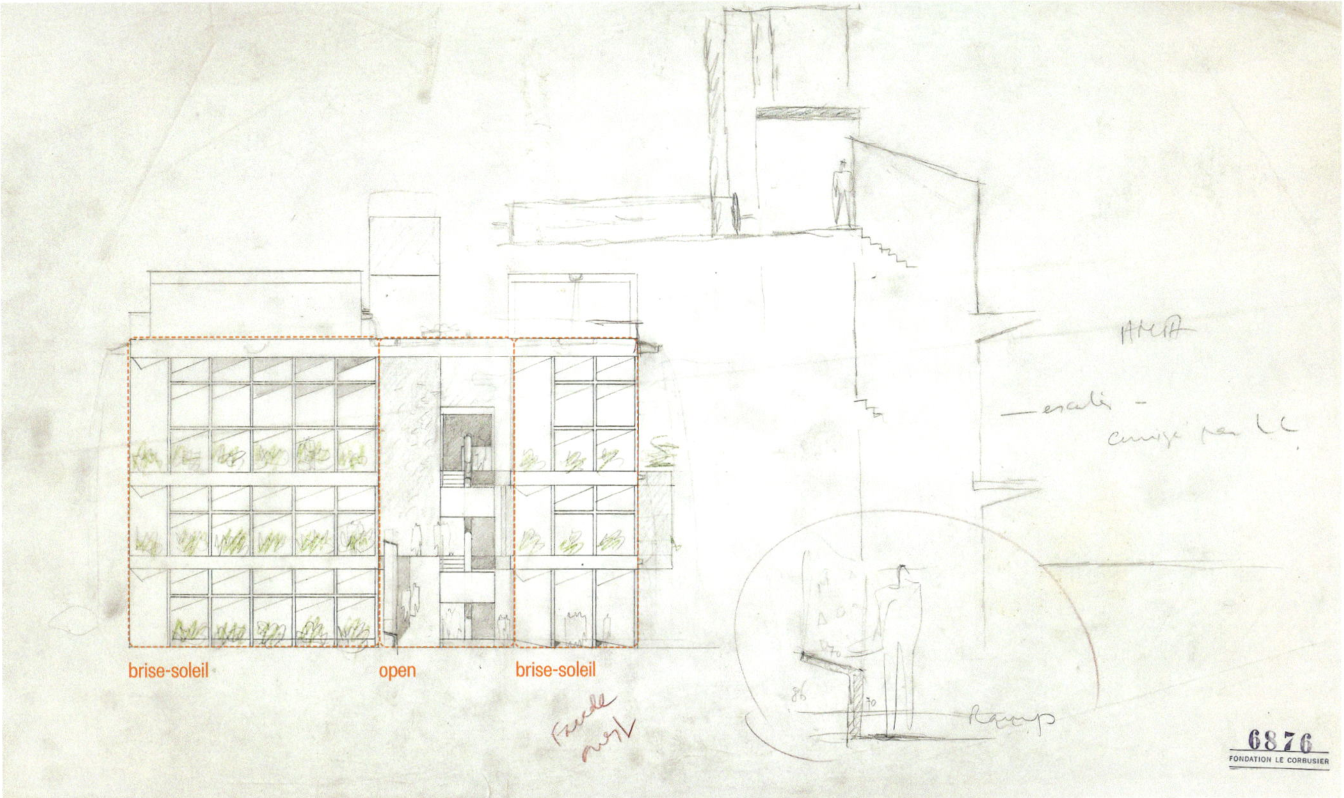

↑ January afternoon photograph from first floor breezeway, facing west towards the ramp and Ashram Road, showing how deep the afternoon sun penetrates the building.

↓ Study of the west elevation with brise-soleil, interrupted by an open space (highlighted) that houses the ramp and the stair (highlights by author).

breezes, is paired with their aesthetic presence on the west façade. Despite multiple studies that express the open interior spaces and breezeways on the façade by eliminating brise-soleil, the final version provides a clear, formal identity for the brise-soleil; however, not always related to the spaces they serve inside the building. *(ill. p. 166 top)* Two northern bays and one southern bay include brise-soleil from the ground to the roof, and the bay immediately to the south of center is left open from the ground to the roof. This invites the late-afternoon sun into the depth of the open spaces of the building yet the brise-soleil provides unnecessary shading for an already enclosed meeting hall concrete wall. On the ground floor, the breezeway is shaded, but on the first and second floors, the sun can penetrate into the open breezeway.

In other words, despite all the sun and wind studies that guide the size and orientation of the brise-soleil, their final form is sculpted aesthetically. This is not to say that the brise-soleil do not play a role in the environmental conception of the building, rather that their shaping is not only due to environmental concerns but also heavily influenced by aesthetic ones. Here again, we see a tension between utilitarian and aesthetic concerns. Together, and in their push-and-pull and tension, they shape the building.

5 COLUMN-WALL (THE BUILDING'S STRUCTURE)

The building's structure is a concrete frame, essentially a three-dimensional linear grid made of reinforced concrete. However, this grid system is not presented as such and incorporates several deviations that serve structural, formal, and aesthetic purposes. The building plan shape, as built, is an absolute square,[164] leading one to imagine a uniform grid of columns equally distanced. This is not the case. On the east and west façades, brise-soleil are present, which offsets the column line into the building by 4 meters on the west side and 3 meters on the east. So, quickly, the square plan shape turns into a rectangle. Despite the change of plan shape from March 1952 to May 1952, from an original rectangle to the final square, the structural grid remained the same: a 5 × 4 grid, five in the north-south direction and four in the east-west. Column spacing is also not uniform, despite any assumptions one may have had about the square plan. There are many different column spacings present throughout the development. However, final drawings and as-built conditions present two column spacings. The central north-south bay is wider than others and so is the off-center east-west bay that includes the circulation. This highlights the circulation spine and gives it more space as it leads the visitor into the core of the building.

The columns themselves remain round and uniform in size, suggesting an equal load uniformly distributed on all sides. Of course, we know this not to be the case. Circular columns in a square-

164 The first set of drawings from March 7, 1952 records a rectangular-shaped plan. But by May 6 of the same year, two months later, the site plan records a square-shaped plan which was maintained through the building's completion.

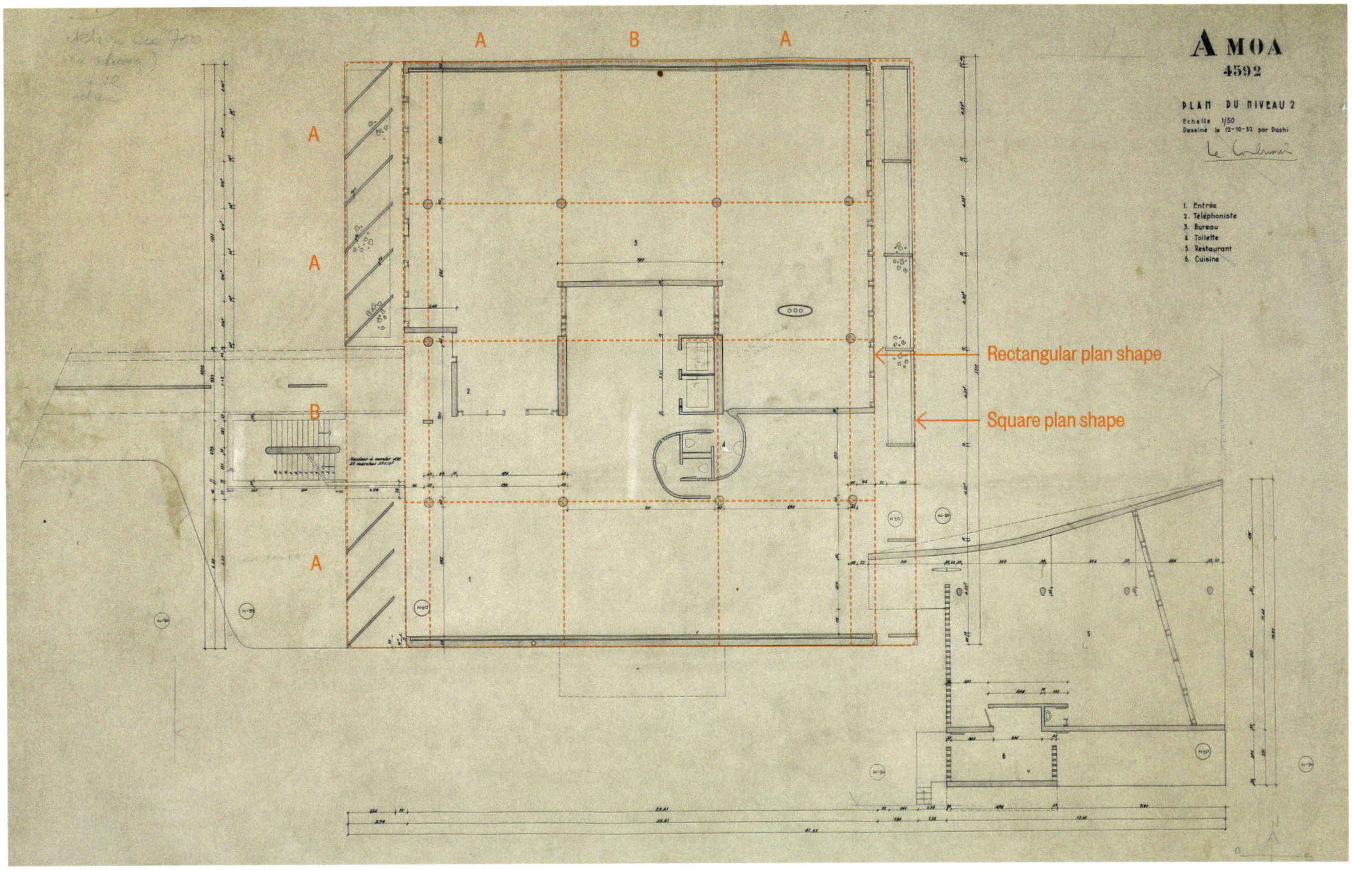

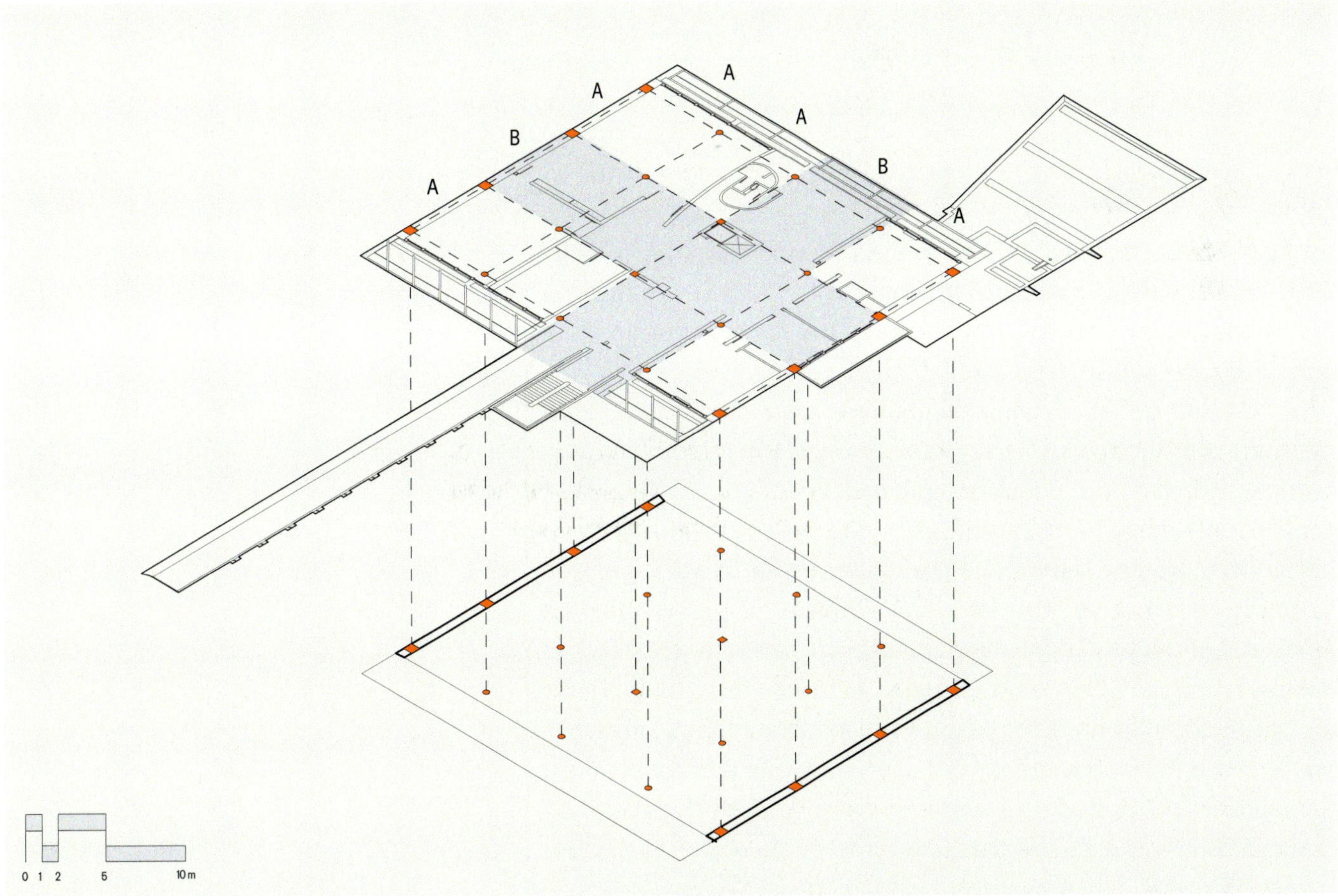

↑ Ground floor plan with dimensions, October 12, 1952. Structural grid and the two different bay sizes are highlighted. Also documented are the square exterior and the rectangular interior building shapes.

↓ Column spacing diagram marking the wider circulation bays in gray.

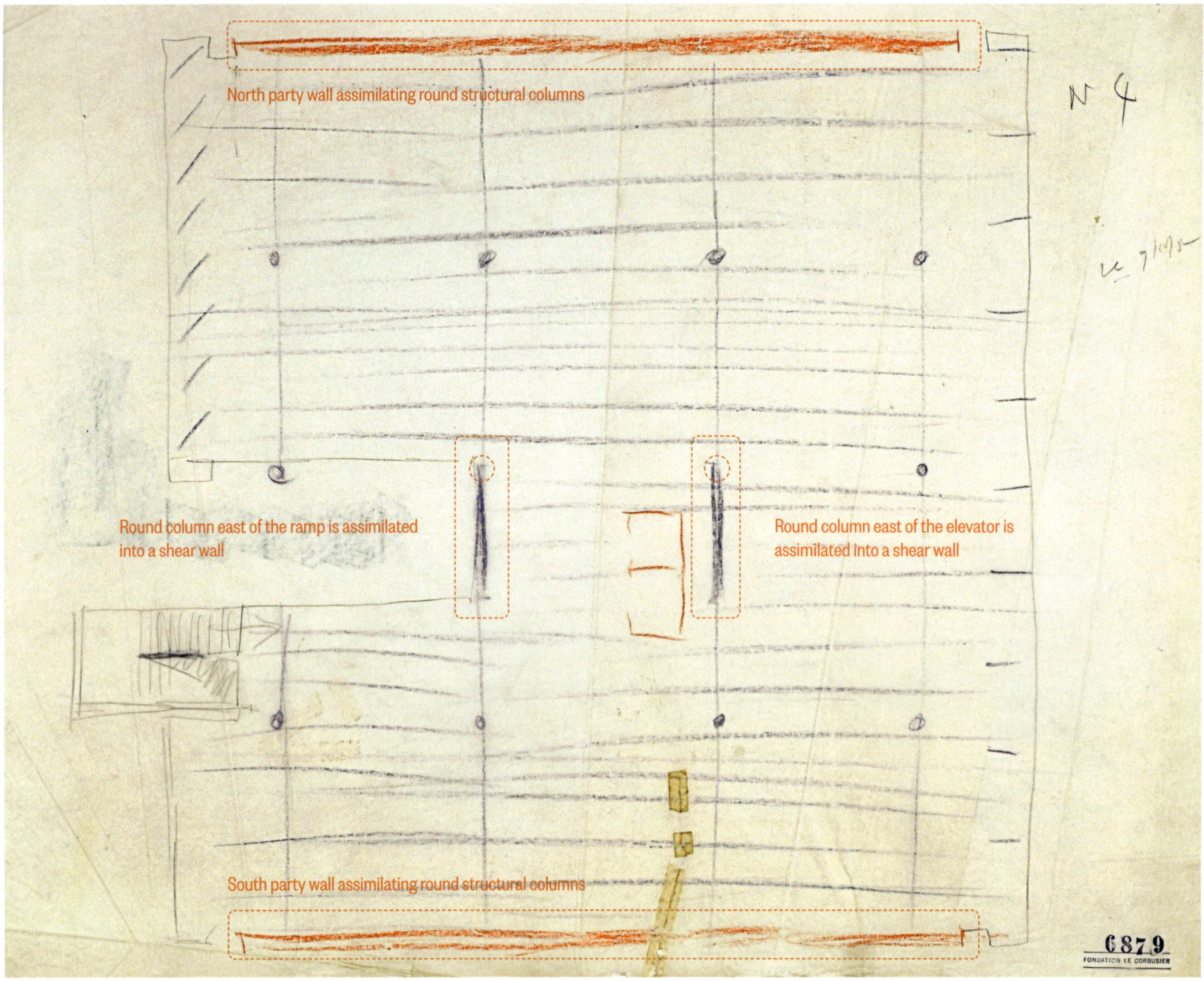

Early structural study, showing columns, north-south beams, and east-west joists. Later revised to east-west and north-south beams and slabs (highlights by author).

shaped building present an idea of structural uniformity which is here present only as a proclamation and not as a reality. In fact, of the twenty columns, only a maximum of two have similar loading conditions. *(ill. p. 89)*

In the first iteration of the building from March 1952, both internal and external east-west walls assimilate the columns, so they are no longer visible as columns; they read as walls. In the final 1954 version, only the perimeter north and south walls (party walls) incorporate the columns and the internal east-west walls are separated from the columns, so their columnar aesthetic is preserved. The north and south party walls appear as brick from the outside and incorporate stone facing on the interior. In other words, the columns are completely obscured and have no structural or aesthetic presence on the two north and south party walls – although the floors do. In the interior spaces, however, their presence is carefully preserved, except for a few critical aesthetic/structural moments.

1 The column directly in front of the ramp is incorporated into a concrete wall. The round concrete column thus disappears into a rectangular concrete wall. The concrete wall, with its

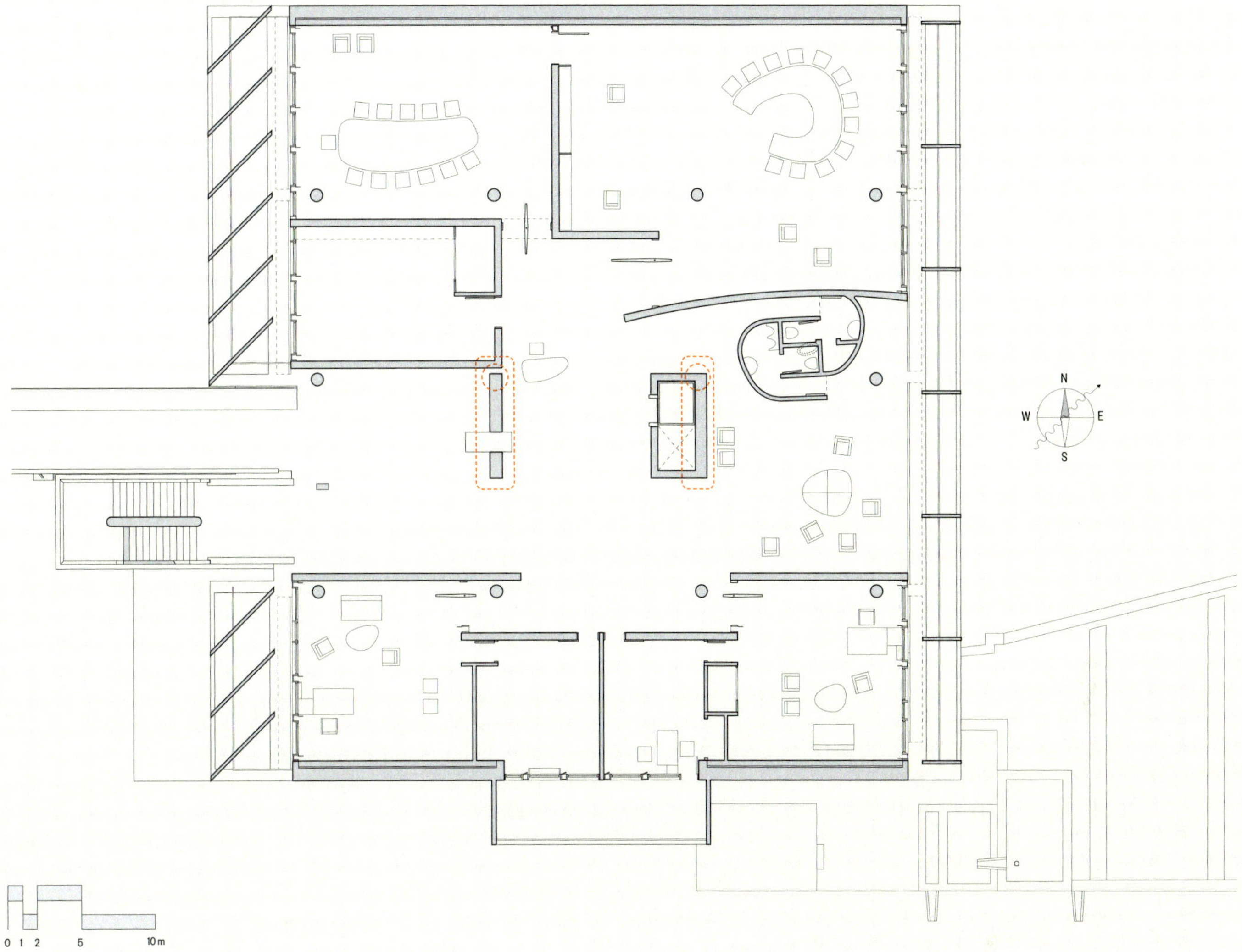

First floor plan, highlighting two shear walls with assimilated columns.

substantial and massive appearance, certainly exudes structure but in fact is also an aesthetic device working with the ramp and the stair, marking where a typical building's vertical-circulation system would have been had it not been drawn out of the building. This same wall, although without vertical load-bearing responsibility, acts as a shear wall, resisting lateral loads. So, despite its lack of vertical load bearing, it does serve a structural purpose but one that is different to that of the other columns.

2 The column directly east of the one mentioned above has been treated similarly, as a part of a rectangular concrete wall, but it does not carry the same aesthetic proposal as the first. This one is in play with the elevator. Since the very first drawings of the building, the elevator is imagined as a separate element disconnected and separated from other walls and the columnar structure of the interior – in essence, a kind of legible building element on its own: a figure within the space of the interior. Late in 1952, there are drawings that combine the elevator and the structural wall mentioned above. However, later, the two separate again. Clearly, there

is an aesthetic desire to maintain the figural legibility of the elevator as a vertical architectural element. In the final iteration, however, the elevator and the wall merge into one and their identities fuse. A round column is assimilated into the east wall of the elevator shaft, thus obfuscating the formal and elemental legibility of both the column and the elevator in favor of the reduction of individual elements. As in Point 1 above, this wall also serves a lateral-stability purpose in addition to a vertical load-bearing responsibility. It is reminiscent of elevator cores we know today, which serve as lateral shear walls.

3 On the second floor (top floor below the roof), there is a large "meeting hall," also described as a congregation space. As a large space, it simply does not fit within the column grid and spans the area of almost two column bays in the north-south direction. If the column spacing had been maintained, this would have meant two columns appearing in the middle of the meeting hall – something very undesirable from a functional standpoint. Le Corbusier eliminated these two columns. Given there are no additional floors above the space, the missing columns only needed to carry the weight of the roof. In a very clever move, Le Corbusier lifted the roof of the meeting hall, providing the depth for a thicker beam to span the two open bays. This also permitted a very desirable clerestory, lighting-from-above condition for the meeting hall. It is the most breathtaking lighting situation in the entire building. The added weight of the inverted-arch concrete roof is supported by the structure of the north wall and the two concrete walls mentioned above (in Points 1 and 2). Here, we see why it was important to assimilate the round columns into the two concrete walls: so they may support the added load of the meeting hall roof in addition to serving as shear walls.

Additionally, structures not only carry loads down to earth but they must also resist lateral loads, sideways forces from the wind, earthquakes, and such. The two long east-west party walls, in addition to carrying loads vertically, also serve as lateral shear walls and resist lateral forces in the east-west direction. The two concrete walls mentioned above (Points 1 and 2) serve the same role in the other direction, resisting lateral north-south forces.

What initially appear as aesthetic decisions that do not follow the logic of the structure in fact turn out to be nuanced approaches to both aesthetic and structural concerns and solutions, whereby the two are so intertwined and layered that they can no longer be taken apart. The tension between the two – the utilitarian, structural logic and the aesthetic, sculptural logic – holds the entire building together.

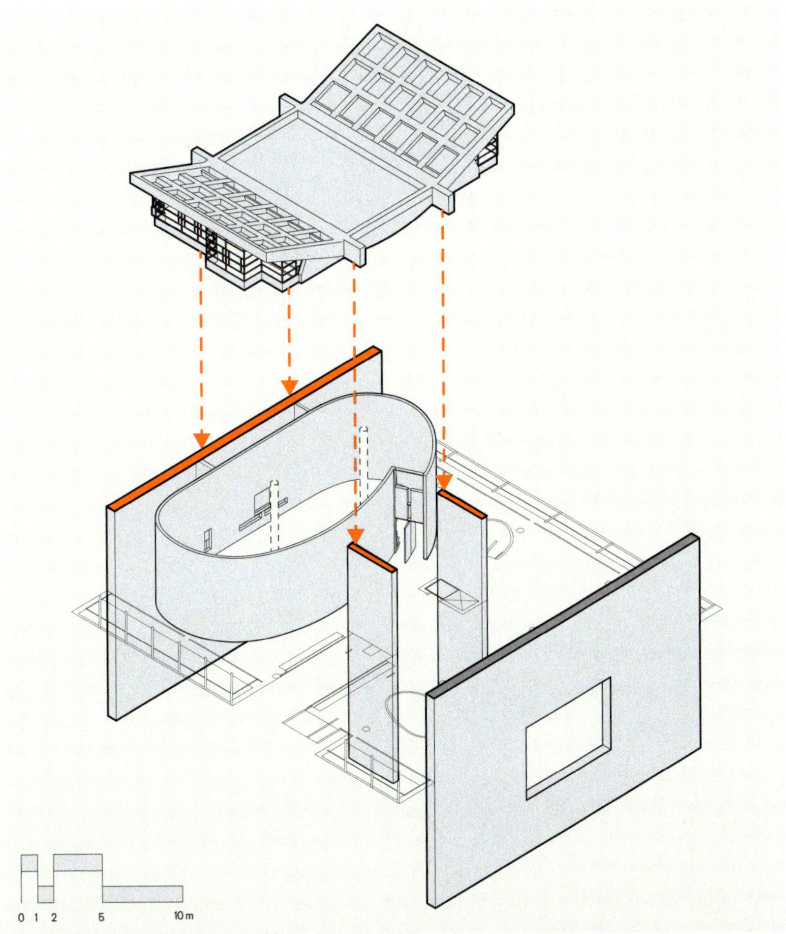

← Second floor meeting hall structural diagram demonstrating the role of the north party wall and the two concrete shear walls.

↓ Second floor plan. October 31, 1952. Location of two eliminated columns and the necessary beams to carry their loads are highlighted by the author.

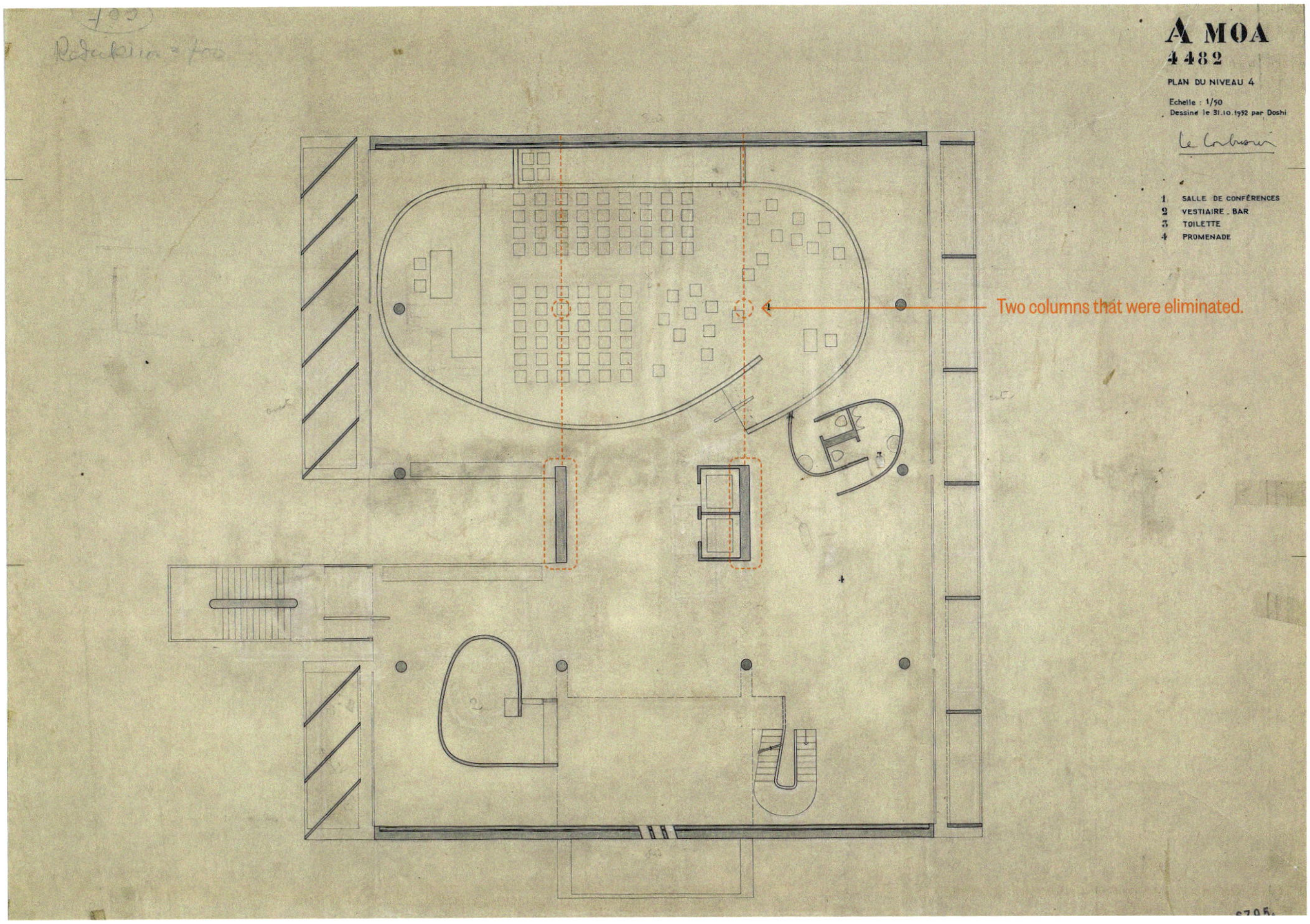

6 PUSH-PULL 1 (RAMP AND STAIR)

The first set of Ahmedabad Millowners' Association Building drawings document a straight-run ramp from the street (west) side arriving on the first floor of the building, as discussed in Section 2 of this chapter. Just to the north of it is a stair. The two appear as a pair and both intrude into the building volume, with the stair completely housed within it. In later iterations, the entire organization of the building is flipped against an east-west axis, relocating the open-to-air half from the north to the south and the enclosed part to the north. The ramp and stair appear within the next bay to the south of the first scheme with their relationship switched north to south. Between June 5, and July 31, 1952, the stair is moved outside the building volume and the elevator moved to the north to be in play with the ramp rather than the stair, a critical move which I will discuss in Section 9 below.

This push-pull defines so much of the Ahmedabad Millowners' Association Building. The ramp pushes into the building volume, carving out a massive space that is present both horizontally and vertically, and is literally contained by the concrete wall discussed in Section 5 Point 1 above. This forceful action both records the "ghost" of where the vertical circulation system could have been - and was, in earlier iterations - and also has a corresponding reaction, pushing the stair out of the volume of the building and creating a sculptural volume on the west façade. In addition, the push-pull defines the circulation system of the building. Starting from the street at grade, the ramp rises with a straight run to the first floor, where the main open lobby of the building (breezeway) is located, as well as all the offices and the committee rooms. A continuous right-hand turn takes the visitor to the second floor, from ramp to stair seamlessly.[165] However seamless, we must recognize the dual condition - both its continuity and its division - and the tension that holds it together. From the street, one rises gently on the ramp with the entire main façade of the building in view, taking it in slowly while gradually changing one's vertical perspective until one is in the building volume, in the three-story subtracted volume: the ghost of the stair, carved by the ramp. From this perspective, one is only able to see entirely orthographically organized walls, with one possible exception if one catches a glimpse of the top of the meeting hall on the second floor. Otherwise, all is north-south or east-west. Within this realm, the concrete wall ahead serves a critical, figural role to stop the ramp and turn attention away from the interior and back to the outside. One may continue straight, almost, with a slight jog, to the outdoor covered lobby, the breezeway, and through to the east side and the Sabarmati River views. Yet, the wall encourages a right-hand turn and continuation on the stair, with different rise and speed than the ramp, once again outside the building volume and in the sun (and rain), continuing up to the landing, with a view back to the street

165 This strategy of utilizing a continuous direction of motion through multiple modes of movement and circulation is a common trait of Le Corbusier's buildings. It is most famously noted in the Villa Besnus of 1922 at Vaucresson.

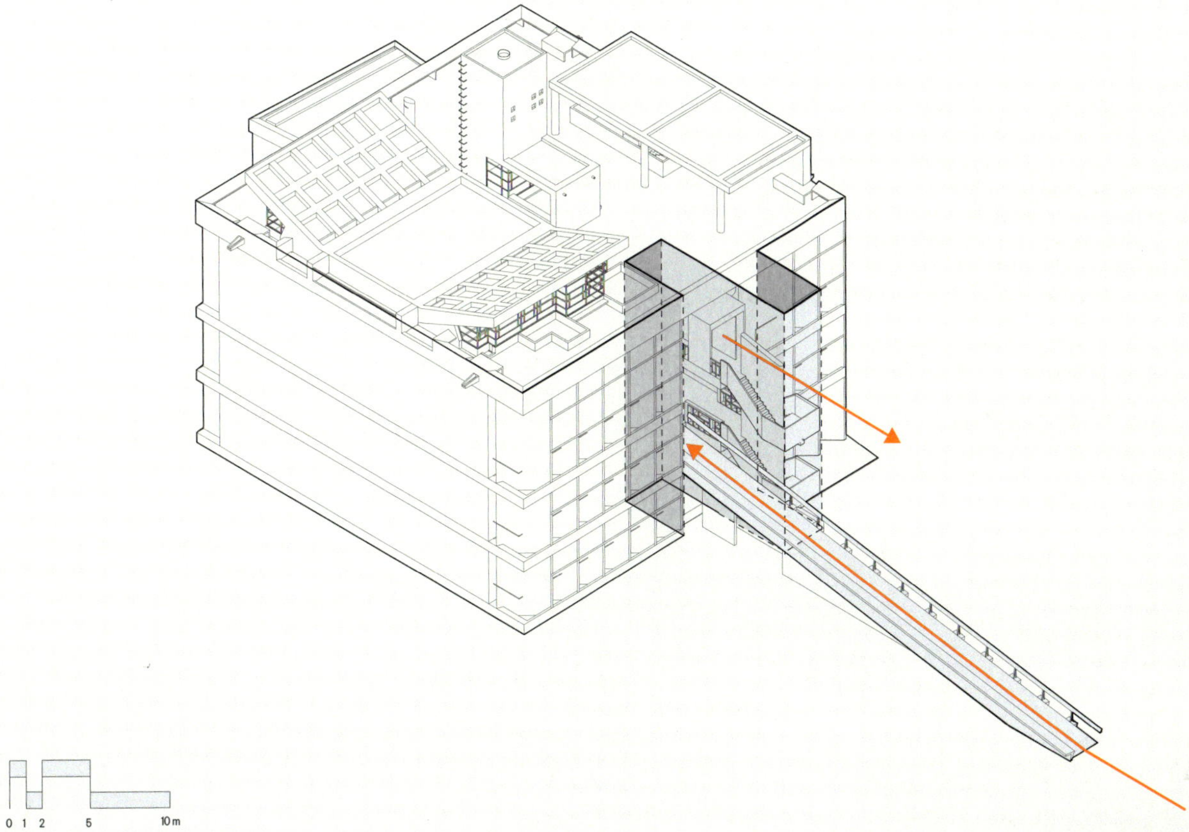

↑ Push-pull ramp-stair diagram. The ramp pushes into the building, creating a three-story volume (a cavity within the building envelope). In reaction, the stair is pushed out of the building volume.

↓ West façade, describing the push-pull ramp-stair relationship. The ramp pushes into and the stair is pulled out of the building volume.

← Detail of stair landing and second floor gate beyond.

entrance where one had started: a kind of orienting device. Here, one must again make two right turns to face the main façade of the building at an acute perspective and continue up the stairs to the second floor.

The second floor, unlike the first, has few rectilinear walls and is full of figural volumes that define space by juxtaposition and spatial tension. The only rectilinear things on this floor, except for the elevator core, are either floor or roof cut-outs – it is a 28 square meter "sea" with a set of objects floating in it. Perhaps this is better described in the context of Le Corbusier as a 28 square meter Purist canvas with a set of juxtaposed (found) objects.

Here, we are faced again with the dual condition between the utilitarian and the sculptural. Had the stairs remained where their memory is marked, where they existed in the March 7, 1952 drawings, within the volume of the building and without sculptural presence on the façade, we would not have a dual condition. Le Corbus-

→ Partial view of the three-story open-air breezeway, describing the volumetric relationship between the ramp pushing into the building volume and the stair projecting out.

ier carefully and precisely pulls the stair out of the building volume as a reaction to the push of the ramp and redefines it as a sculptural volume that not only provides for the utility of vertical ascent but also marks the west façade of the building with a figural, sculptural element. The tension between the utilitarian and the sculptural is nowhere more visible than in the relationship between the ramp and the stair.

7 PUSH-PULL 2 (RAMP AND CAFETERIA)

The push-pull described above makes itself visible and can be experienced by the visitor in one fell swoop; the entire thing is visible on one face of the building and must be experienced if one is to go up to the second floor. A different way of considering push-pull or action-reaction in this building is to examine the "push" of the ramp into the building with the "pull" of the cafeteria out of the building on the

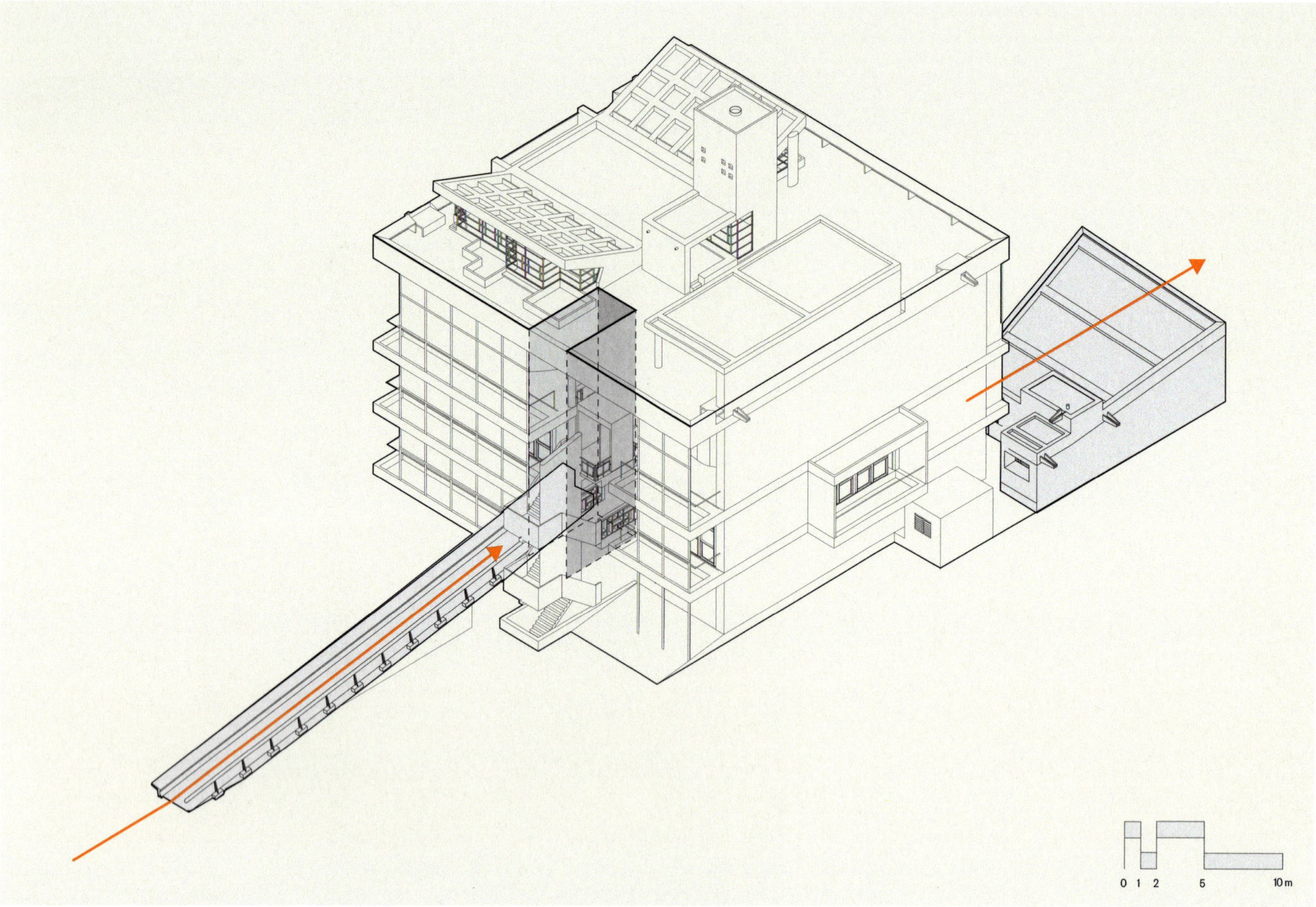

Push-pull ramp-cafeteria diagram, emphasizing the volumetric relationship between the ramp pushing into the building volume on the west side and the cafeteria projecting out of the building volume on the east side.

ground floor. So, a push into the building volume from the west side pulls a volume out of the ground floor on the east. This pairing is only visible in plan and as a conceptual device, not experienced as one does the relationship between the ramp and stair as a continuous promenade through the building. These are two independent building elements, one could argue, almost unrelated. However, formally, we see an absolute relationship between the two sets of volumes. Here, the relationship is entirely non-utilitarian and aesthetic. It is formal.

In the earliest set of building drawings from March 7, 1952, *(ill. p. 86 bottom)* the ramp pushes into the building volume but does not yet cause a reaction, either in the stair or the cafeteria. In the May 6, 1952 set, the stair is still within the building volume and the action of the ramp is countered with the volume of the cafeteria on the east side. Though all of this is mirrored later along an east-west axis, the volumetric play remains. It is not until July 31, 1952 that we see the "push-pull" between the ramp as it penetrates the volume of the building, pulling out the stair volume on the west façade, and the cafeteria, which it pulls out from the east side. Of course, there is also a pragmatic angle to the location of the cafeteria as it extends as far as possible towards the river and its views, containing the garden with its northern brick wall. The open space of the ground floor serves as the lobby for the cafeteria and the current auditorium.[166]

166 B. V. Doshi's office undertook the alteration of the building in the 1970s that included the transformation of the ground floor clerical offices into an air-conditioned lecture hall.

↑ South façade looking west, describing the relationship of the cafeteria volume to the building. The south wall of the cafeteria is located outside the main volume of the building, while its north wall projects from within the building volume.

↓ Interior view towards the east showing the relationship of the cafeteria volume penetrating into the main building. Also shown is the north brick wall of the cafeteria which helps define the garden to the east of the building.

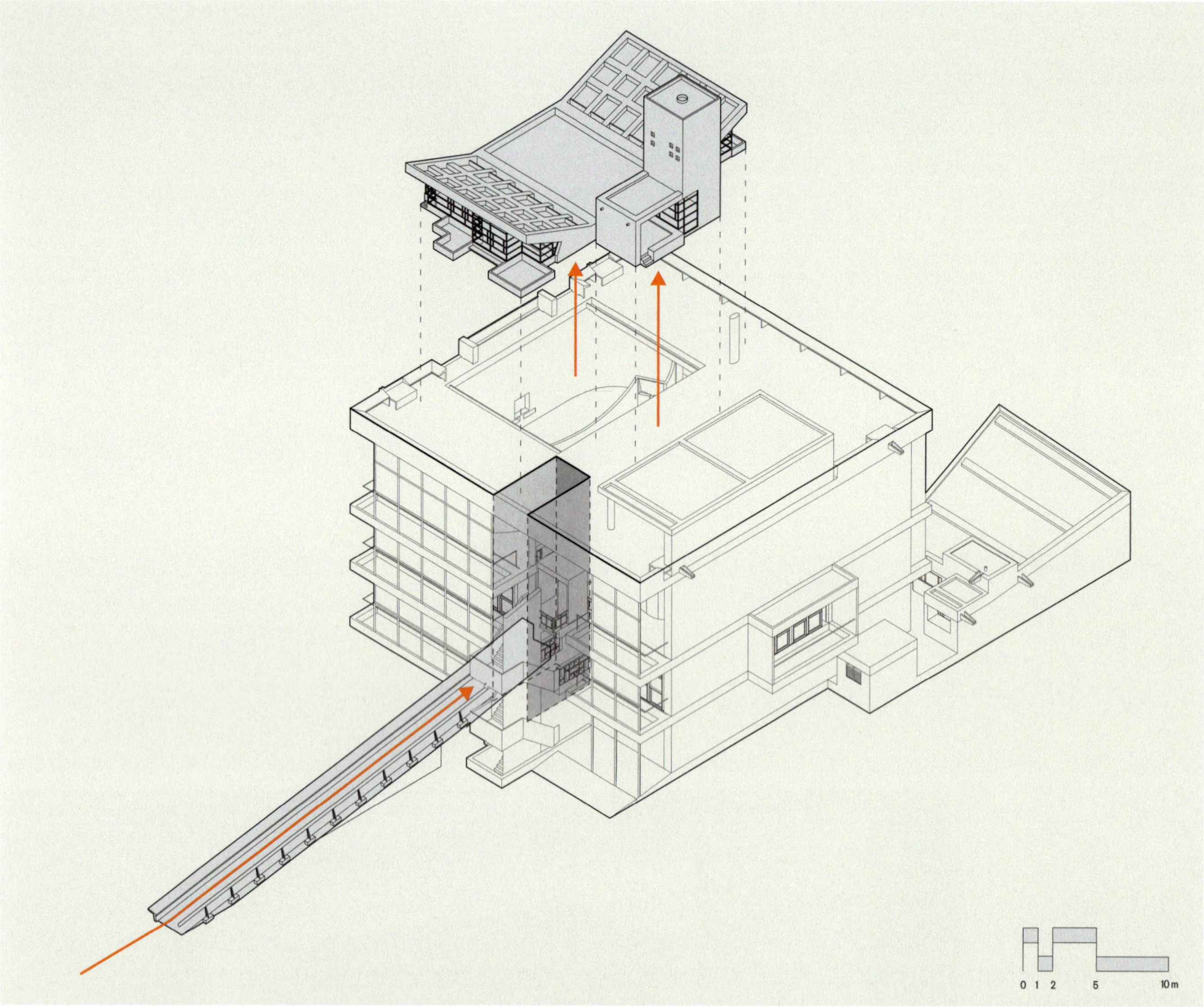

Push–pull ramp–roof diagram. The push into the building volume by the ramp carves out a three-story volume. In reaction, the roof of the meeting hall pushes up through the roof of the main volume.

8 PUSH–PULL 3 (RAMP/ROOF ELEMENTS)

A third version of this conceptual device used by Le Corbusier in the Ahmedabad Millowners' Association Building is the countering of the horizontal push with a vertical pull. This occurs in two ways, both volumetrically and in organizing the building circulation. The square shape of the building plan is complemented by the proportion of each of the four façades, all "golden-section" rectangles. In other words, the building height was made to align with the prescriptions of geometry: a formal utility, if one may use that term. Thus, the protrusions above the roof line express a decisive move: they are significant in the building's geometric configuration. They emphasize the perimeter of the "golden-section" rectangle at the roof-slab by protruding beyond it. The push into the building volume by the ramp carves out a three-story volume, the memory of where the stair would have been, which in turn pushes several other volumes up, through and above the roof, beyond the "golden-section." One is the roof of the meeting hall, discussed earlier, and another is the roof above the mezzanine, which also accommodates the circulation to

→ West stair, brise-soleil, and second floor gate, describing the main elements of the building's circulation.

the roof. The volumes above the roof line also, in turn, produce aesthetic effects – in this case, sculpting by light. In addition to shaping the building volume to geometric precision, they introduce light from above into the building volume. This light is most dramatically experienced in the meeting hall as the shadows of the curved roof line are cast upon the curved walls, producing a double curve only visible as a shadow line. Also shown is the north brick wall of the cafeteria which helps define the garden to the east of the building.

9 IN-OUT (CIRCULATION)

On his first trip to India, Le Corbusier recognized that, unlike buildings in Paris where everything needed to be enclosed, the Indian climate permitted and encouraged outdoor living, so the relationship between indoor and outdoor spaces had a more fluid nature. The

Ahmedabad Millowners' Association Building is thus organized as a large, roofed shelter that protects the building's occupants and its spaces from the sun and rain. Almost half of the building is sheltered but not enclosed. All the horizontal building circulation occurs within these roofed but open-to-air spaces. Specifically, on each floor, no horizontal circulation is enclosed, while workspaces are. For example, the president's office is enclosed and has an internal and enclosed connection to the secretary's office. However, to get to the vice-president's office, the president must exit the enclosure and venture into the outdoor air. The same holds for the relationship between offices, the managing committee room, and the sub-committee room. On each floor, so long as one communicates with other spaces within that floor, the circulation is covered but open-air. However, if communication requires a change of floors, then the access is via the stair, which is not roofed.

The main stair on the western façade connects the basement to the second floor with a stop on each floor. It may be used as a simple, continuous stair between floors, as one would in any building. So, in one way, there is a simple and straightforward mode of vertical movement in the building that involves the stair. However, at each point in the building one is always faced with a dual condition of movement. From the street entrance, the ramp calls one up to the first floor. But, in fact, one could simply not engage with the ramp and go straight into the ground floor, continuing through to the cafeteria or the east gardens. This is something documented decisively by Le Corbusier in the first site sketch in sketchbook E25,[167] where he notes "garden parties." *(ill. p. 71)* He imagined that there would be instances where the visitor would go directly to the garden without entering the rest of the building.

If one chooses to go up the ramp, there is another dual condition at the top of it: whether to continue up via the stair or to move straight through to the breezeway/lobby and the Sabarmati River views. At the top of the stairs on the second floor, the visitor has two options: one, to move around the two-story opening and to the left to the meeting hall, the programmatic climax of the building, or two, to the right and up to the mezzanine, and from there whether to continue up through the raised roof to the rooftop terrace or stay under the roof. These are clearly dual conditions that are not of the conceptual nature previously discussed but are instead dual choices. They do, however, emphasize Le Corbusier's interest in the dual condition.

The designed promenade of the building (shown in the eight images on *pp. 104–107*) from the ground to the roof includes four sets of vertical movement systems, each different, with different cadences and different rises, but always guiding the visitor to turn right: ramp to the main stairs; to the right, boomerang stairs up to the mezzanine; to the straight-run stairs to the roof. *(ill. p. 104 left, 105 bottom, 106 top and bottom)* Then, there is another promenade,

167 Le Corbusier and Fondation Le Corbusier, *Le Corbusier Sketchbooks,* Volume 2, 675.

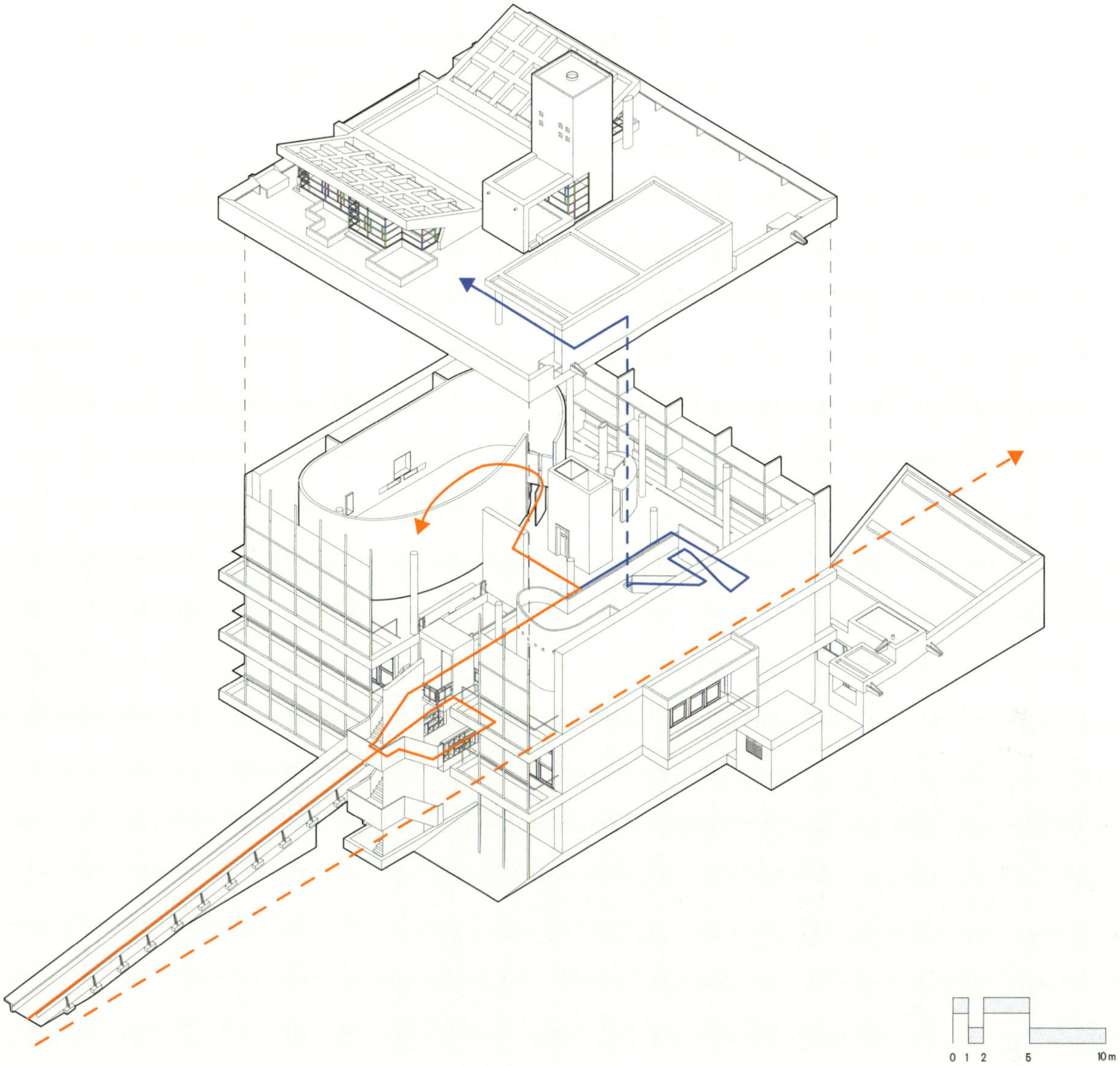

In-out circulation diagram, showing the two paths of movement in the building and the architectural promenade.

perhaps the one used most often, leading to the meeting hall: once on the second floor from the ramp and the stairs, the right-hand turns end and the left-hand turns start, leading to the entrance and following left into the hall and around the curvature of the space, facing back towards the congregation stage (west and the street). *(ill. p. 107 top and bottom)* A singular, continuous circulation system would engage the building and its elements in ways that are consistent from floor to floor. At the Ahmedabad Millowners' Association Building, however – given the multiple, discontinuous systems montaged and adjacent to one another – one never experiences the building or its elements in a singular manner. One is always turning and facing different directions, different light, different textures; passing through different spaces; moving horizontally to move vertically; and so on. None of the elements of the circulation are formally unique on their own. We have seen each of them somewhere as a mode of circulation, but usually not together as different parts of the same system; could one even call it a system? Here, we see the method Le Corbusier used as a Purist painter by juxtaposing "found" ele-

← Partial view of ramp, stair, and breezeway, describing the continuation of the sequence in the architectural promenade.

↑ View east from the second floor interior of the Ahmedabad Millowners' Association Building. The ramp-stair sequence plays an important role in the architectural promenade.

→ View towards the east from the second floor, looking back at the ramp.

↘ View from the mezzanine of the second floor, looking down at the boomerang stair, showing the right-hand turn in the sequence of the architectural promenade.

ments – in this case, with the building as canvas. He juxtaposes a series of "found," building-related, utilitarian elements such as bathrooms, kitchen, elevators, ramps, and stairs in an unfamiliar context to create a spatial experience never before seen: a series of utilitarian elements juxtaposed on a sculptural canvas.

We see the lessons of the Acropolis at work here: the balance between asymmetrically organized objects in an ensemble; the privileging of oblique views over frontal ones; different modes and speeds of movement; the anticipation and surprise of spaces and views; and, finally, climactic spaces/forms. Le Corbusier's architectural promenade, which he described in the context of a cinematic experience while in motion, finds its canvas here. The four different modes of vertical ascent – each with their own direction, cadence, speed of movement, rate of rise, and changing views – constitute cinematic clips that have been montaged together to create the entirety of the movement experience. The collage of the Purist canvas

depicting space has been transformed into a montage of experiences in space and time: the cinematic promenade.

An entirely different means of vertical ascent at the Ahmedabad Millowners' Association Building is provided by the elevator, a singular and enclosed experience. From the very first set of drawings, an elevator is present. *(ill. p. 86 bottom)* It is initially imagined as a single elevator and one that appears as a figure within the large open space of the floors, connecting basement to roof. This single elevator changes to two cabs but remains as an object in the open space. One of the most important developments in the design sequence is the decision to keep the elevators separate from the concrete structural shear wall that was immediately to their east. All the drawings that were prepared in the Atelier Le Corbusier document the elevators as such, identifiable as a separate elements, unconnected to any other building element. Late in 1952, we see sketches and drawings that unify the east wall of the elevators with the column line and the concrete shear wall, essentially using the wall of the elevators as a shear wall for lateral support and assimilating the identities of both the elevators and the concrete shear wall. It is not until the on-site drawings prepared by B. V. Doshi, dated October 8, 1954, that the elevator is returned to a single cab accompanied by a mechanical chase to its side.[168] This chase also permitted the elimination of the basement access to the mechanical services. *(ill. p. 108)*

There are no drawings that document the removal of this lower-level access, but the as-built condition verifies the elimination of the basement elevator. As built, the basement is not accessible by elevator and is confined to one north-south bay on the westernmost edge of the building, accommodating all the building utilities. *(ill. p. 155 top)*

In the early sketches, we see the elevator, the column, and the shear wall as unique and identifiable architectural elements, each legible on their own. However, the final, as-built condition verifies a unification of these three elements, losing individual legibility yet gaining formal cohesion so that the entirety may read as a figure on the ground of each floor. Clearly, as documented by two years' worth of drawings, aesthetically and sculpturally, Le Corbusier preferred to maintain the identity of the three elements as separate, yet structural and economic utility brought them together.

10 FIGURE-GROUND

The open, outdoor, covered spaces at the Ahmedabad Millowners' Association Building occupy almost half of the building's floor plans. Starting from the very first drawings, certain building elements are conceived as figural elements, those that appear as objects in space, identifiable as architectural elements and separated from the rest of the building. These consist of the ramp, stairs, elevator(s), and the bathrooms. The ramp consistently appears in all the drawings over

168 In US parlance, a mechanical chase is the volume of space provided in a building for the passage of pipes, wires, and ducts.

↑ West façade from the ramp, marking the start of the sequence in the architectural promenade.

↓ View from the mezzanine of the second floor, looking west at the straight-run stair leading to the roof.

↑ View from the second floor breezeway, looking east at the entrance of the meeting hall.

↓ View from the stage of the meeting hall looking east towards the entrance. The meeting hall serves as the culmination of the architectural promenade.

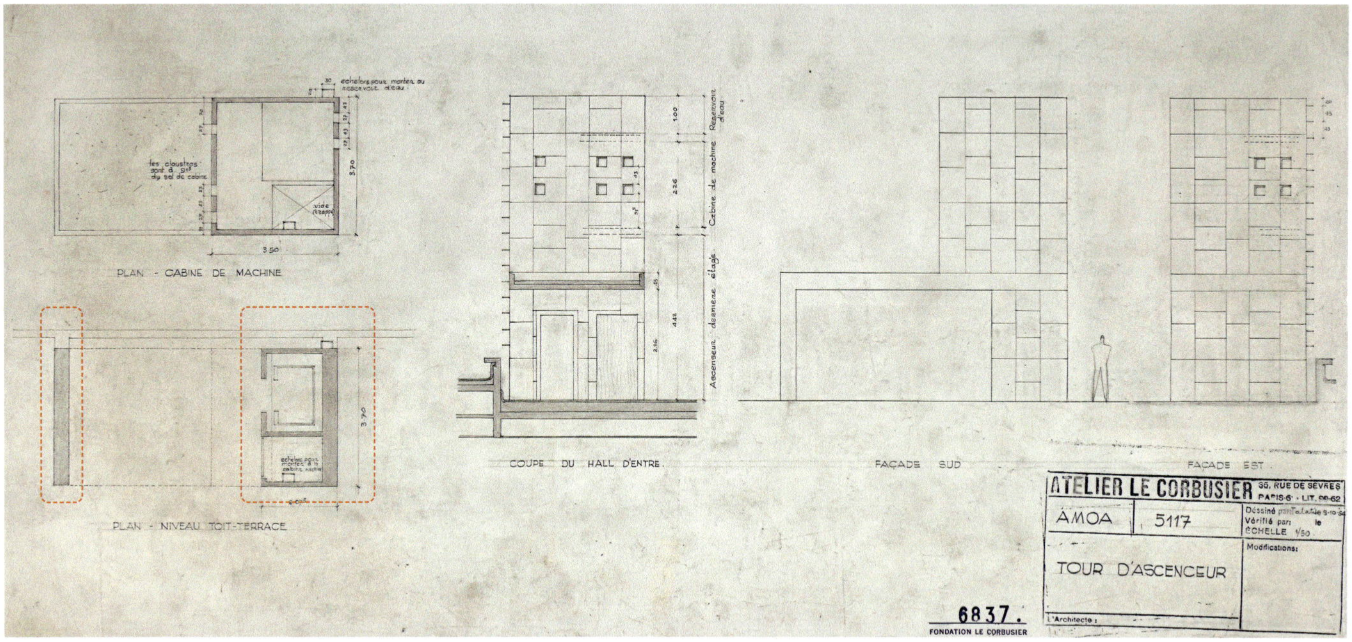

Atelier Le Corbusier on-site drawing for the final elevator configuration, with one cab and a mechanical chase to the side, October 8, 1954 (highlights by the author).

time and is built as drawn and conceived, an identifiable architectural element. The stairs are mirrored from their initial location and pulled out from the building volume then reconfigured as a sculptural element, an identifiable architectural figure on the west façade and in the plan. The elevator starts as a separate, identifiable element disconnected from all other elements of the building, but at the end is co-joined with the concrete structural wall. Although it loses its "pure" programmatic function, it remains identifiable as a figure. On the ground floor, its configuration blends with the walls of the clerical offices (now the auditorium). However, on the first and second floors it truly reads as a figure within the large expanse of the open floors. It differs from the other figural elements as it is rectilinear in form.

On the ground floor, the stair and ramp project out of the building and become character-defining elements on the west façade. Once under the cover of the building, the bathrooms read as an object within the open half of the ground floor. In addition, straight ahead, looking east towards the Sabarmati River, is the cafeteria – another independent figure, which juts out from under the first floor and defines the garden space to the east of the building. The first floor is defined primarily by the push of the ramp into the building and by the carved, unenclosed three-story space. The elevator and the bathrooms read as objects in the open breezeway/lobby space, defined by the walls of the offices and the committee rooms. *(ill. p. 110 bottom)* On the second floor, the culmination of the stair, there are only objects. In addition to those visible throughout the building – the elevator, stair, and bathrooms – we also have the large meeting hall, the cloakroom/bar object, the boomerang stair, and the mezzanine above. All these objects are carefully distinguished from one another with reveals, small gaps, and other architectural details to ensure a floor full of figural elements, one whose composition is

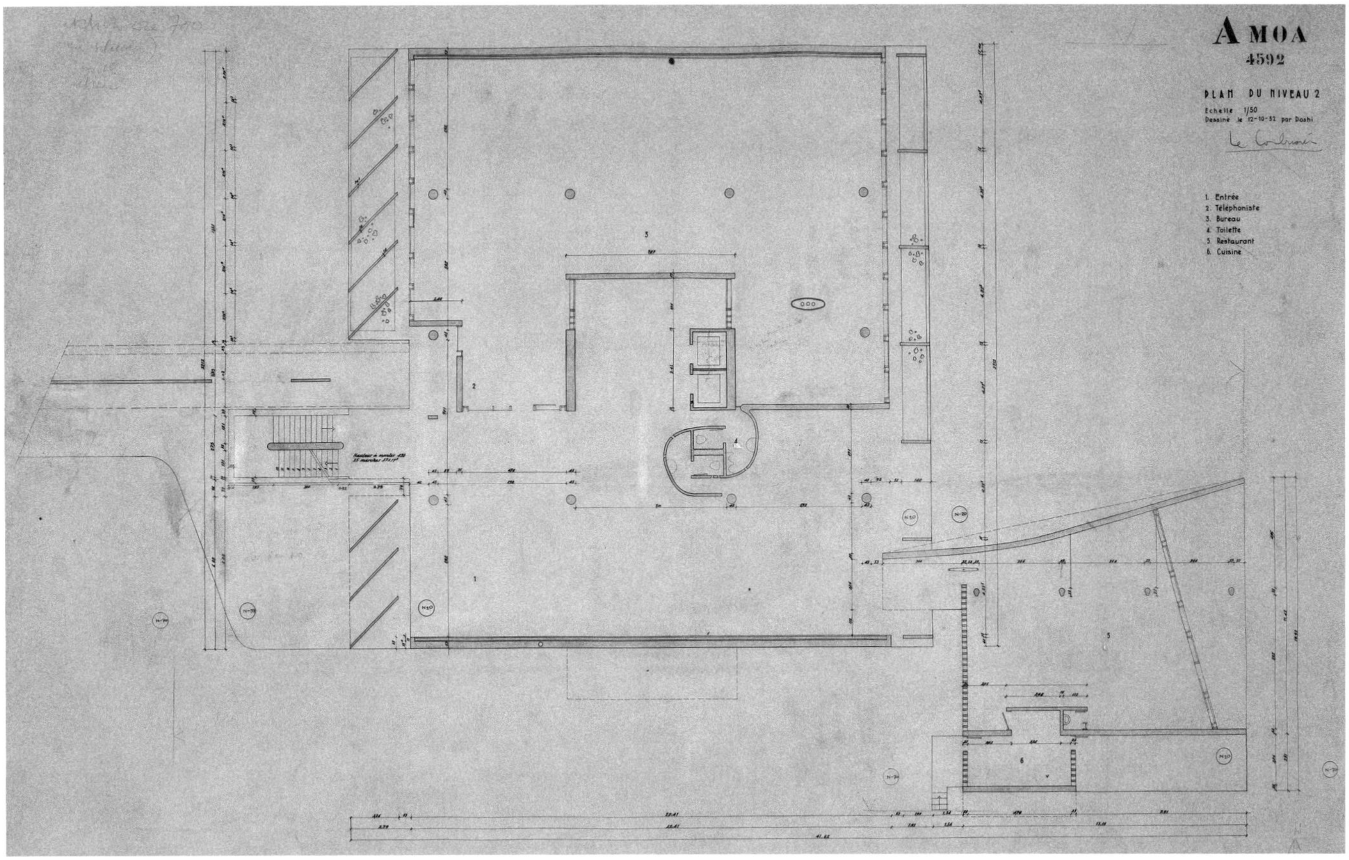

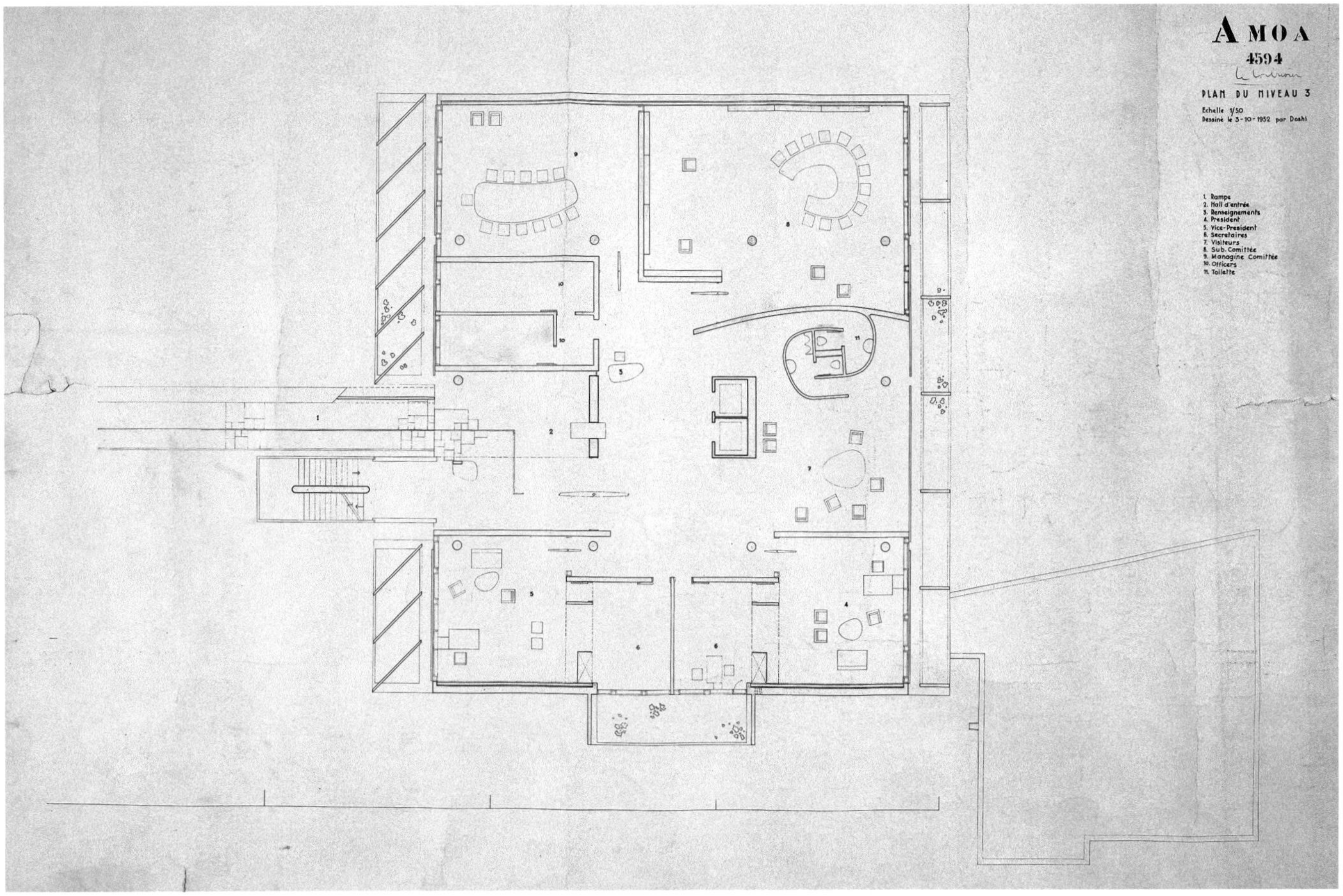

↑ Ground floor plan showing the elevators blending into the clerical offices and not reading as a figure. Plan as designed by Atelier Le Corbusier and constructed.

↓ First floor plan showing the elevators as a figural element in the breezeway space. Plan as designed by Atelier Le Corbusier and constructed.

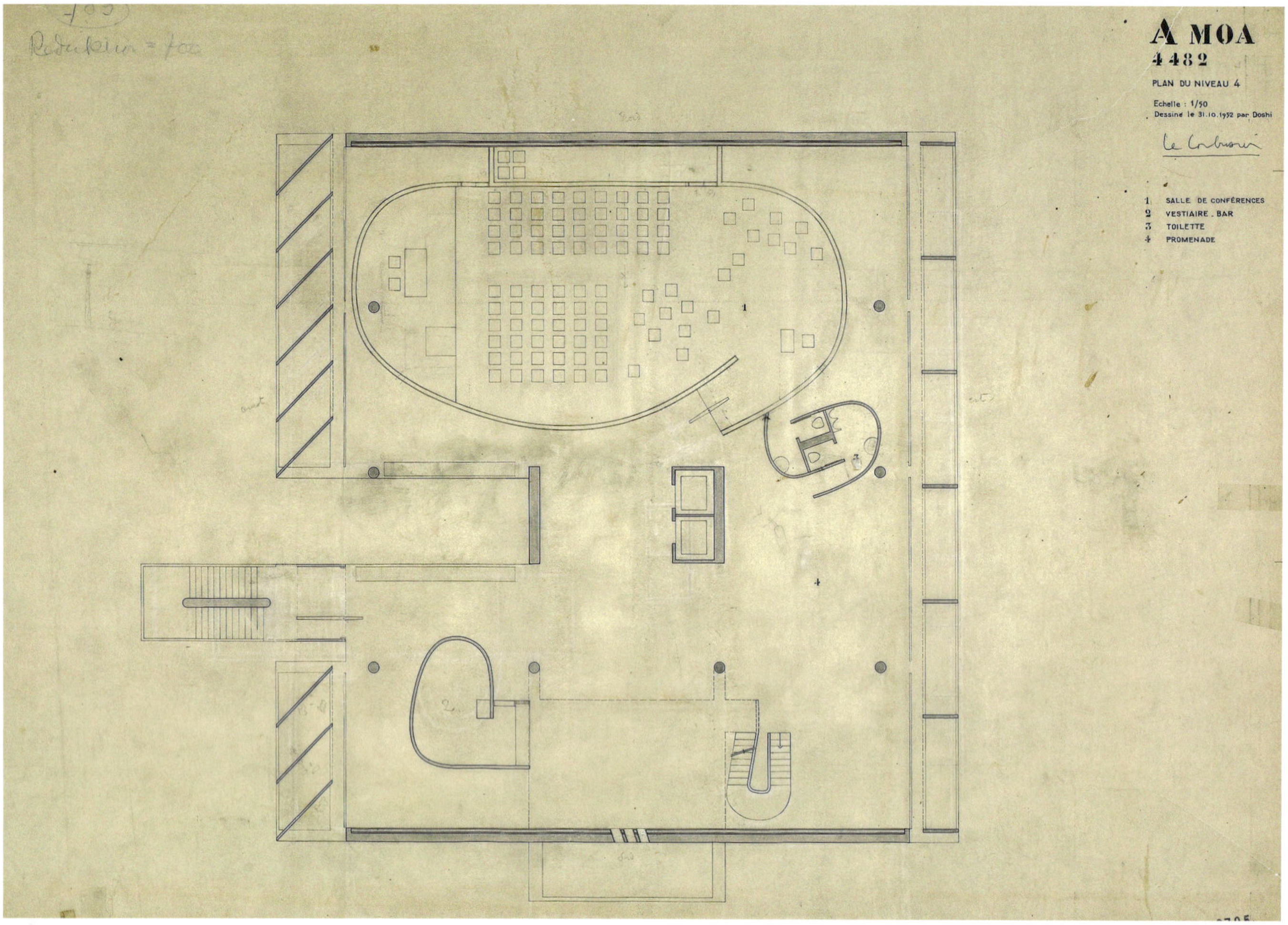

↑ Second floor plan showing the elevators as a figural element in the milling space. Plan as designed by Atelier Le Corbusier and constructed.

↓ View north from the first floor breezeway highlighting the figural nature of the architectural elements.

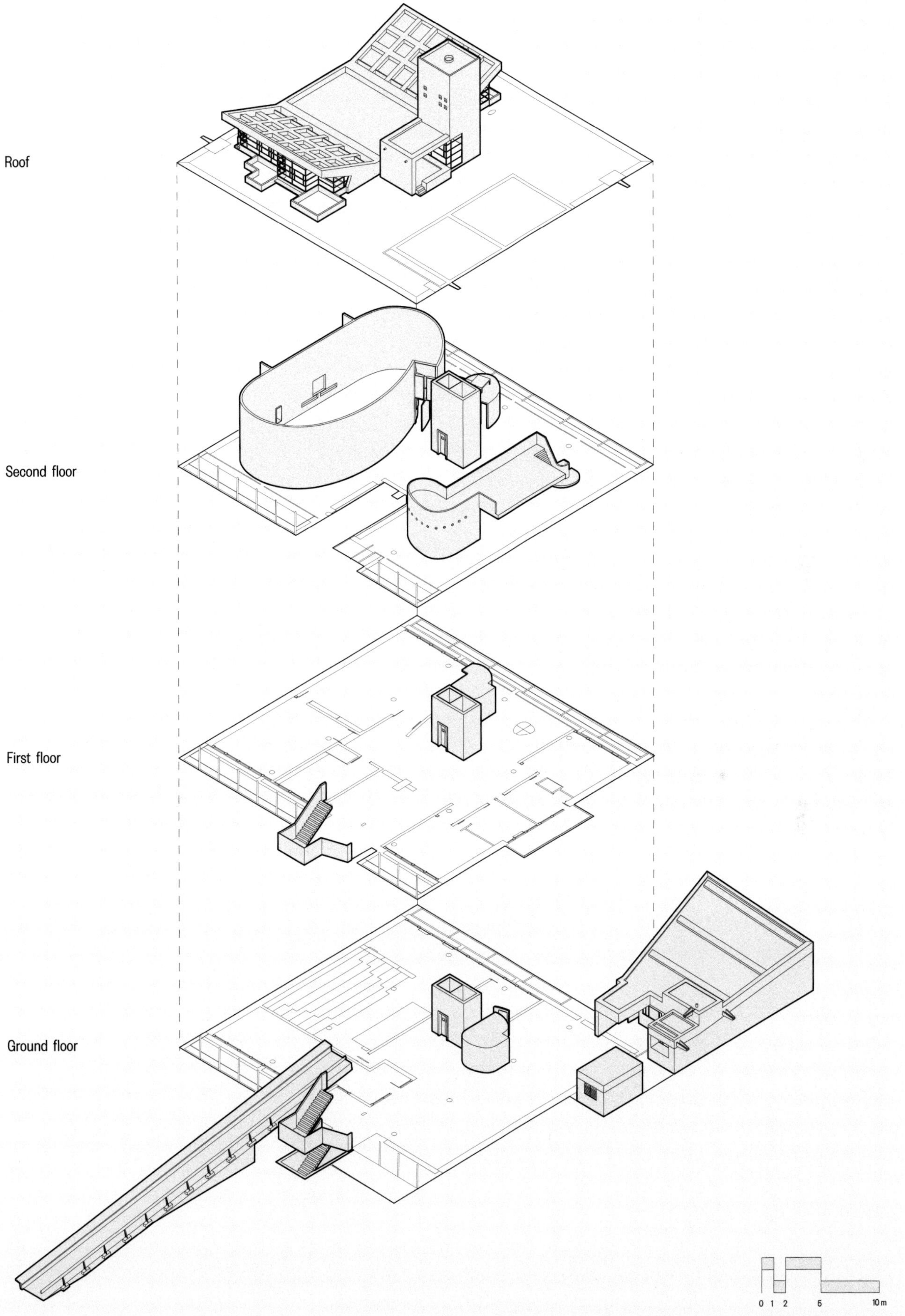

↑ Figure-ground diagram of three floors and roof, emphasizing the figural volumes on each floor.

entirely about the juxtaposition of unrelated building elements that are made legible as such. A truly Purist canvas.

Almost all of these elements have a distinct utilitarian program and many are not identifiable as figures in the earlier versions of the building, where they were made to dissolve into the background of walls and enclosures. As the project developed, these utilitarian elements – ramp, stairs, elevator, bathrooms, cloakroom/bar, cafeteria – took on a sculptural, space-defining role. Their utility and identifiable character were used to define them in contrast with other elements juxtaposed in their context. Once again, we are in this "tense space" between utilitarian and sculptural elements.

11 UP-DOWN (PLUMBING SYSTEM)

One of the figural elements in the Ahmedabad Millowners' Association Building is the set of male/female bathrooms that exist on each floor. The March 7, 1952 drawings document a pair of bathrooms together within a singular, figural shape (a rounded rectangle) on the ground and second floors. *(ill. p. 72)* The first floor had the bathrooms between the committee rooms, blending into a wall, undetectable. Later schemes, including those shown in a complete set of building drawings from July 27, 1952, had the male/female bathrooms in an embracing plan shape around a wet-wall chase that continued vertically throughout the building. In addition, the bathrooms on all three floors had independent and lower roofs and did not reach up to the floor above. This made them read clearly as objects that did not belong to the structural vocabulary of the walls and columns, but that also necessitated the continuation of the plumbing chase vertically and beyond the bathroom figure.

The plumbing chase itself is another figural element: it is a vertically extruded, ovoid-shaped object that takes water to all floors, brings waste down from all floors, and also vacates fumes from pipes through its uppermost vents through and above the roof where it is marked by a tall, concrete, ovoid-shaped tower rising above the roof.[169]

The continuous vertical alignment of the three bathrooms, however, was not maintained in the final set of drawings. Already in a July 29, 1952 study of the ground floor, the bathrooms are moved south from their vertical alignment with the upper bathrooms.

Although they maintain their vocabulary and continue the appearance of the two other sets on the first and second floors, including the white-painted ovoid plumbing chase, they do not align vertically. In other words, the basic laws of physics were overruled to accommodate the desired programmatic necessities and the aesthetics of an "object-in-a-field" reading. The ovoid chase below the upper bathrooms continues through the ground floor offices and into the subterranean infrastructure. A second set of water and waste lines had to be constructed to accommodate the ground floor bath-

→ This on-site drawing shows the lavatories with plumbing chase highlighted by the author.

↘ Ground floor plan, study from July 29, 1952. The ground floor lavatories were relocated out of alignment with the upper lavatories, thus requiring two different plumbing chases (highlights by the author).

169 The "vent stack" housed in the ovoid-shaped, concrete tower above the roof is also misaligned with its sources below. The vent pipes, by necessity, jog within the roof space in order to accommodate the misalignment. Had it been aligned it would penetrate through the inverted-arch roof of the meeting hall.

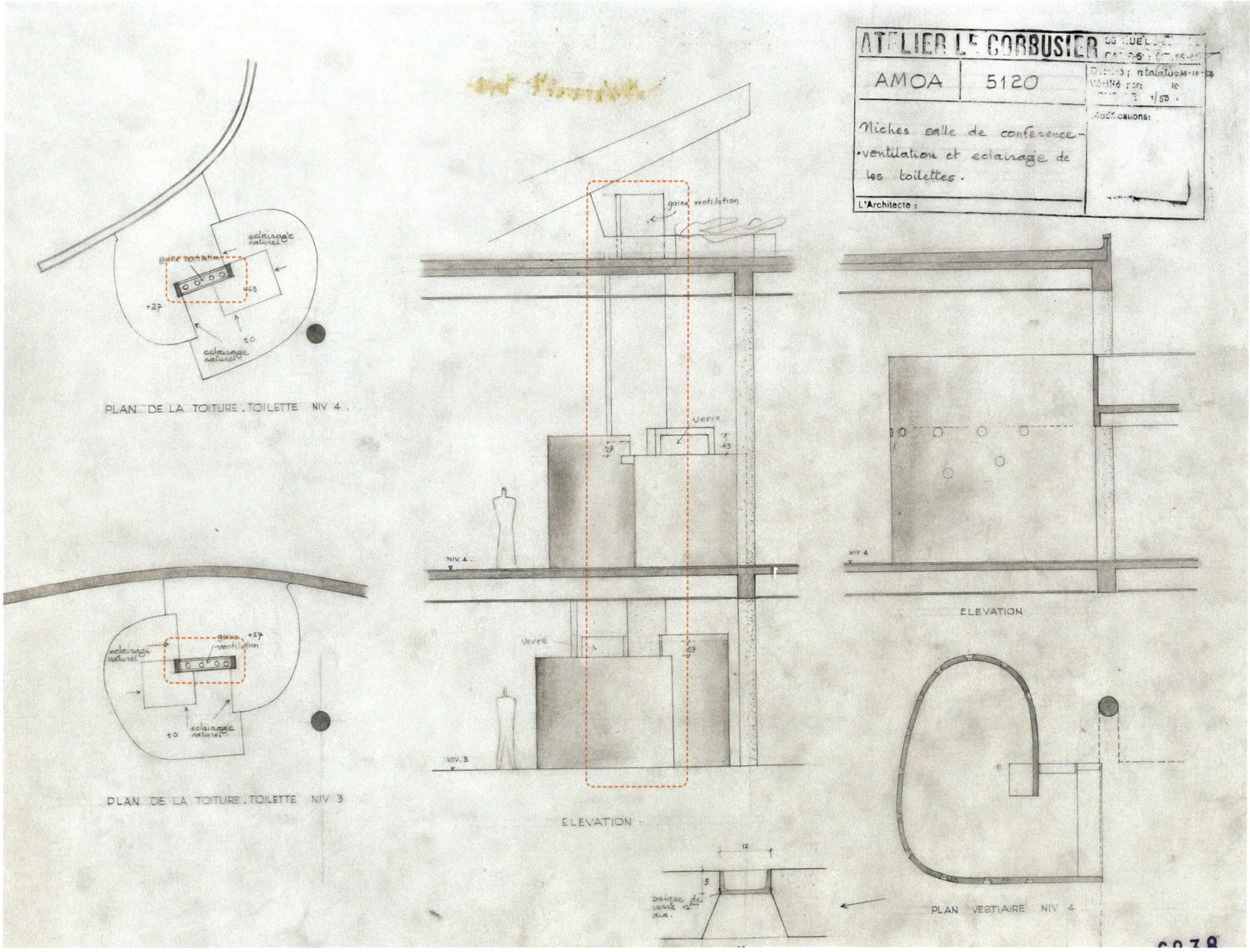
ATELIER LE CORBUSIER
AMOA
5120
Niches salle de conférence - ventilation et éclairage de les toilettes.
L'Architecte :
gaine ventilation
éclairage naturel
PLAN DE LA TOITURE . TOILETTE NIV 4 .
verre
NIV 4
ELEVATION
PLAN DE LA TOITURE . TOILETTE NIV 3
NIV 3
ELEVATION .
PLAN VESTIAIRE NIV 4

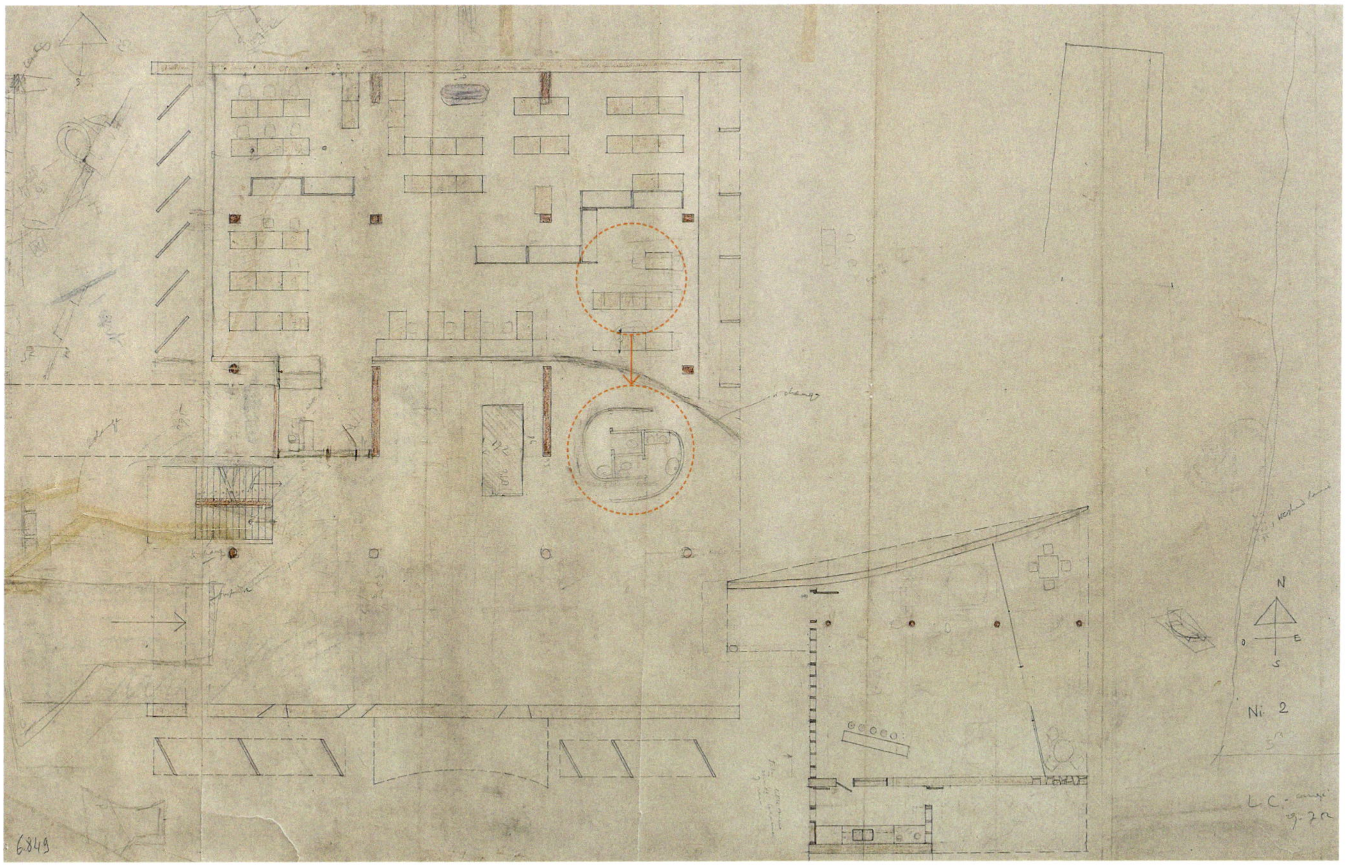
N
E
S
Ni 2
6849

↑ First floor breezeway/entrance hall with view of concrete table and the lavatories beyond. The ovoid plumbing stack is visible above the bathroom volumes in white.

← Ovoid-shaped vent stack appearing above the roof.

→ Diagram of the plumbing chase for waste, water, and ventilation and its vertical misalignments.

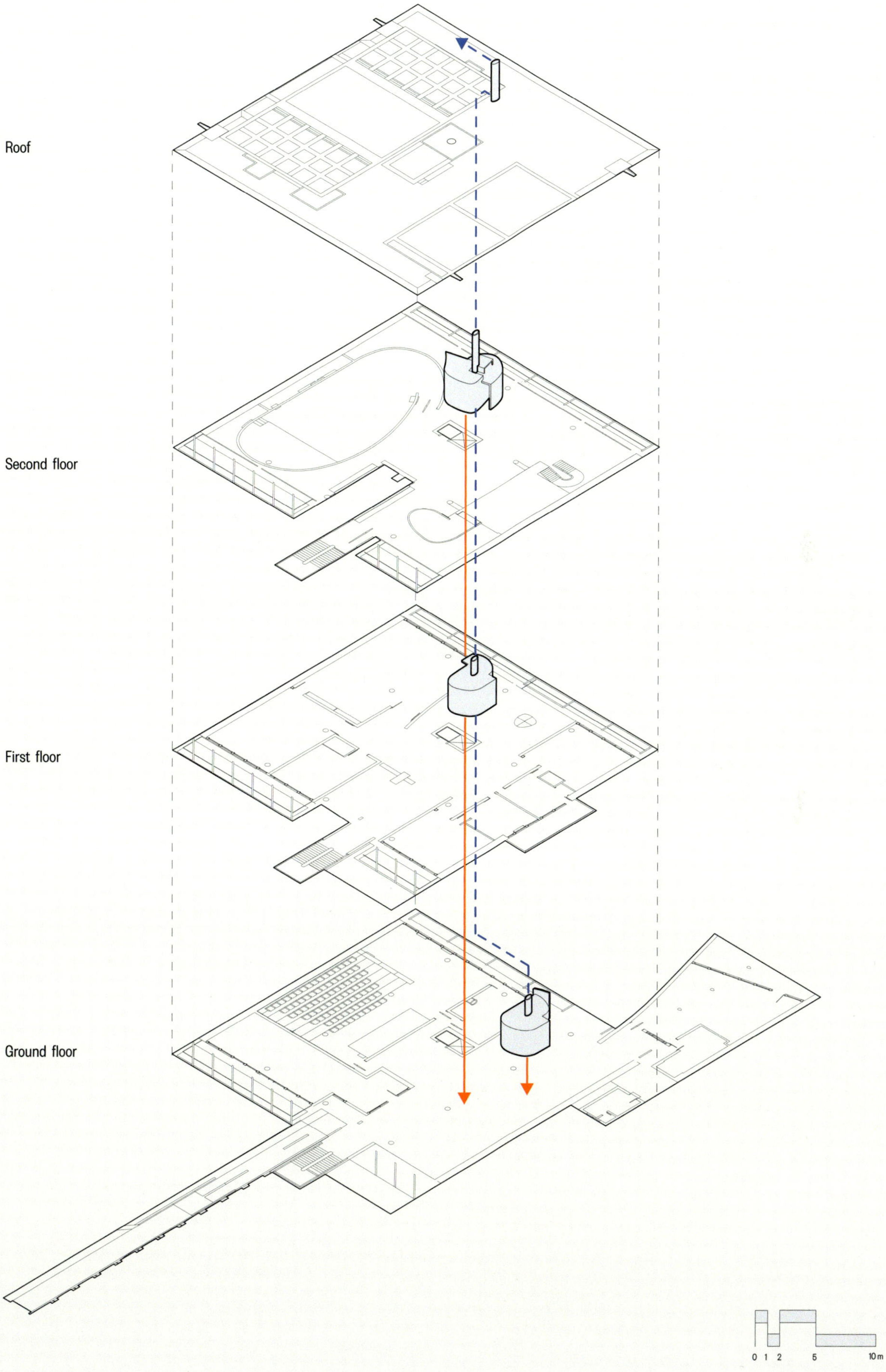
Roof
Second floor
First floor
Ground floor
0 1 2 5 10m

rooms. It is not clear how Le Corbusier dealt with the necessity of the ventilation of the waste vapors, as there is the open lobby immediately above the ground floor bathrooms.

The bathrooms, like most of the other figural elements in this building, transform from utilitarian elements to sculptural ones. The bathrooms, as sculptural elements, require plumbing "gymnastics" to allow them to function with the physics of water, vapor, and waste. Here, the tension between the utilitarian and the sculptural pushes building physics to extremes.

CONCLUSION

It is clear from the eleven analytical points above that Le Corbusier was decisively engaged in this tension between the utilitarian and the sculptural. The Ahmedabad Millowners' Association Building is, on one level, a simple and straightforward building: a concrete-framed 4 × 5 meter structural grid with two party walls and a main circulation stair. However, we see that in bringing this simple building to a constructed reality, Le Corbusier strives to create tension between a structure organized by the regularity of the building systems and the formation of plastic experience. This is visible everywhere. The earlier analysis is limited to a certain scale of building elements. We could conduct a much more detailed examination of elements down to the scale of a doorknob and we would find similar tension between its utility and sculptural quality. The Ahmedabad Millowners' Association Building is the manifestation of constructed and decisive tension between these two realms: reason and poetry, the systematicity and rationality of building systems (such as structural, plumbing, sun-shading, and circulatory ones), and the plasticity and malleability of space and form in light, shadow, color, and texture, experienced through movement.

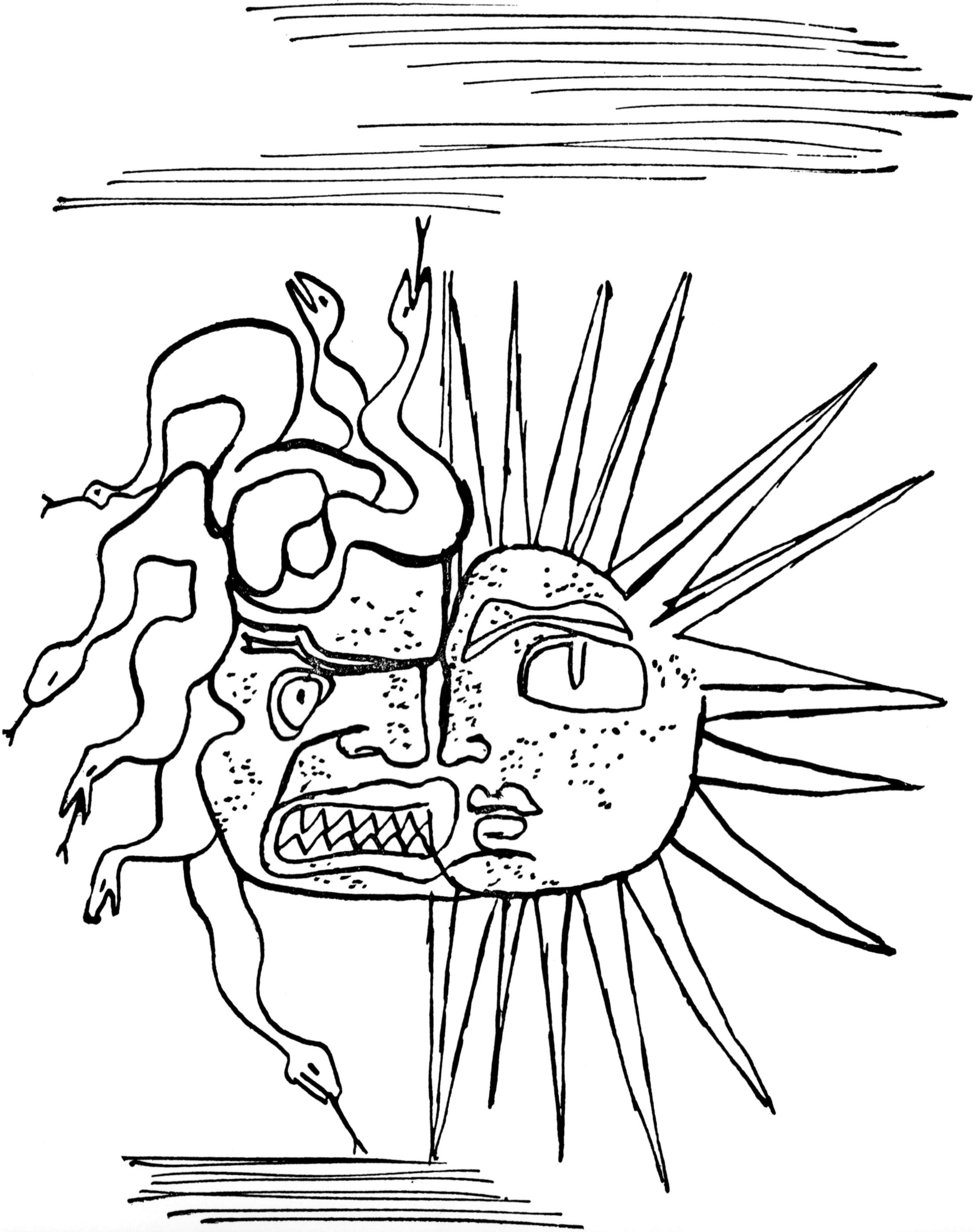

IV
APOLLO AND MEDUSA: LE CORBUSIER AND NIETZSCHE

← Le Corbusier, *Apollo and Medusa*, 1945, black ink on paper.

Charles Jencks, in his 1973 book titled *Le Corbusier and the Tragic View of Architecture,* established a connection between Le Corbusier and Friedrich Nietzsche's writings.[170] Le Corbusier annotated and dated a copy of Nietzsche's *Thus Spoke Zarathustra* in 1908.[171] Jencks provides a penetrating look at the person, Le Corbusier, and how he might have become who he was – a kind of self-fashioning that is described much later by Catherine Malabou in the context of Nietzsche.[172] In this sense, the tragic view of which Jencks speaks is that of Le Corbusier's personality: a personality built of and on conflict, Jencks argues. Jencks does not speak of the work of his subject as a work of conflict, one that uses conflict strategically, but rather that he tries to provide logical trajectories that define and determine the work based on the training, upbringing, and self-fashioning of the individual, of Le Corbusier.

Jencks examines Le Corbusier's life and proposes four distinct eras in his career, each presented in a chapter:

1 "Jeanneret's School for Le Corbusier 1887–1916": his youth; schooling; apprenticeships with the Perrets, Behrens, Garnier, and others; international travel; his stay in Paris; and a few houses in his hometown based on the local Swiss building traditions and Art Nouveau. This, Jencks calls the period of self-fashioning, Le Corbusier trying to see who he is and who he wants to be. Already at an early age, Jencks argues, he is attached to the Nietzschean way of life as Jencks defines

170 Charles Jencks, *Le Corbusier and the Tragic View of Architecture* (Cambridge, Massachusetts: Harvard University Press, 1973).

171 Friedrich Nietzsche, *Thus Spoke Zarathustra*. Translated by Walter Kaufman (New York: Modern Library, 1995). Jencks establishes this connection through references made to Paul Turner's dissertation ("The Education of Le Corbusier") recorded on page 186, note 11 in *Le Corbusier and the Tragic View of Architecture*.

172 Malabou has argued the plasticity of the self, a kind of self-(trans)formation that she reads in Nietzsche. This is critical in the way that Le Corbusier shaped himself into the architect/person that he became, without ever being schooled in the discipline. Catherine Malabou, "Nietzsche's *Ecce Homo*," COL 711: Philosophy and Writing (Class lecture, University at Buffalo, Buffalo, New York, Spring 2011).

it: to the conflict of the tragic hero, the artist who aspires for absolute truth and with the highest unattainable ideals, always resulting in failure.

2 "The Hero of the Heroic Period 1917–1928": Le Corbusier's move to Paris; the "Heroic Period"; Ozenfant and Purism; the publication of the journal *L'Esprit Nouveau* in twenty-eight issues; and four seminal books: *Towards a New Architecture, Urbanism (The City of Tomorrow), Decorative Art of Today,* and *Modern Painting.* This is the period when he reaps the fruits of the self-fashioning of his youth and is able to make a "heroic" mark on both painting and architecture. He manages to invent a Purist vocabulary through painting, which he perfects in the architecture of the Villa Savoye and the Villa Stein-de-Monzie at Garches.

3 "At War with Reaction 1928–1945": the years leading to the Second World War are spent refining his social ideals as they pertain to city planning. Le Corbusier proposes many of his city plans during this period, as there are few commissions (except the Swiss Pavilion and the Salvation Army "Cité de Refuge"). He marries. He is dragged towards political ideologies but remains steadfastly without a partisan affiliation and refuses to join any political movements – although he is both celebrated and criticized by leaders of both communist and fascist movements.

4 "Other Languages of Architecture 1946–1965": Le Corbusier develops a new vocabulary that Jencks refers to as "brutalism," which presents the aesthetic effects of reinforced concrete. He has a number of international commissions, some of which are built, such as ones in New York City and India – including the building being studied here. This is also the period in which he builds the "Unités," which gives him the opportunity to explore many of his social agendas at a smaller scale than city plans. This period is also marked by the enigmatic Ronchamp. Later, he develops a steel vocabulary for the Heidi Weber Pavilion in Zurich and even a tensile one for the Philips Pavilion in Brussels.

Despite Jencks's clean and clear subdivisions of Le Corbusier's life in the context of "tragedy," he does not make direct and strategic connections between Le Corbusier's work and the duality conjured by Nietzsche in the context of *The Birth of Tragedy.* Given this focused research into Le Corbusier, Jencks insists on an almost psychological analysis of the personality without a comparable analysis of the work. He writes:

> Le Corbusier continually tried to realize his goal of "harmony" for an industrial civilization, but was repulsed so often that his incessant efforts appear to be literally mad,

> insane, pragmatically futile. What was the meaning of an idealism which would only fail again? Perhaps symbolic. Perhaps Le Corbusier, like the tragic hero, saw the conflict between his ideals and society as being of equal importance as the attainment of these ideals. He certainly enjoyed these conflicts. And he presented "joy" in many key parts of a building: the "three essential joys", sun, space and greenery; the colour and crisp materials which would contrast with brutal concrete.[173]

Nietzsche speaks of "tragedy" as a mode of intense creative production, as a way of both creating culture (art) and exploring the human condition within the culture: a dual work. Nietzsche's *The Birth of Tragedy* is dual in many ways; first, in that it is a historical study, befitting of an academic in the field of classical philology: a historical study of the origins of Greek tragedy. It is, however, also a manifesto and a critical examination of Nietzsche's contemporary German culture. Second, it presents the human condition through the lens of individuation and unification. Third, tragedy is explored in the context of the Apollonian and the Dionysian, each associated with a Greek mythic figure: Apollo, the god of light, "one who appears shining"; and Dionysus, the god of intoxication. The Apollonian and Dionysian are further explored in the context of visible form vs. formlessness and flux, dream vs. intoxication, moderation vs. excess, and rational knowledge vs. mysticism.

For Nietzsche, all representational artistic practices, including painting and sculpture, belonged to the realm of the Apollonian, that of the visible form which also connected it very closely to the plastic arts including architecture. Music, however – because it is not representational, has no physical, visible form, and produces heightened states of mind without representing phenomena – belonged to the Dionysian realm. Nietzsche not only outlines the division in the dual condition but also describes the simultaneity of the two realms in "Greek tragedy": "every artist is an 'imitator,' that is, either Apollonian dream-artist or Dionysian artist of intoxication, or finally – as for example in Greek tragedy – artist of dream and intoxication."[174] In fact, Nietzsche proposes that the only productive artistic practice is one that is able to fuse the two, simultaneously to work with both, to utilize the form-giving powers of the Apollonian to present the formlessness of the Dionysian. The creative production is where Nietzsche's Apollonian and Dionysian are held in tension, in the creative process and the work. This is not to say that there is no relation between the work and the artist. On the contrary, Jencks's analysis is quite sharp and to the point about Le Corbusier's personality. Yet, the interest in the current study remains the work and the analysis of the work itself, and not Le Corbusier's personality, upbringing, education, etc., although clearly, they influence one another.

173 Jencks, *Le Corbusier and the Tragic View of Architecture*, 182.

174 Friedrich Nietzsche, *The Birth of Tragedy.* Translated by Douglas Smith (Oxford: Oxford University Press, 2008), 23–24.

Charles Jencks connects Le Corbusier and his ideas of the order of the universe, nature, and geometric harmony to Plato. Nietzsche, on the contrary, sees Socrates (and Plato) as the end of "Greek tragedy." Nietzsche notes that the struggle between the two forces (Apollonian/Dionysian) was genuinely creative and the two forces would not allow a simple, positivistic resolution; they would keep one another in tension, suspended. Nietzsche also posits that post-Socrates, artistic production is resolved through a positive, formulaic affirmation of life, and a code is followed for the production of beauty wherein the work of art is no longer challenged or challenging. In fact, Nietzsche claims that this dual struggle (Apollonian/ Dionysian) is what is needed for artistic endeavors in his contemporary society and uses the music of Richard Wagner as an example. Jencks's analysis does not engage with this dual condition as a prerequisite for the production of works of art. In fact, he side-steps the entire question of the production of the work and speaks directly to Le Corbusier's psychological state as a "tragic hero." Moreover, Jencks does not resolve the conflict between two claims that are made in *Le Corbusier and the Tragic View of Architecture:* 1) Le Corbusier is attuned to Nietzsche in the context of "tragedy," and 2) Le Corbusier is attuned to Plato. Given Nietzsche's analysis that Socrates/Plato ended the Dionysian and foregrounded the Apollonian, the two claims cannot simply coexist without a proper theoretical contextualization, a model of which Nietzsche provides in *The Birth of Tragedy,* to which Jencks does not attend.

Jencks and, prior to him, Paul Turner have clearly established Le Corbusier's familiarity with Nietzsche from an annotated copy of *Zarathustra* dated 1908. Jencks also cites a 1945 sketch that Le Corbusier made "while he was struggling with the authorities over the 'Unité at Marseille.' It is a double portrait perhaps of himself: part Apollo, part Medusa, part the smiling sun god of reason, part the Dionysian, sensual figure of the underworld – a dark bitterness just barely balanced by joy and light."[175] *(ill. p. 118 bottom)* Although a copy of *The Birth of Tragedy* has not been recorded as owned or read by Le Corbusier, the two documents above and Jencks's book-length analysis provide convincing evidence of Le Corbusier's awareness of Nietzsche's exploration of Greek tragedy in terms of Apollo and Dionysus. The question remains how Le Corbusier addressed the conflict between his Apollonian/Platonic views of geometric beauty and harmony and Nietzschean views of the Dionysian.

Nietzsche places architecture squarely with the representational and plastic arts, along with painting and sculpture. Of course, he is right in the context of the plastic arts as architecture is always, by nature, material – and therefore visually present form. However, the complicating factor lies in architecture's relationship to representation. Architecture does not necessarily represent anything. Over time, with an established culture of architecture, it may begin to refer to its own history and associations, and thus represent politics,

175 Jencks, *Le Corbusier and the Tragic View of Architecture,* 182.

governments, the power of a church, wealth, and so on. But this appears to be a secondary layer of readings over architecture's primary concern: idea as material. In this context, architecture can also belong to the Dionysian, as it can conjure awe-inspiring emotions like the sublime would. So, already here, within itself, architecture has access to the Apollonian and the Dionysian. This, I argue, is one of Le Corbusier's aims: to present (the Apollonian/Platonic) ordered beauty that is codified through harmony and geometry, yet, at the same time, to present space, light, and texture as the sublime and powerful – thereby creating intense emotions. In Le Corbusier's context, the Apollonian is the engineer's realm: the realm of the laws of economy and the universal laws of nature, geometric harmony, and the organization of the building systems based on systemic order. The Dionysian, on the contrary, is the realm of the architect, affecting the senses acutely through space, light, and texture, reaching heightened emotion that moves the senses:

> Architecture has graver ends; capable of the sublime, it impresses the most brutal instincts by its objectivity; it calls into play the highest faculties by its very abstraction. Architectural abstraction has this about it which is magnificently peculiar to itself, that while it is rooted in hard fact, it spiritualizes it, because the naked fact is nothing more than the materialization of a possible idea.[176]

THREE MODELS FOR THE DUAL CONDITION

In *The Birth of Tragedy,* Nietzsche gives us three models that help conceptualize the Apollonian/Dionysian dual condition:

FINITE AND LIMITLESS

Apollonian as finite and Dionysian as limitless. Codified notions of beauty, geometric proportions, and harmony rely strongly on the finite and limited. How can one have symmetry without limit? How can we have geometric proportions without forms defined by the exactitude of geometry. Architecture's relationship to finitude and limit is clear. The complicating factor is the "limitless." Sites are bounded, materials have limits, rooms are contained. How does architecture engage the limitless?

On the one hand, the Ahmedabad Millowners' Association Building very much abides by the logic of geometry – only possible through the finitude of definition: a square-shaped plan; a golden-rule rectangle defining the building's heights; a 4 × 5 meter grid of circular columns defining its structure; a single, vertical stair tower connecting all its floors; and almost vertically stacked lavatories.

176 Le Corbusier, *Towards a New Architecture,* 27–28.

↑ Exterior street view in 2019, across the ramp.

← View of the Ahmedabad Millowners' Association Building from the Sabarmati River, photograph by Lucien Hervé, ca. 1956.

All are visible and experienced as they are finite and their shapes and forms defined and static.

On the other hand, the ramp, the cafeteria, the roof elements, and the river play an important role in exploding the finite limits that define the building. The entrance ramp, an element already not contained within the building geometry, projects the building limits to the street on the west side and to the infinitude of the Sabarmati River on the east. *(ills. p. 95 top, p. 98)* The inverted-arch roof of the meeting hall explodes the space of the hall to the sky and projects intense light and shadows into the hall. *(ill. p. 100)* These are two examples of "infinitude" as imagined by Le Corbusier in the Ahmedabad Millowners' Association Building. Additionally, the finitude defined by the north and south party walls is paired with the open nature of the building's east and west sides. Space, air, views, breezes, and aromas are projected beyond the limit of the building volume and into space not contained by the geometry, yet still within the domain of the building. In the north-south direction, the building is contained by the party walls, but in the east-west direction, the building belongs to a continuity of space from Ashram Road to the river and the opposing bank. This condition is perhaps best evidenced by

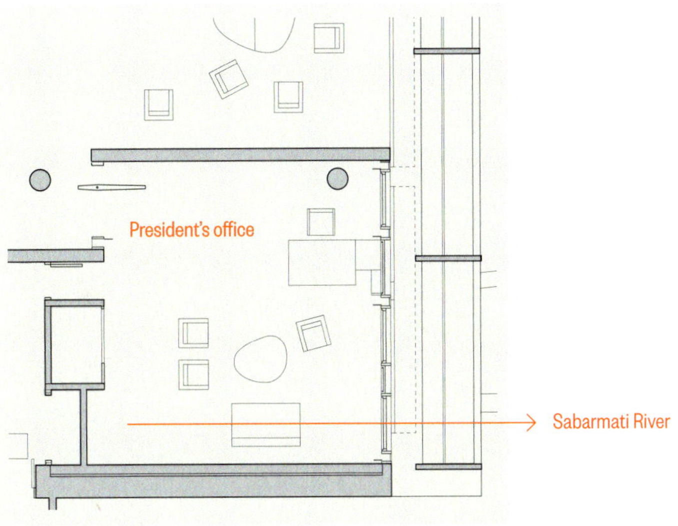

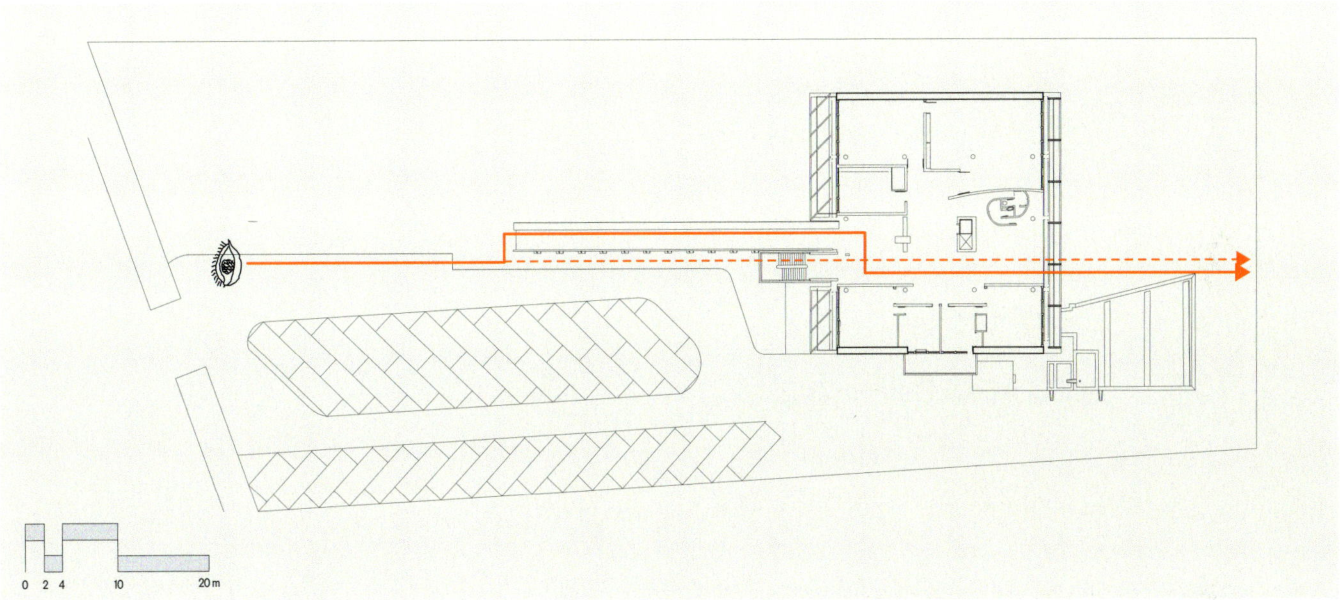

↑↑ President's office on the first floor. Infinitude is the spatial strategy here as all north–south enclosing walls have been removed and corners dissolved, thus allowing the space of the interior to continue uninterrupted to the river.

↑ Diagram of infinitude as a site strategy. The visitor can travel from Ashram Road to the Sabarmati River, through the building, without entering an enclosed space.

the two most widely known images of the building: one taken from the street along the ramp with the west façade in view and the other from the opposite bank of the river with bulls and mules in the foreground and the concrete retaining wall and building beyond.

In both images, we are held captive by the grasp of the building, though far from it. In addition, in the interior organization of the building programs, new conceptions of space are developed that do not rely on the conventional containment of each room and instead project a continuity of space, views, and materials beyond the finitude of the room. The president's office, for example, is bound by the glazed north-south wall. However, its space continues through the glass wall and projects beyond – certainly through the brise-soleil, and perhaps even to the river.

This is not a new strategy for Le Corbusier. Already in 1923, in the Maison La Roche, he was reconceptualizing the definition of space and questioning finitude and containment in favor of infinitude and continuity. In the Ahmedabad Millowners' Association Building, he is literally free to remove enclosures as he does not face

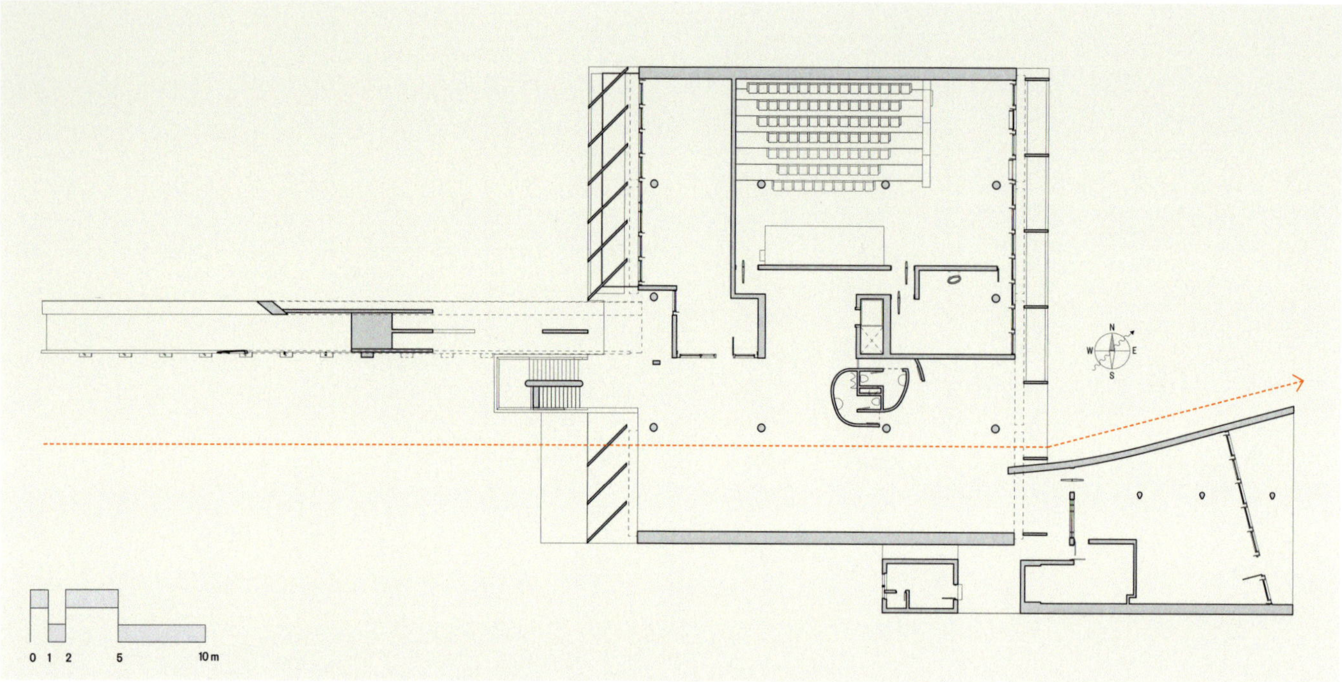

Ground floor plan with path from Ashram Road to Sabarmati River highlighted.

the Parisian climate and is able to push limitlessness and continuity of space to extremes. We can "travel" from Ashram Road to the Sabarmati River through the building on all three floors without setting foot in an enclosed interior space.

STATIC AND FLUXIVE

Apollonian as static and Dionysian as fluxive. The square-shaped plan of the Ahmedabad Millowners' Association Building, the golden-rule rectangle elevations, the column grid, the vertical stair tower, and vertically stacked bathrooms are all elements that are best described in static representations – for example, in a plan or section drawing, or in a photograph. Their relationship to beauty is through the precision of their static geometry and not through the way they would be experienced as architecture. Movement, both orchestrated and free, introduces a variable in architecture that does not exist in the other "representational and plastic" arts.[177] Architecture is experienced through movement. A golden-rule rectangular space that is entered symmetrically on the short side with a window placed symmetrically on the opposite short side is very different from a space with the same geometry entered tangentially on the long side with a source of light from above and behind that turns the visitor around towards the light. As described in Chapter III, Le Corbusier has gone to great lengths to organize movement in the Ahmedabad Millowners' Association Building and create a dynamic, ever-changing, awe-inspiring experience of space, light, and texture: the architectural promenade. The spaces of the breezeway on the first and second floors are not contained within the shape or the static geometry of the plan, but rather within space fluxively defined by the juxtaposition of several independent architectural elements: bathrooms,

177 This, in Nietzsche, refers to the late nineteenth century, before the popularization of moving pictures.

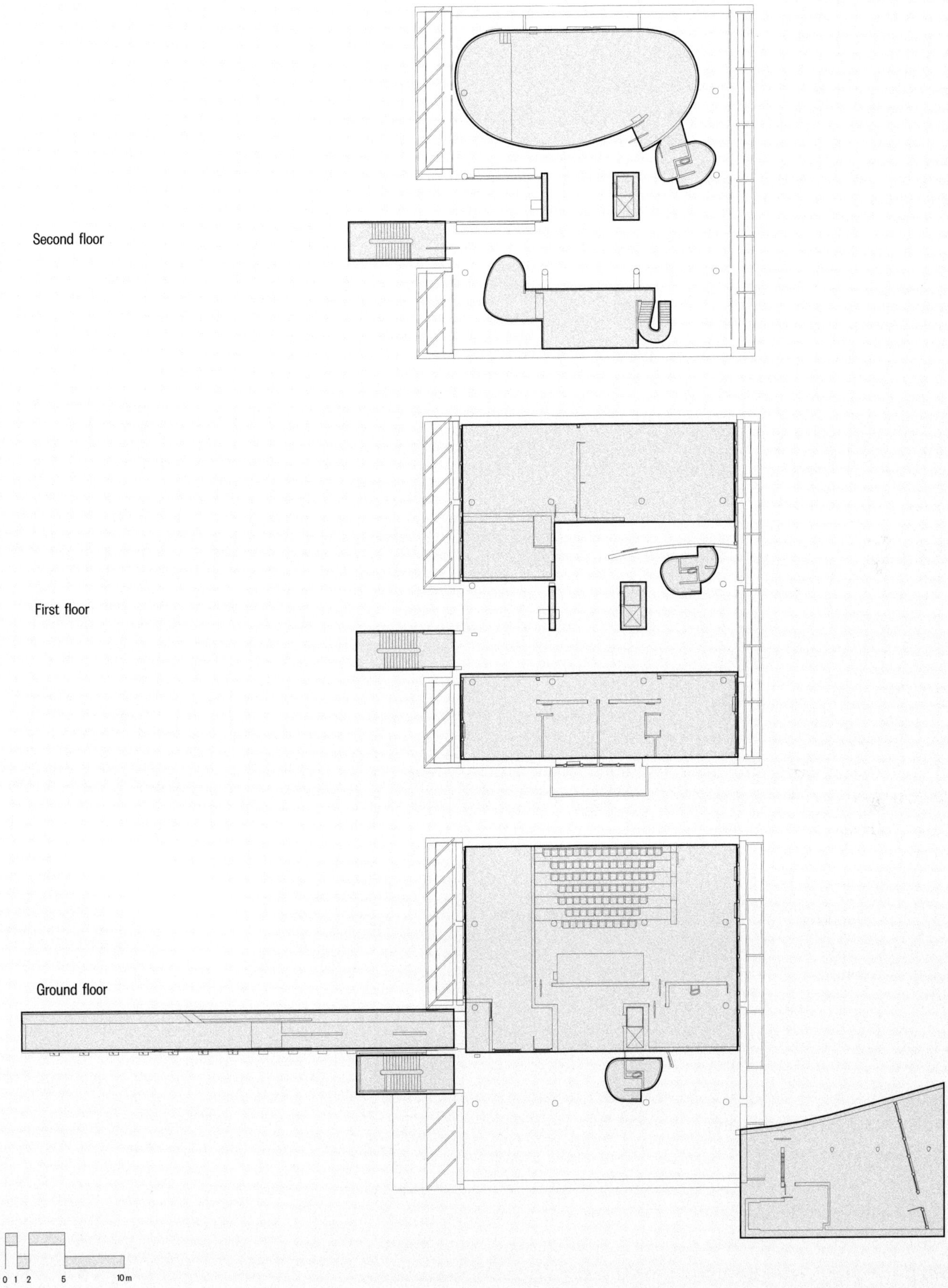

↑ Diagram of fluxive vs. defined space. The breezeways on all floors are not contained within the static geometry of the plan, but rather within space fluxively defined by the juxtaposition of several independent architectural elements.

elevators, walls, columns, stairs. Space is projected and imagined rather than defined, fluid rather than static.

What constitutes fluxive in architecture? All built works of architecture are material and had to have been described as "form" in order to have been built. So, at some point, all is form in architecture. There is no such thing as "formlessness." Given this as the foundation, however, it is important to distinguish between form that is designed to be comprehended as form, with clear delineations, absolute geometry, and proportion - and to be taken in at once and understood in the context of geometry and harmony - and form that is entirely projected from bits and pieces, fragments gathered through movement. In the Ahmedabad Millowners' Association Building, there are both types of form. One's conception of form in the building is governed by a dual condition, one aspect of which is the result of a static encounter with the squarish building volume defined by the geometry of the form. The other is informed by movement to, within, and through the building; glimpses of forms juxtaposed against one another; and the experience of spaces defined by those juxtapositions. Could one call this "formless?" Maybe! It certainly presents us with a very different conception of how we comprehend form. It does not present us with a complete form that can be understood as a designed shape with specific geometry; rather, we are asked to assemble forms and spaces as we move through them. Movement through the building aggregates spaces and forms. These two experiences of form in the Ahmedabad Millowners' Association Building, together, construct the experience of the building. Neither one is complete without the other and the tension between the two readings - one static and fixed; the other dynamic, fluxive, and changing - keeps us suspended. The fixity of one and the flux of the other create a tense space, which is the Ahmedabad Millowners' Association Building.

CONSONANCE AND DISSONANCE

Apollonian as consonant harmony and Dionysian as dissonant. And finally, the third conceptual model that Nietzsche presents is a compositional and strategic one. He opposes harmony and consonance with dissonance and argues for harmony belonging to the Apollonian and dissonance to the Dionysian. He describes the human condition as one that is marked by division and separation, torn, and fragmented from an original unity. Nietzsche suggests that dissonance is the human condition: "man" as dissonance.[178] This is significant in architecture because until the beginning of the twentieth century, architecture was generally wedded to consonance and harmony. Even Le Corbusier's early buildings did not project dissonance. Beginning with the "Dom-ino," Le Corbusier declares the possibility of the independence of elements: structural, enclosing, partitioning, circulating. They were fragmented from a whole and presented as in-

178 Nietzsche, *The Birth of Tragedy,* 130.

dependent elements, but dissonance was not yet in play in their composition. In the Ahmedabad Millowners' Association Building, we see not only the fragmentation of building elements but also dissonance as the compositional strategy that holds everything together.

For example, the structural grid of round columns and rectangular beams at the Ahmedabad Millowners' Association Building does not define the interior spaces. Each system (structure and interior partitions) belongs to its own organization and the relationship between them is completely dissonant. Not only is the structural grid not regular, but it also meets the interior partitions in compositionally dissonant ways. If we examine a typical pre-nineteenth-century building, we immediately recognize that, by necessity, all walls were structural and had to be laid one above the other, and they also had to define the interior and exterior partitions. So, in effect, all building systems were aligned, harmonious, and in consonance by necessity. In the Ahmedabad Millowners' Association Building, all walls and the structural columns are offset from one another, and to different degrees. If we start at the south wall moving north, the first row of columns is offset to the south of the first east-west set of walls, bringing the columns into the interiors of the programmed spaces. The next row of columns and walls to the north have a similar relationship in plan but the opposite in experience, as the columns are outside the programmed spaces rather than inside so they are a part of the vocabulary of the breezeway/entrance halls. (Two columns in this row have been assimilated into two concrete walls that provide lateral stability.)

We see a similar dissonance between the structural grid and the brise-soleil grid. On the west and east façades, there are four column bays – three of equal size, one larger. On the east façade, there are six equally spaced brise-soleil bays set against the four unequal structural bays with no alignment, in a state of complete dissonance. The west side is complicated by the oblique brise-soleil, the entrance ramp, and the stairs. Despite a beautifully configured, geometrically precise locating of the western brise-soleil, they appear dissonant from the structural column bays. The western end of the angled brise-soleil, which is the side most visible from the outside, appears randomly located in relation to the building's structural grid. However, the eastern end of the same appears completely in alignment with the column grid. Each of the three equal bays houses two brise-soleil bays plus the orthographic projection of the oblique angle. There is the appearance of three different harmonic systems, two governing one each of the two brise-soleil and one the structural grid. In addition, the east and west glazing systems have yet another rhythm of their own. There is a regular glazing dimension of 113 centimeters horizontally measured; however, there are also added ventilation screens of 19 centimeters that complicate the organization and put the rhythm of the glazing in dissonance with both the structure and the brise-soleil.

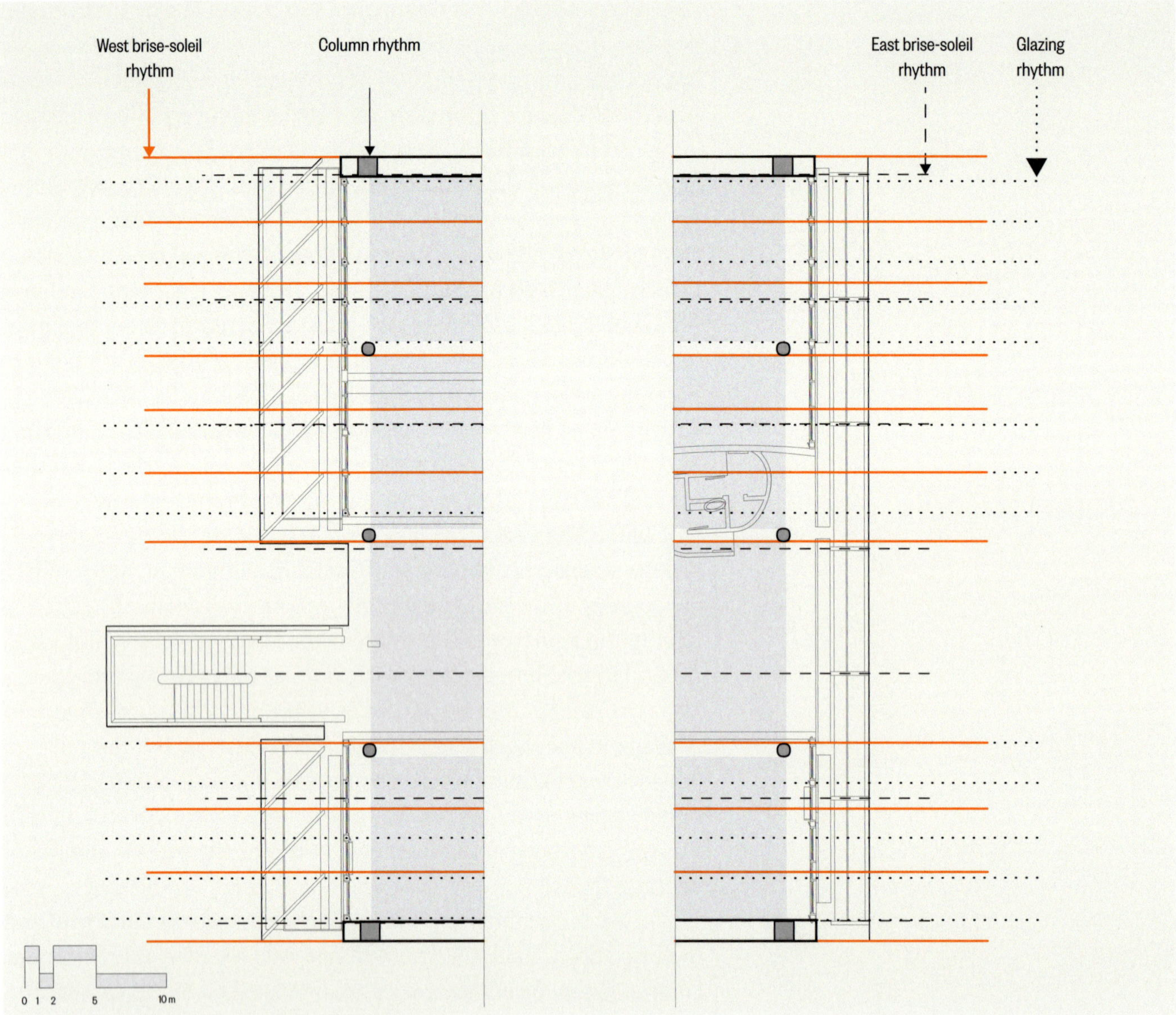

First floor plan with east and west edges described. The dissonance of the rhythms of architectural elements, such as brise-soleil, glazing, and columns are described with dashed and dotted lines.

↗ First floor isometric showing eight different column/wall relationships.

→ First floor plan with column/wall relationships highlighted.

The same dissonance exists between the many architectural elements that have been fragmented, separated, and identified from the unity of the building. These elements are the ones already discussed in Chapter III: lateral structural walls, the elevator, stairs, the ramp, bathrooms, the meeting hall and its roof element, two sets of mezzanine stairs, the mezzanine deck, the thirdfloor gate, and other elements. *(ill. p. 111)*

What holds them together and with the rest of the building is dissonance. First, they are fragmented from the unity of the building and then they are presented in juxtaposition to one another and the rest of the building elements in decided dissonance. What keeps the building and its elements together is the tension between its overall geometric harmony - expressed in the square-shaped plan, golden-rule-rectangle façades, and structural grid - and the ramp, stair, elevator, bathrooms, cafeteria, etc. with which it is set in dissonance. The Apollonian/Platonic, codified, static beauty achieved through harmony and geometry is set in tension with the Dionysian flux of space, light, and texture achieved through movement, creating sub-

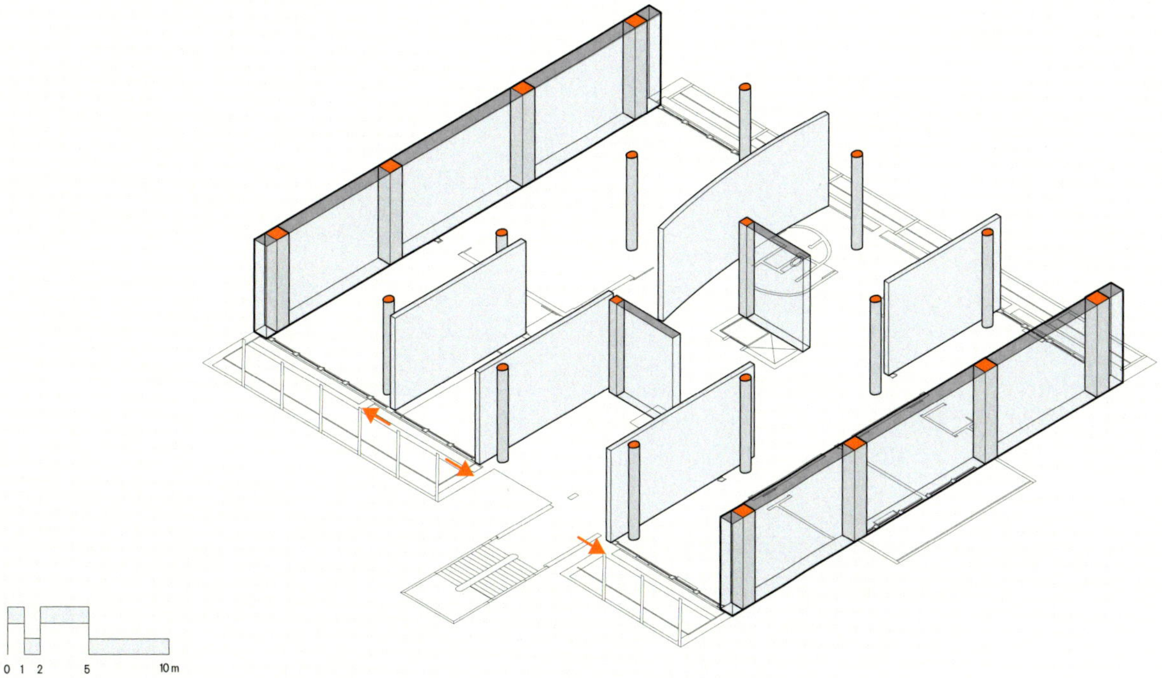
0 1 2 5 10 m

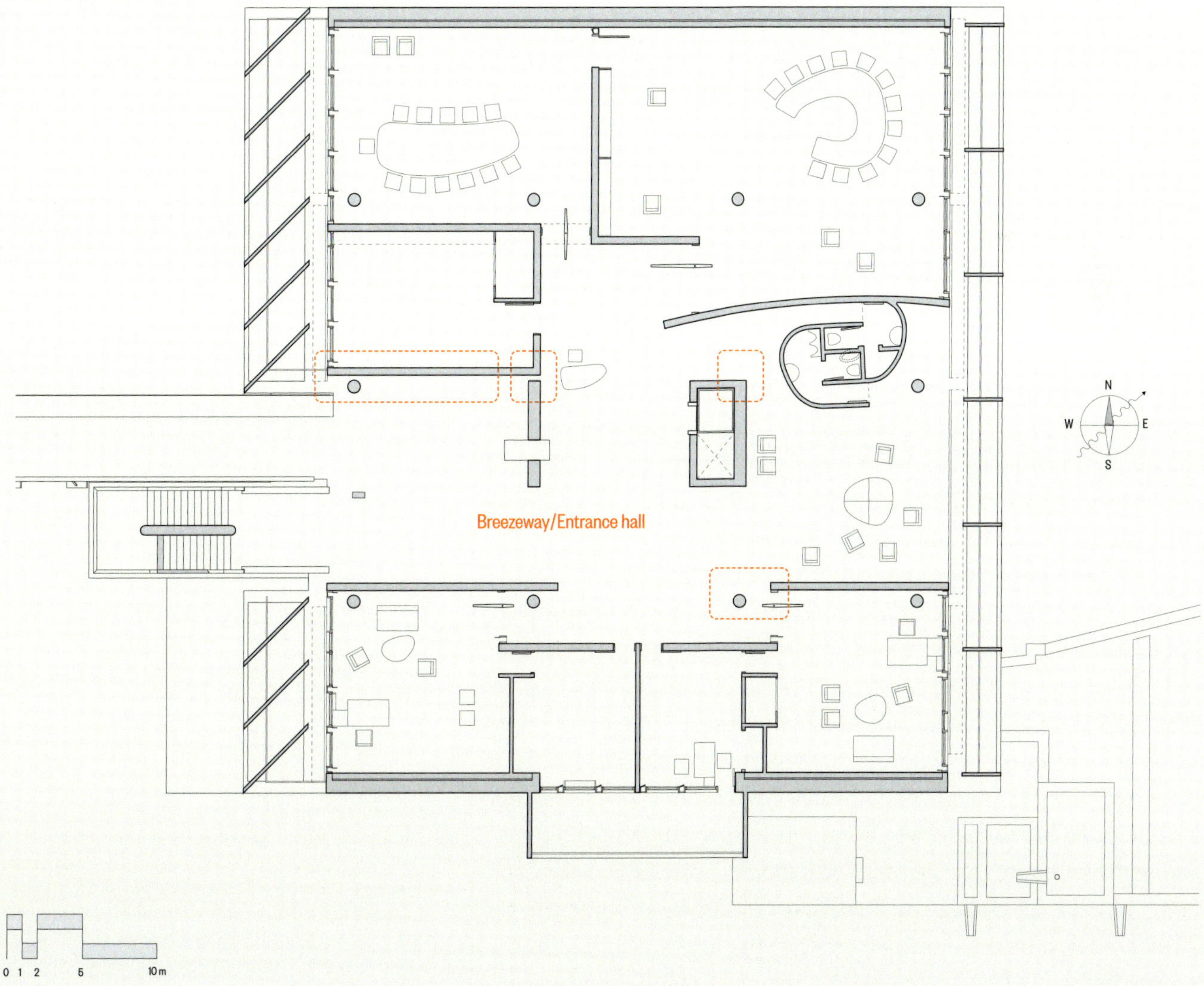
Breezeway/Entrance hall
N
E
S
W
0 1 2 5 10 m

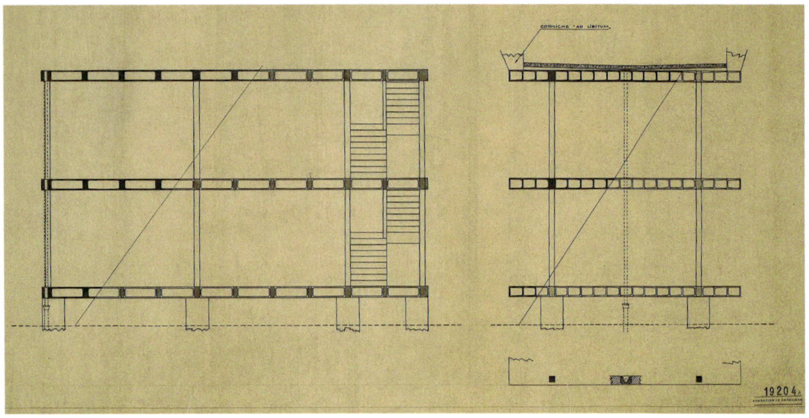

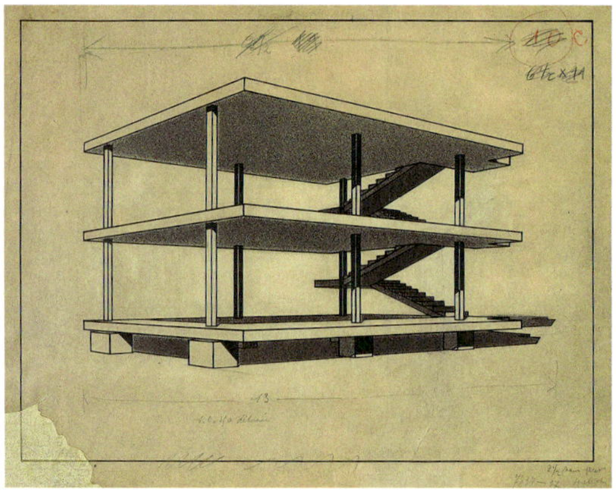

Maison Dom-Ino. Sections and perspective view.

lime and intense emotions – or, as Le Corbusier put it, "the Architect, by his arrangement of forms … affects our senses to an acute degree and provokes plastic emotions; … he wakes profound echoes in us, … it is then that we experience the sense of beauty."[179]

The argument here is not that Le Corbusier was following these three conceptual models developed by Nietzsche and putting them into practice in the Ahmedabad Millowners' Association Building. Rather, there are intellectual affinities between Nietzsche and Le Corbusier, and this, more than anything else, affects the formal and compositional strategies utilized by the latter in Ahmedabad. The proposal is that these affinities have translated into ways of working, conceptualizing, and composing architecture.

Despite these affinities, there are differences. Nietzsche saw the fusion and simultaneity of the Apollonian and Dionysian in Greek tragedy, and also saw it in Wagner's music. Architecture, for him, belonged to the Apollonian and the consonant, perhaps because he always saw it in the context of the "representational arts," as a part of which he considered all plastic arts such as sculpture and architecture. Le Corbusier would undoubtedly disagree with Nietzsche on the consideration of architecture as representational.

Le Corbusier focused on things that could be proclaimed and prescribed and things that belonged to a knowledge system that could be measured and quantified. Maison "Dom-Ino" focused on the structural frame and slabs, and the "five points" on what was made possible by the concrete structural frame.

His geometric proposals focused on plans and elevations abiding by rules of geometry. However, he, along with all prior architectural theorists, never theorized the aesthetics of space beyond geometry and quantifiable concerns.[180] From Vitruvius onwards, architectural theory has been wedded to the trinity of firmness, commodity, and delight – and delight was always held to derive from geometric proportion and beauty. The prescriptions and proclamations belonged to the realm of the engineer, as Le Corbusier defined it: the realm of geometry, systems, and quantifiable knowledge. But clearly, there is something else at work in Le Corbusier's practice. He has referred to it as the ineffable quality; the indescribable, plastic emotion, affecting our senses to an acute degree; and the sublime.

179 Le Corbusier, *Towards a New Architecture*, 7.

180 Even in the realm of geometry, as previously noted, Vitruvius, Alberti, and Ruskin have all presented aesthetic theories that have large conceptual gaps in them; inconsistencies that privilege an architecture that adheres not only to geometry and proportional systems, but also to a particular kind of geometry that belongs to a mythical origin of the discipline.

These all refer to something that lies outside the bounds of the prescriptions and proclamations yet that is achieved along with them and through them. All these references are shrouded in a mist of mysticism and are never codified; indeed, they are not explained. Le Corbusier follows in the footsteps of architectural theorists so long as he is in the realm of prescriptions and proclamations. However, the moment he ventures away from that definable, finite, and static realm, he is in a territory that is, at best, at the margins of the traditions of architectural theory. His capacity as an architect allows him to formulate these indescribable spaces and forms in material, but as a writer and a theorist he remains in the mist of mysticism once he leaves geometry and harmony. How could he describe the west façade of the Ahmedabad Millowners' Association Building in terms of geometry and harmony? The overall shape fits within the golden-rule rectangle, therefore abiding by the prescriptions of geometric harmony – the same ones that have existed and been prescribed by Vitruvius, Alberti, and others. The rest of the façade, however, will be difficult to describe in terms of geometry: brise-soleil across two equal bays to the north, followed by a larger bay to the south defined as a cavity that houses the end of the ramp and the stairs, a large multi-story opening, and multiple other architectural elements (gates, lateral concrete walls, openings, columns) followed by a small bay of brise-soleil at the southernmost section of the façade.[181] Intersecting the vertical lines are four concrete slabs (including the ground floor slab) that divide the façade into three unequal, horizontal segments, each with its own brise-soleil divisions, with the roof element being the heaviest of all four. This is truly a collage of architectural elements juxtaposed against one another and against the building geometry. In this context, the brise-soleil serve as a field that provides a ground through which fragmented, identifiable building elements can play as figures, push and pull, act and react, open and close, cast light and shade, and circulate in and out, resulting in an intertwined composition of tensions.

181 I have already described the dissonant nature of the relationship between the rhythm of the brise-soleil and the remaining building systems, columns, walls, and glazing.

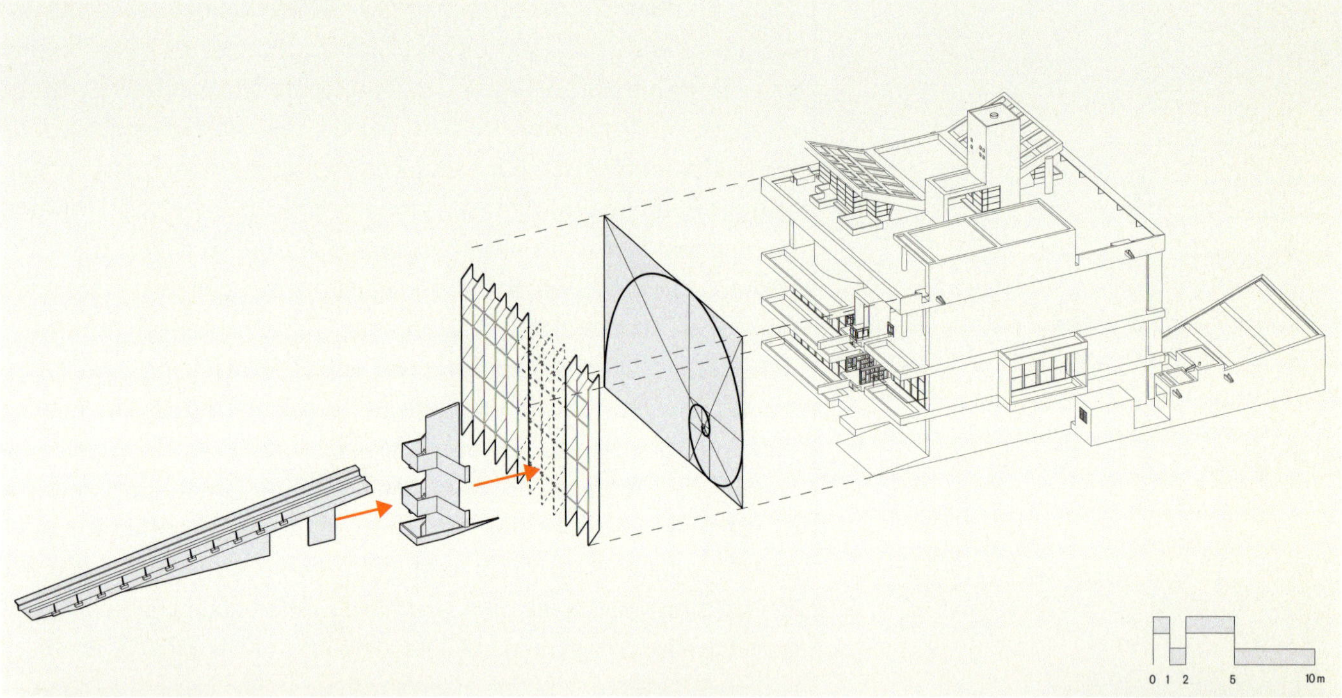

↑ Exploded isometric drawing showing the west façade geometry and its proportions against the geometry of the golden-rule rectangle.

↓ Partial west façade with brise-soleil and the three-story volume.

V
CONCLUSION

← West side three-story open-air volume, looking northeast from the first floor ramp/stair landing, catching the last of the evening sun rays.

The questions being explored here by examining one of Le Corbusier's mature, later projects are whether the theoretical foundations of his buildings belong to the classical history of architectural theory dating from Vitruvius onward and, if so, how Le Corbusier's unparalleled formal inventions fit within that classical theory? If not, then where exactly do his theories fit?

Undoubtedly, Le Corbusier steadfastly believed in the absolute beauty of pure geometric forms:

> Our eyes are made to see forms in light; light and shade reveal these forms; cubes, cones, spheres, cylinders or pyramids are the great primary forms which light reveals to advantage; the image of these is distinct and tangible within us and without ambiguity. It is for that reason that these are *beautiful forms, the most beautiful forms.* Everybody is agreed as to that, the child, the savage and the metaphysician. It is of the very nature of the plastic arts.[182]

He adds, "Primary forms are beautiful forms because they can be clearly appreciated."[183] We see this not only in his writing but also in his buildings. In fact, in the same book as the quotations above, Le Corbusier cites François Blondel's Porte Saint-Denis,[184] the façade of the Arsenal of Athens's Piraeus, Achaemenian cupolas, Paris's Notre Dame, Rome's Capitol, and Versailles's Petit Trianon – all with regulating lines traced over images and drawings of the buildings, proving their adherence to geometry: circles, squares, and golden-rule rectangles.[185]

182 Le Corbusier, *Towards a New Architecture,* 31 [emphasis in original]. This appears in the first of three chapters titled "Three Reminders to Architects", this one is subtitled "I. Mass." The other two chapters are "II. Surface," and "III. Plan." These essays had originally appeared in the journal *L'Esprit Nouveau* in volumes 1, 2, and 4 respectively. Note that the primary forms Le Corbusier names as "beautiful forms" are the forms commonly referred to as Platonic solids.

183 Le Corbusier, *Towards a New Architecture,* 26.

184 Blondel served as the first architecture chief of the French Academy system. He tried, in vain, to establish a precise set of dimensions for the classical orders that could be used by all architects to design "beautiful" buildings.

185 Le Corbusier, *Towards a New Architecture,* 63–75.

The visual citation is continued with three of his own buildings. At first glance, they appear like the historical examples with over-drawn geometric regulating lines. However, upon closer inspection the geometry as described in these three buildings is different from that of the historical examples Le Corbusier cites. In his own buildings, he develops a proportioning system from the geometry of the building, which he then uses to proportion and locate windows, doors, sections of the building, and so on. In other words, there is an adherence to geometry, but one that is developed within the building rather than imposed from without. Geometry and proportion still rule, but they do not necessarily belong to primary geometric forms; they are instead invented as harmonic systems internal to the building, much closer to Alberti's edict than Vitruvius's.[186] We see how Le Corbusier completely adheres to the history of architectural theory yet is able to manipulate the rules of that history in such a way that would permit him formal and spatial innovations outside primary geometric forms.

Clearly, Le Corbusier has a complex relationship to geometry. He can neither simply let go of it nor absolutely adhere to its primary forms and relations. He calls out the "necessity of order" and explains that "the regulating line is a guarantee against willfulness."[187] Most importantly, that "it brings satisfaction to the understanding,"[188] engaging the intellect in the way that Plato would suggest for a discipline involving precision, such as architecture.[189] Nonetheless, Le Corbusier adhered to geometry as the language of "man": "For all these things - axes, circles, right angles - are geometrical truths, and give results that our eyes can measure and recognize; whereas otherwise there would be only chance, irregularity and capriciousness. Geometry is the language of man."[190]

Undoubtedly, Le Corbusier also believed steadfastly in architecture's ability and responsibility to acutely affect the senses in a manner that he could name only as sublime - something that was impossible to achieve through harmony and geometric proportions alone: "Architecture has graver ends; capable of the sublime, it impresses the most brutal instincts by its objectivity."[191] The object of architecture - its very physical material forms and spaces - what Le Corbusier called the "naked fact of architecture," also has the ability to move the human spirit. The architect spiritualizes the material facts.[192] Le Corbusier points to the simultaneity of these dual conditions: the adherence to conceptions of systemic order and geometric harmony, and the aspiration to move the human spirit in a way that exceeds the possibility afforded by order and harmony to achieve beauty and sublimity at once. For Le Corbusier, the question is not whether to reference Apollo or Dionysus but how to construct Dionysus from Apollo, how to construct the Dionysian through the language of the Apollonian, how to create spaces and experiences that acutely affect the senses but are constructed through reconceptualizing the language of the systemic order of the building systems.

186 Le Corbusier, *Towards a New Architecture,* 76–79.
187 Le Corbusier, *Towards a New Architecture,* 64.
188 Le Corbusier, *Towards a New Architecture,* 64.
189 Plato acknowledges that the master-builder has a share in theoretical knowledge, but only offers an ambivalent relationship to architecture. He calls it an art which is therefore involved in judgment, yet it cannot exist outside of the material world, precision, and mathematical calculation. It is also closely associated with theoretical knowledge and aspires to beauty and the promotion of good in society. It is a discipline that swings between the representational arts and theoretical knowledge, never able to belong to one exclusively. Perhaps best described by Plato via his term *khora,* as the *ground* on which the distinction between form and formlessness, and between constructed space and "mere" space, takes place. It is the ground for the distinction between what can and cannot be thought - hence, Plato's use of "bastard reasoning": not completely "reason," but also not outside "reason."
190 Le Corbusier, *Towards a New Architecture,* 68.
191 Le Corbusier, *Towards a New Architecture,* 27–28.
192 Le Corbusier, *Towards a New Architecture,* 28.

THE MEETING HALL

The second floor meeting hall in the Ahmedabad Millowners' Association Building provides a succinct example. This is a large space on the top floor of the building, just below the roof. It is also the culmination of the architectural promenade. The meeting hall is programmatically of a size that could not be accommodated within the structural grid of the building. Its space occupies almost six bays: three long in the east-west direction and two wide in the north-south. Had Le Corbusier simply abided by the order of the building system – in this case, structure – there would have been two columns in the middle of the space, something very undesirable from a functional standpoint for a meeting hall with a stage. Le Corbusier eliminated these two columns. Given there are no additional floors above the space, the missing columns only needed to carry the weight of the roof. This could have been addressed structurally by adding deeper beams to carry the load of two bays. This is a typical engineering solution and is referred to as a transfer beam. These beams could have been hidden from sight, so one would never have known how the roof was held up. Le Corbusier, however, in a very clever move, lifted the roof and exposed it as an independent and expressive element which allowed clerestory lighting into the meeting hall, an otherwise dark space. Rather than the flat roof which covers the rest of the building, the meeting hall received an inverted-arch concrete roof cantilevered at its eastern and western ends. This arched roof compresses the space towards the middle of the meeting hall and expands it at the eastern and western extremes, towards the entrance and the stage respectively, and towards the sky and light. The arch is a stable structural shape and its smooth, curved bottom surface creates a reflective texture off of which light bounces. The depth and type of structural members that permit the concrete arch to span two bays in the north-south direction and to cantilever one bay each towards east and west are above the arch and invisible from below. The roof is an upside down, structural waffle slab, curved to the shape of a shallow arch, with varying thickness: thickest in the middle and thinning as it gets to the cantilevered extremes. The added weight of the inverted-arch concrete roof is supported by the structure of the north party wall and two concrete walls that have assimilated the round columns to the south: the eastern shear wall of the elevator and the wall in front of and east of the ramp. *(ill. p. 93 top)*

The interior of the meeting hall is clad in dark walnut plywood in a diagonal pattern. The darkness of the interior is contrasted with the white ceiling and the light of the sky penetrating from the clerestory opening, making the roof appear as a featherlight element floating above the space with all horizontal and vertical structure invisible. Nowhere else in the building do we see this level of genius in addressing the logic of the building systems yet making the same systems present unprecedented spaces and textures in light, shadow,

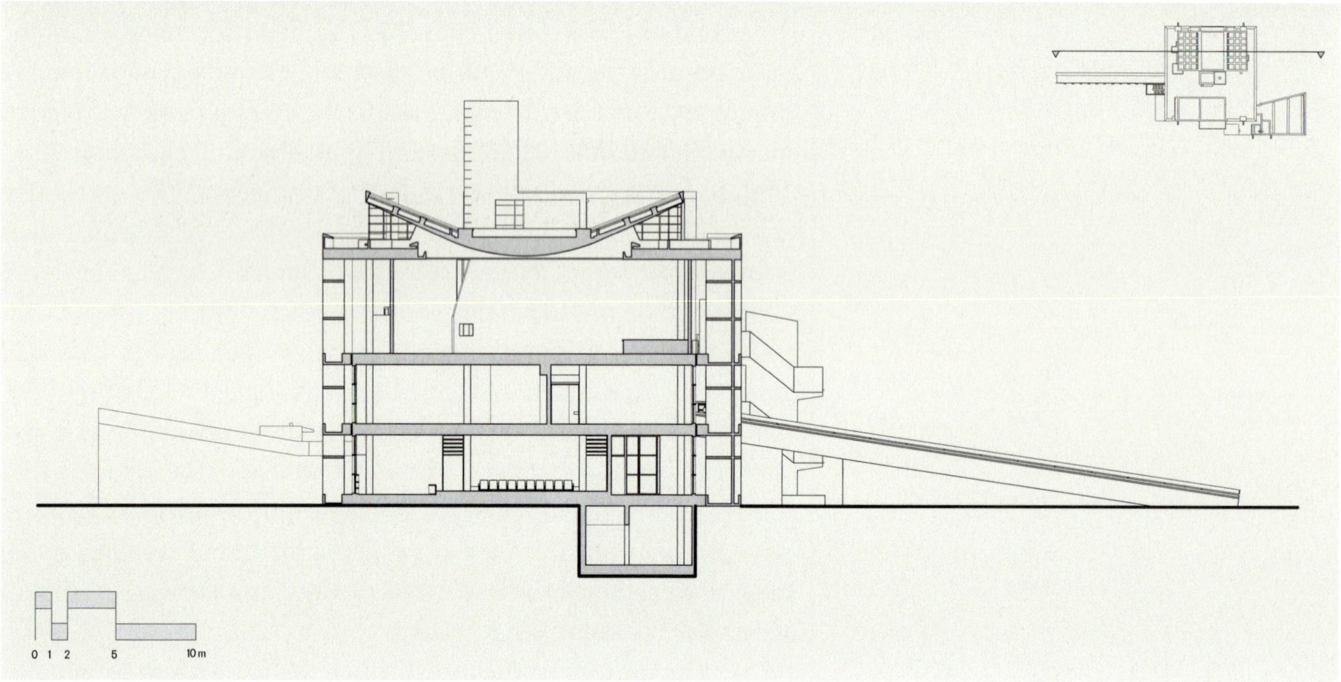

↑ Interior of second floor meeting hall looking north.

↓ East-west cross section through the meeting hall with inverted-arch roof.

→ Interior of second floor meeting hall looking south towards entrance.

and color. The meeting hall at once belongs to the building systems and defies their prescriptions. It utilizes the language of the building systems to express a space which is not imaginable within that language. The meeting hall is suspended in tension between the logic of the building's systems and its formal/spatial proposition: Corbusian beauty and Corbusian sublime constructed together in tension and presented one through the other.

EPILOGUE

The meeting hall on the second floor of the Ahmedabad Millowners' Association Building is not a unique instance in Le Corbusier's work. He often uses the regularity of the geometric language of the building systems to construct spaces and forms that do not belong to that language and appear impossible within the codes of its geometric definition. As much as Le Corbusier believed in the harmony of pure geometric forms and the strict geometry of building systems, his relationship to geometry was much more complex. He could neither simply put it aside nor absolutely adhere to its primary forms and relations. He also undoubtedly believed in architecture's ability and responsibility to acutely affect the senses in a manner that he could name only as sublime, desiring architecture to "impress the most brutal instincts."[193] The meeting hall of the Ahmedabad Millowners' Association Building is suspended in the tension between earth and sky, dark and light, and between the logic of the building's systems and its singular, plastic experience.

In his writing Le Corbusier focused on matters belonging to a knowledge system that is measurable and quantifiable. In this, he belongs to a long history of architectural theory. From Vitruvius onwards, architectural theory has been wedded to the trinity of firmness, commodity, and delight – and delight always to geometric and proportional beauty. In distinction from that history, in Le Corbusier's architecture there is something else at work. He has referred to it as the "sublime," the "ineffable quality," the "indescribable," "plastic emotion," or "affecting our senses to an acute degree." These all refer to something that lies outside the bounds of geometric prescriptions and systemic proclamations yet is achieved along with them and, necessarily, through them. On the one hand, Le Corbusier's writings consider architecture as formal, privileging space over time, and static images and their geometric proportions over fluxive experience. His buildings, on the other hand, are plastic experiences that temporalize space through movement, suspending us in the tense space between the building's systems and its sublime experience.

193 Le Corbusier, *Towards a New Architecture*, 27–28.

VI
THE BUILDING TODAY

← The east side at sunset, 2024.

We know from Le Corbusier's sketches that the proximity of the Millowners' Association Building to Ahmedabad's Sabarmati River was both an opportunity and a structural threat – hence, the massive retaining walls and foundations at the eastern edge of the site. Photographs from the 1950s show the building in the context of the river and all its activity. More recently, with economic liberalization in India in full force, Western-style urban renewal has taken hold, with lanes of roadways, a median and a vast zone between the Millowners' Association Building and the river – including, during my visit, an entertainment complex with bouncy castles and trampoline parks. The river boundaries have been redrawn and controlled by constructed concrete banks. The following images are to record the current context and compare it with that of the 1950s.

↑ Comparative view from the Sabarmati River (looking west). The left image is from 1975, the right one from 2024. The natural riverbed was relocated east and bound by a concrete bank.

↓ This view from the east shows the building in its urban context, quite far away from the riverbank now, 2024.

↑ The four-story volume is now dwarfed by its taller neighbors, 2024.

↓ Aerial view with the garden and the mature trees surrounding the building, 2024.

↑ This drone photograph provides a vertical view of the building with its roof garden, 2024.

VII
DRAWINGS AND MODELS

The following set of drawings are based on the drawings produced by Atelier Le Corbusier between 1952 and 1954 for the Ahmedabad Millowners Association Building. Dimensions and physical facts have been checked, verified, and corrected through on-site field measurements in January 2019.

The set of drawings were used to construct a computational model to ensure the three-dimensional accuracy and alignment of the two-dimensional drawings. From these documents a physical model of the building was hand-fabricated in order to permit the study of individual floors, spatial conditions, and views no longer possible within the current context of the building. These models were fabricated by Ryerson Studio at a scale of 1:100.

After the completion of construction in 1954, there were modifications made by the architectural office of B. V. Doshi in the 1970s. These included the transformation of the ground floor clerical offices to a stepped lecture hall, which included the addition of several interior walls. This programmatic change permitted the use of the space by the public, which, even today, serves as a source of income and outreach for the organization. The lecture hall has direct access to the street, allowing the public to enter it without going through the more private parts of the building. The lecture hall was also supplied with a basement-located air conditioning system that introduced cool, humidified air through a trough at the back (north end) of the lecture hall. There were two large cooling ponds introduced at the east end of the yard to accommodate the air conditioning system, in lieu of the smaller system that was installed during construction.

In addition, a lavatory was added to the south side of the building, adjacent, and to the west of the kitchen/cafeteria volume. The lavatory is an independent small building which is only connected to the remainder of AMOA through the floor slab. Both changes remain today. The changes are documented in two floor plans, one as drawn by Atelier Le Corbusier and constructed in 1954, *(ill. p. 156 top)* and the other labeled "as modified in 1970s," which documents the addition of the lecture hall and the lavatory. *(ill. p. 155 bottom)* The cooling ponds have not been included in the drawings. More recently, the 1970s air conditioning system in the lecture hall was replaced with a split system, which has made the cooling ponds and all associated plumbing defunct.

There is also a metal roofed structure at the southeast corner of the site, adjacent to the cafeteria. This appears as a temporary structure and is not recorded in our drawings. Similarly, there are two small, roofed structures on the north side of AMOA that cover the well and pump associated with the 1970s version of the air conditioning system. We have not recorded these structures either.

In addition, there have been other small changes to the building. There are exposed electrical conduits feeding new lights and "split" air conditioning systems in most offices, which have necessitated drilling through the exterior envelope. The original three air conditioners, serving seven rooms on the first floor, are no longer serviceable. Their remains exist in two "closets" where they were originally installed. These minor changes have not been recorded in our drawings.

The Atelier Le Corbusier site plans document housing for caretakers at the northwest corner of the site, shielded from the rest of the site with a sinuously curved wall. These were never constructed and are not included in our drawings.

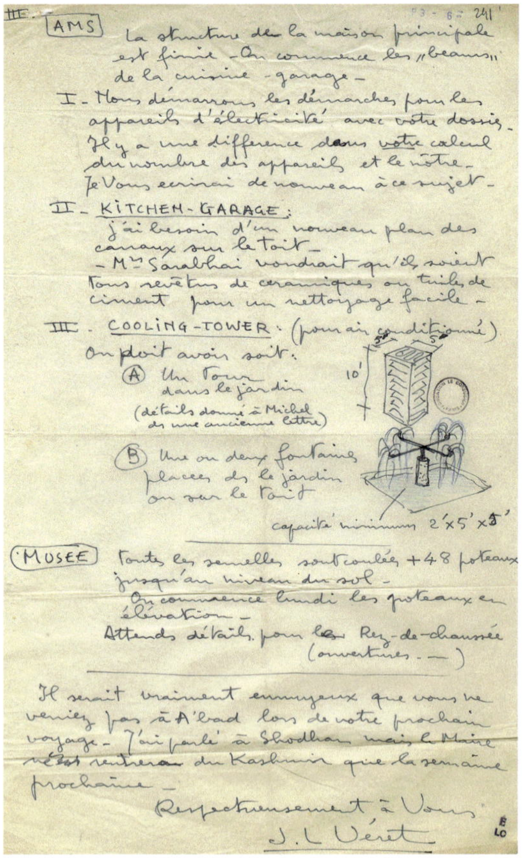
III. P3-6-241

AMS La structure de la maison principale est finie – On commence les "beams" de la cuisine-garage –

I – Nous démarrons les démarches pour les appareils d'électricité avec votre dossier – Il y a une différence dans votre calcul du nombre des appareils et le nôtre – Je vous écrirai de nouveau à ce sujet –

II – KITCHEN-GARAGE: j'ai besoin d'un nouveau plan des canaux sur le toit – Mme Sarabhai voudrait qu'ils soient tous revêtus de céramiques ou tuiles de ciment pour un nettoyage facile –

III. COOLING-TOWER: (pour air conditionné) On doit avoir soit:

(A) Un Tour dans le jardin (détails donné à Michel ds une ancienne lettre)

(B) Une ou deux fontaines placées ds le jardin ou sur le toit

10' 5' 5'

capacité minimum 2'x5'x5'

MUSEE Toutes les semelles sont coulées + 48 poteaux jusqu'au niveau du sol – On commence lundi les poteaux en élévation – Attends détails pour les Rez-de-chaussée (ouvertures. —)

Il serait vraiment ennuyeux que vous ne veniez pas à A'bad lors de votre prochain voyage – J'ai parlé à Shodhan mais le Maire ne rentrera du Kashmir que la semaine prochaine –

Respectueusement à Vous

J. L. Véret

Hand-written instructions about the "COOLING-TOWER," noting either a tower in the garden, or fountains placed in the garden or on the roof.

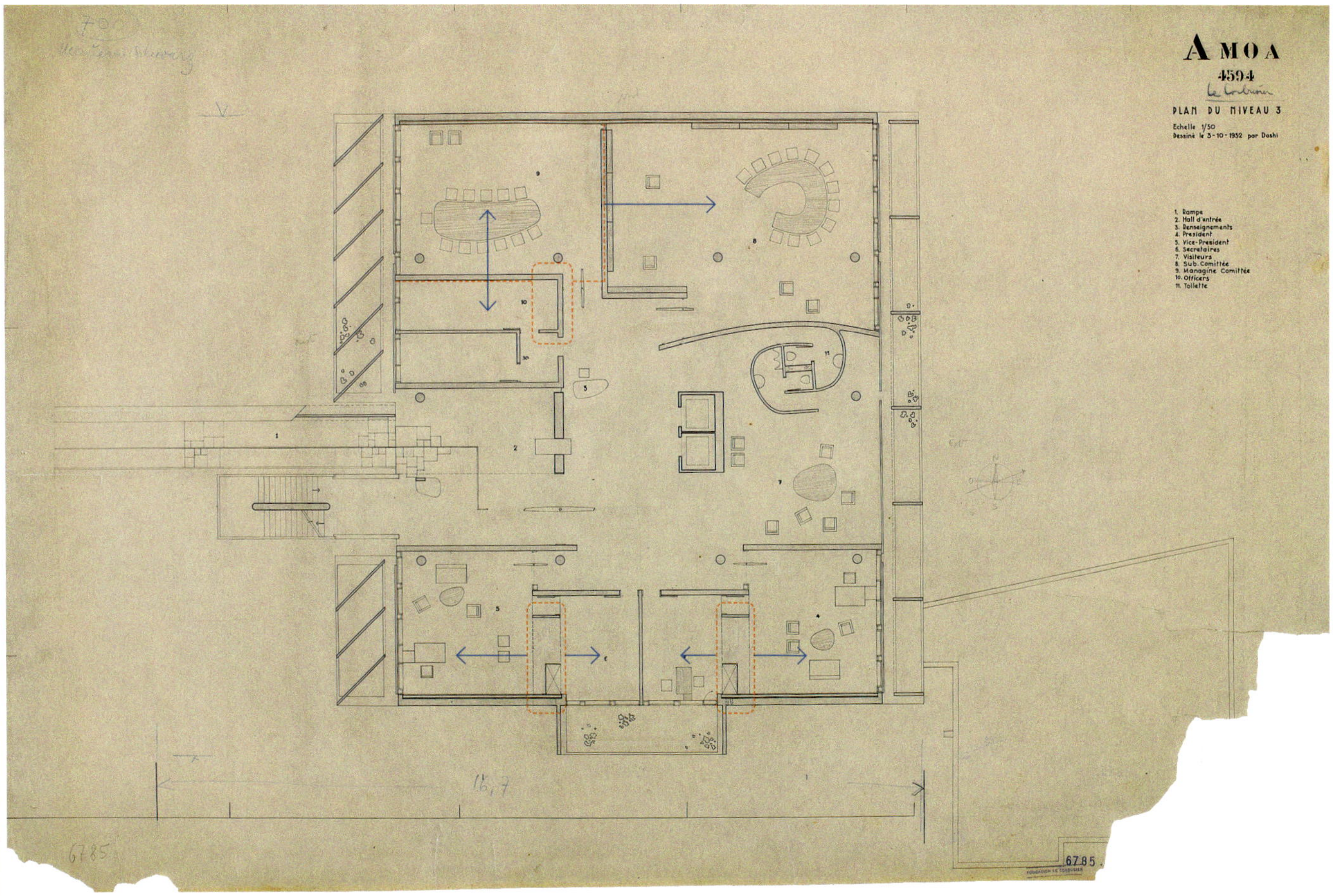

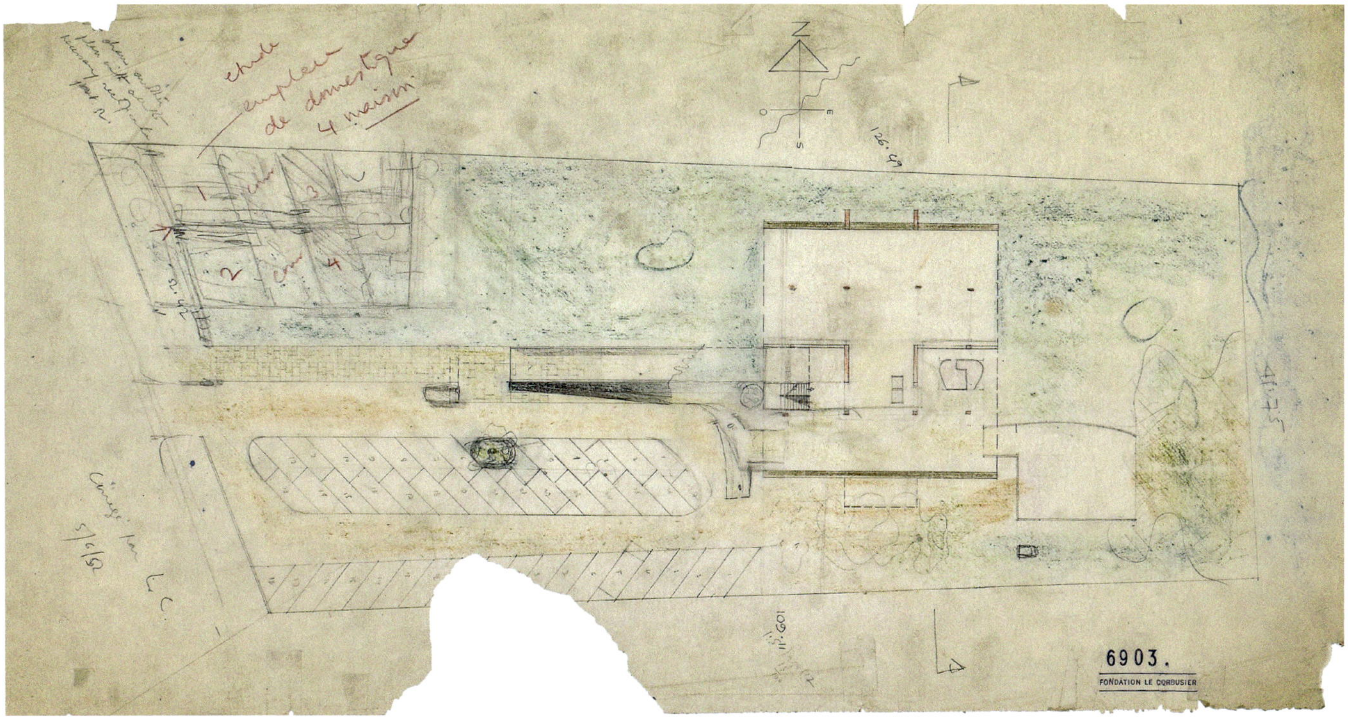

↑ First floor plan dated October 3, 1952. Here, two air conditioning systems are positioned along the south face of the building. A later version, dated November 30, 1953, locates a third system between two meeting rooms (highlights by the author).

↓ Site plan study, June 5, 1952, showing the location of the caretaker apartments that were never constructed..

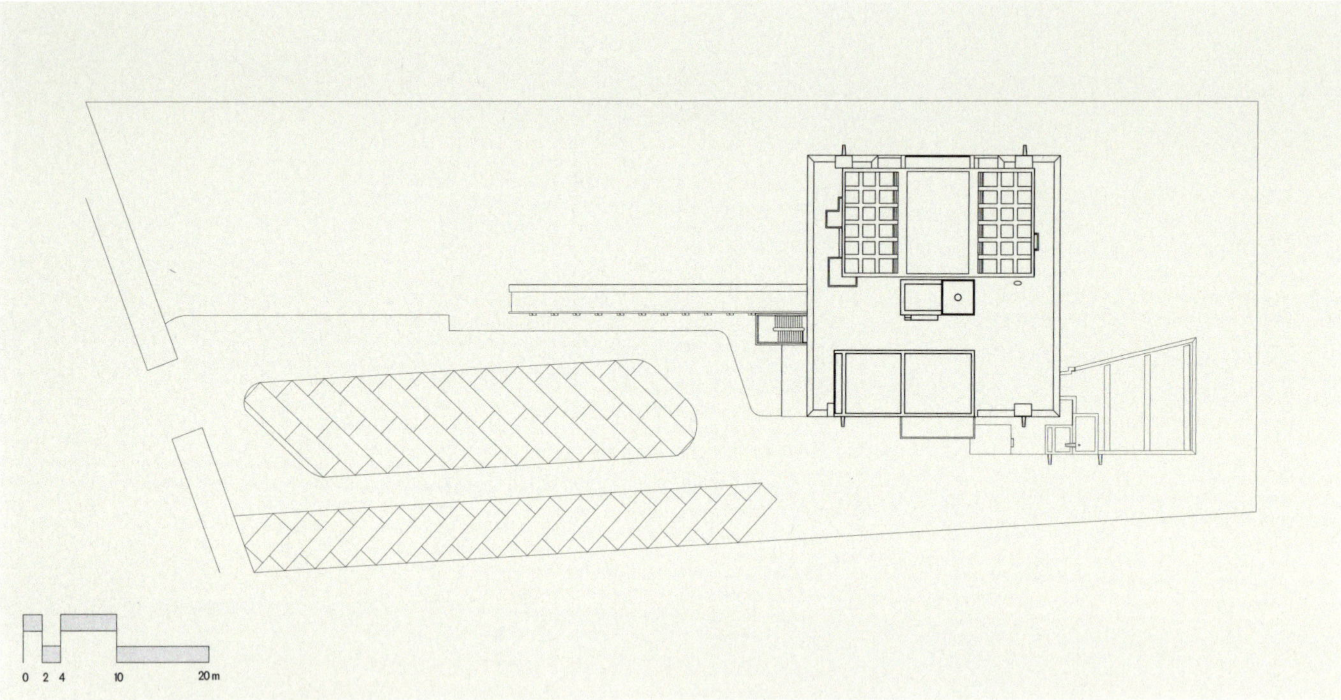

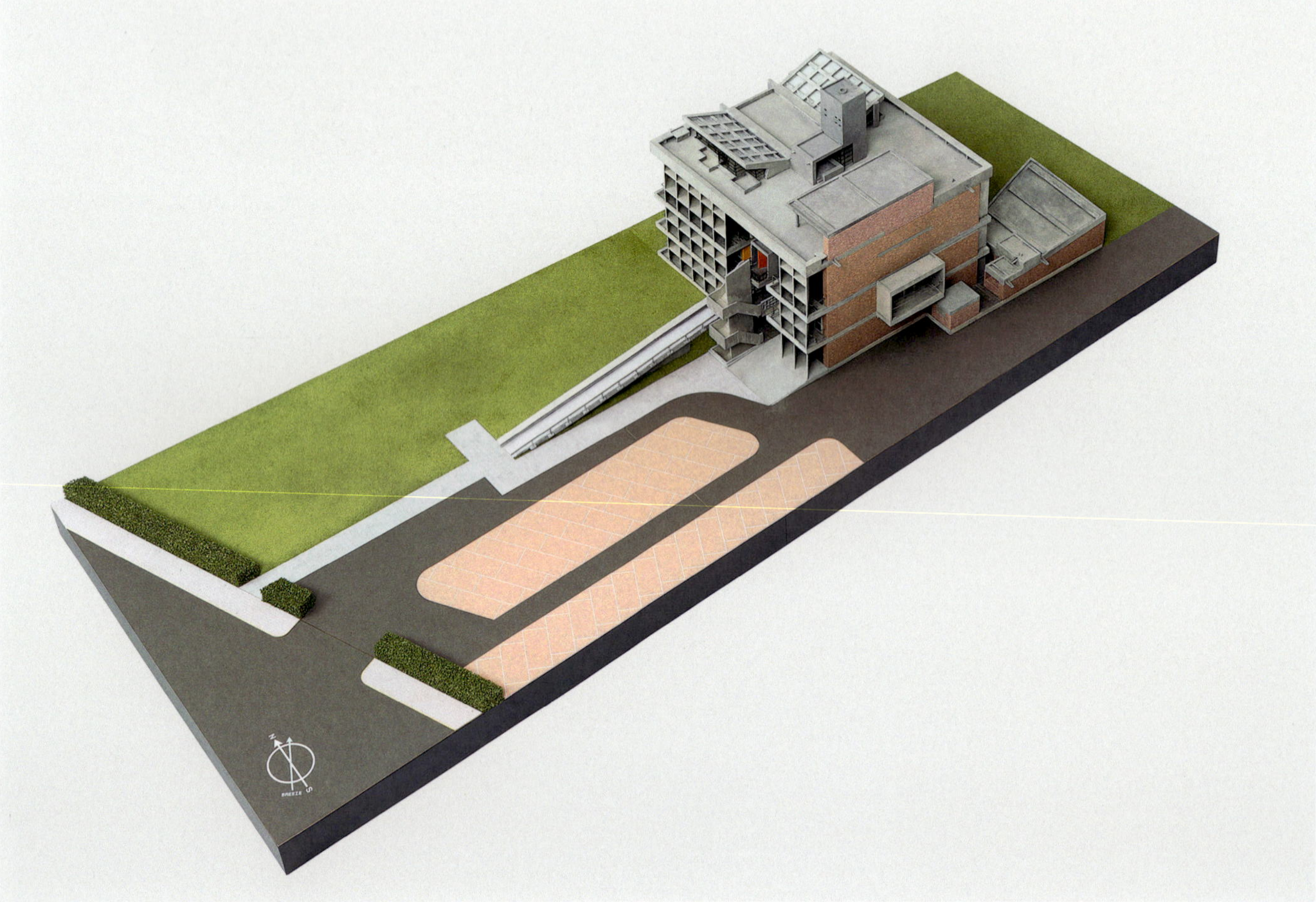

↑ Site plan, as constructed.

↓ Model of building with site, southwest view, including the bathroom added in the 1970s to the south.

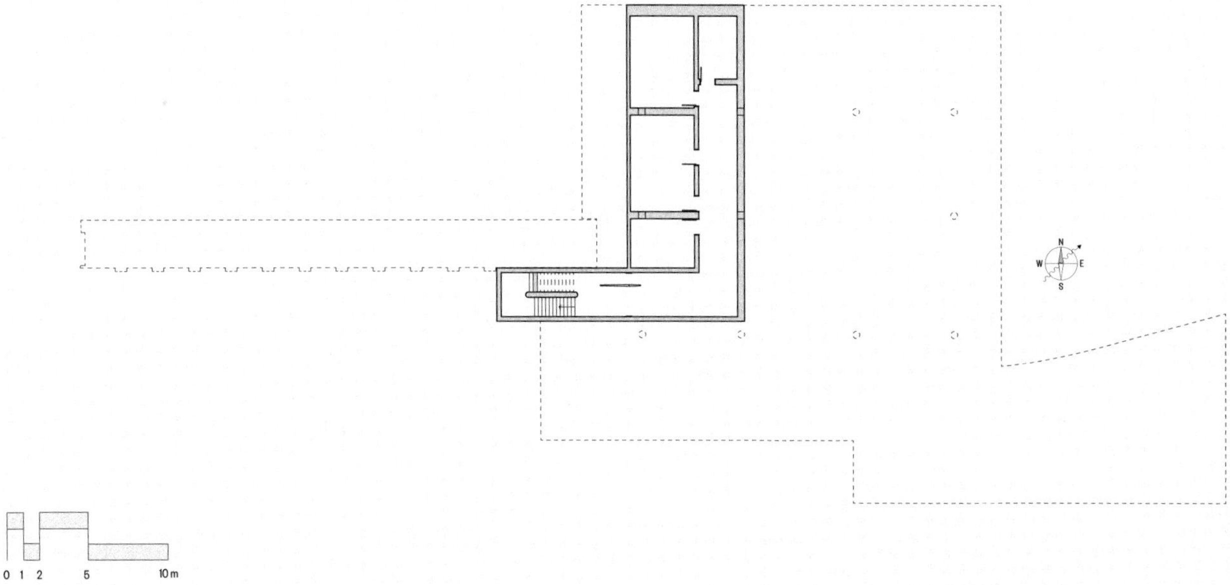

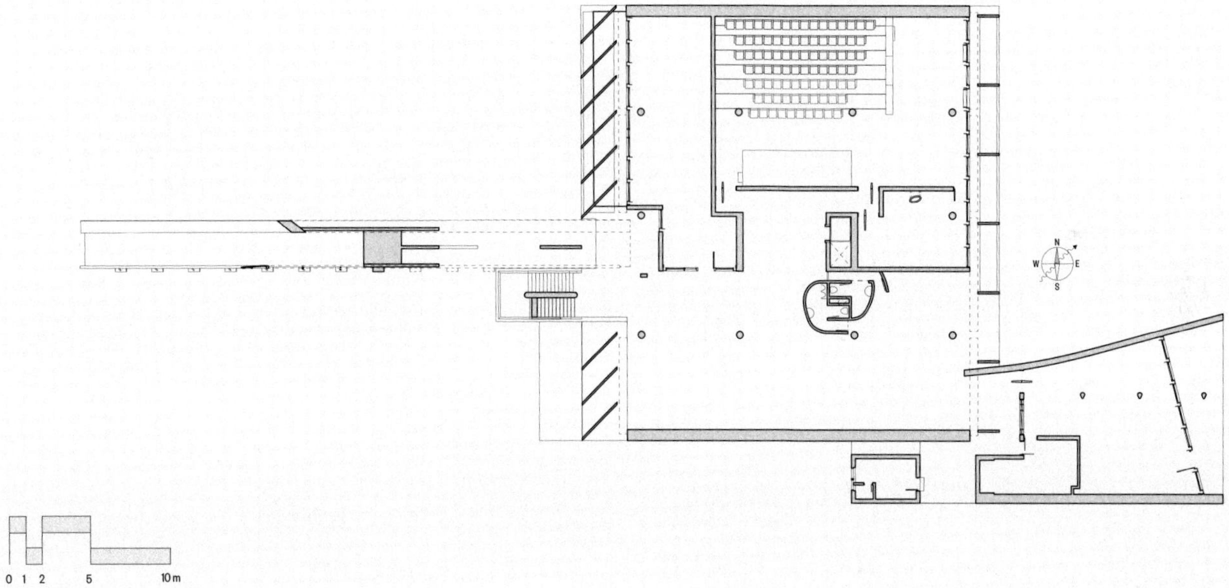

↑ Basement floor plan, as constructed, including changes during construction.

↓ Ground floor plan, as modified in the 1970s, with the addition of the lavatory facilities to the south and the reconfiguration of the clerical offices into a lecture hall.

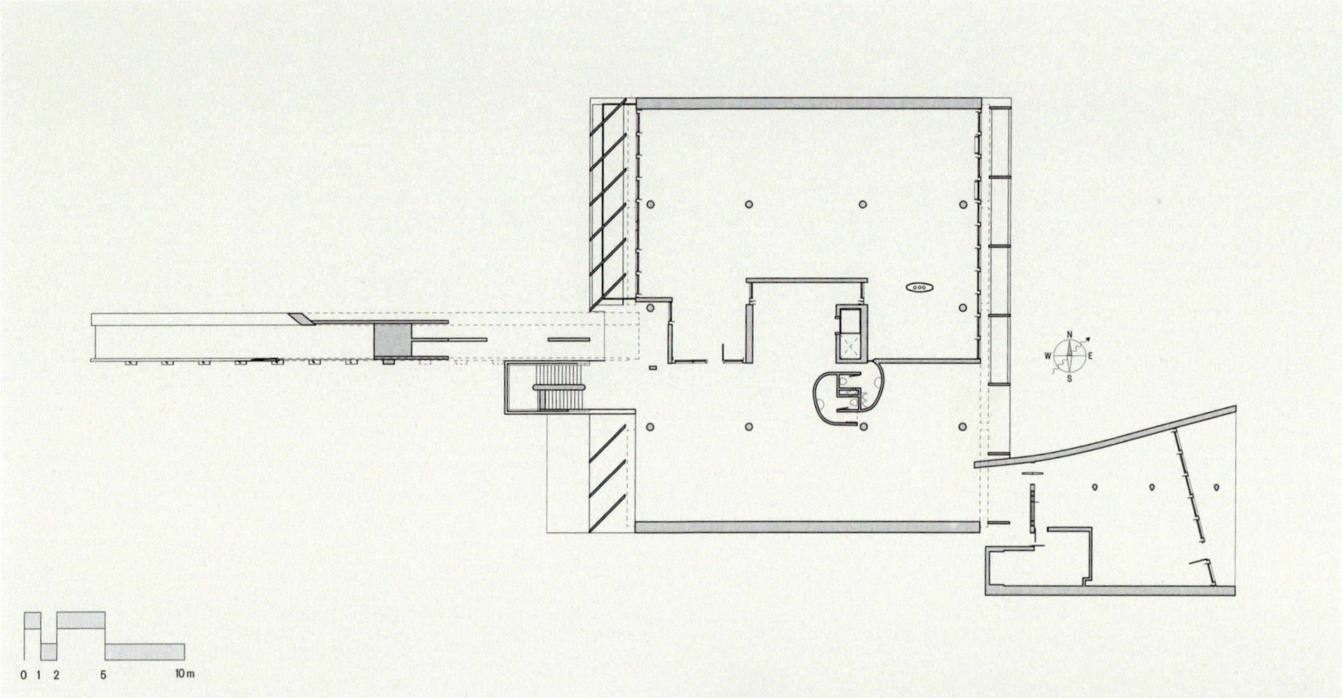

↑ Ground floor plan, as designed by Atelier Le Corbusier and constructed.

↓ Model of the ground floor, southwest view, showing the clerical offices to the north (these were later transformed into a lecture hall) and the open breezeway to the south. To the far right is the cafeteria.

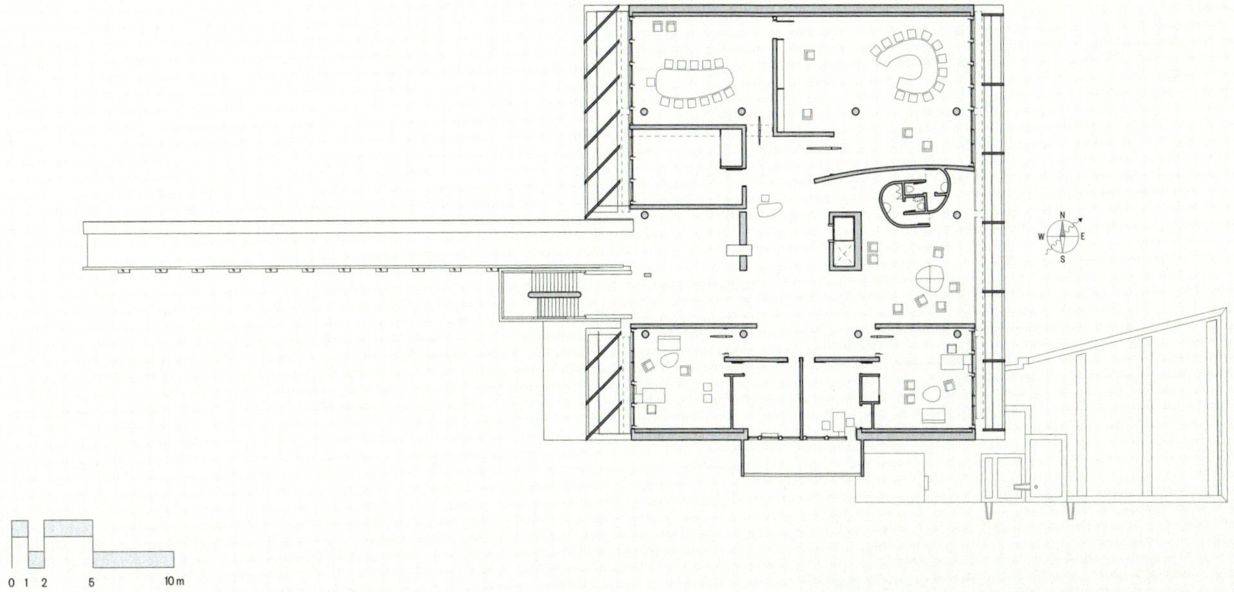

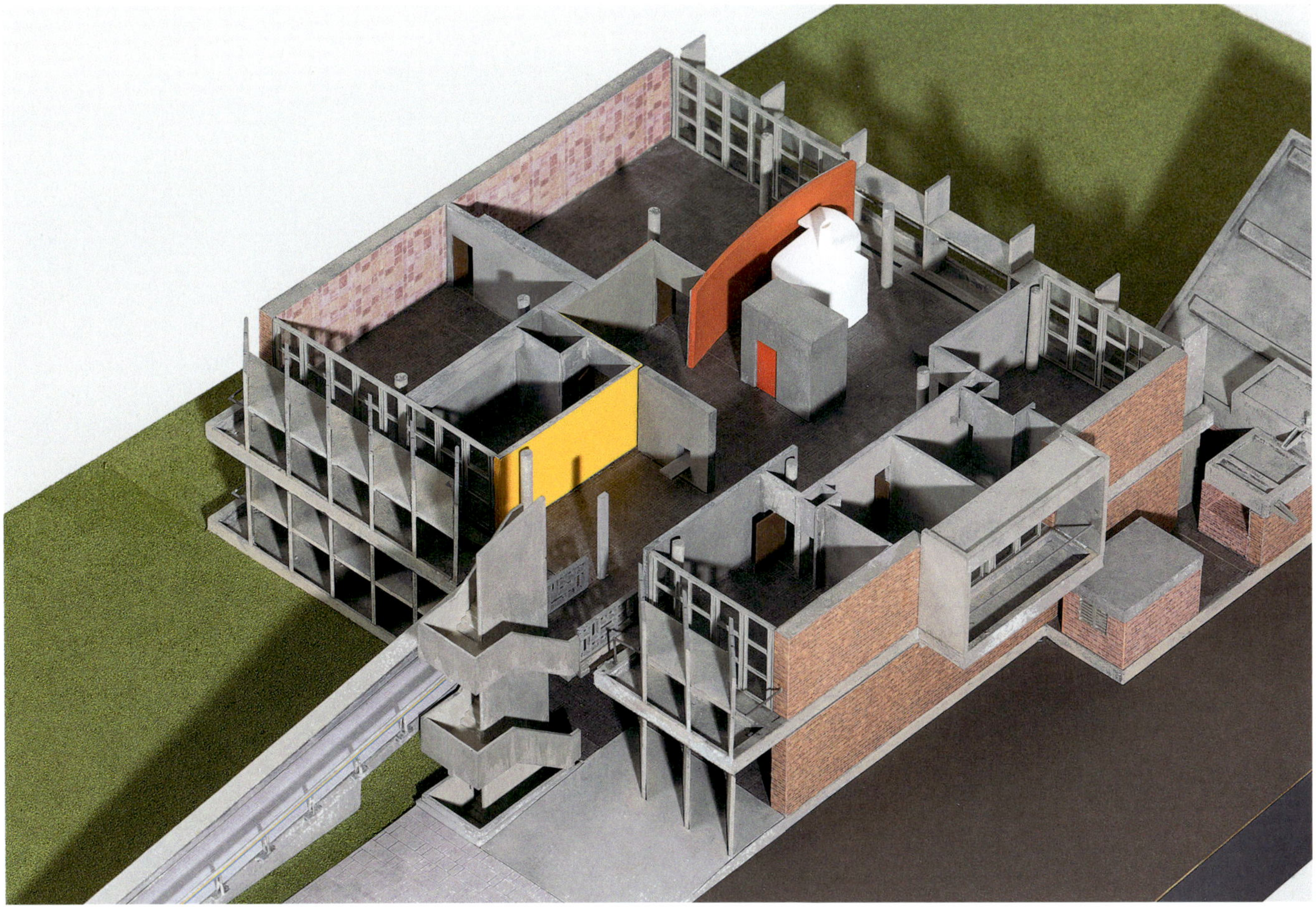

↑ First floor plan showing the meeting and conference rooms to the north of the breezeway and the presidential suite of offices to the south. Plan as designed by Atelier Le Corbusier and constructed.

↓ Model of the first floor, southwest view, showing the culmination of the ramp at the breezeway, with offices to the south and meeting and conference rooms to the north.

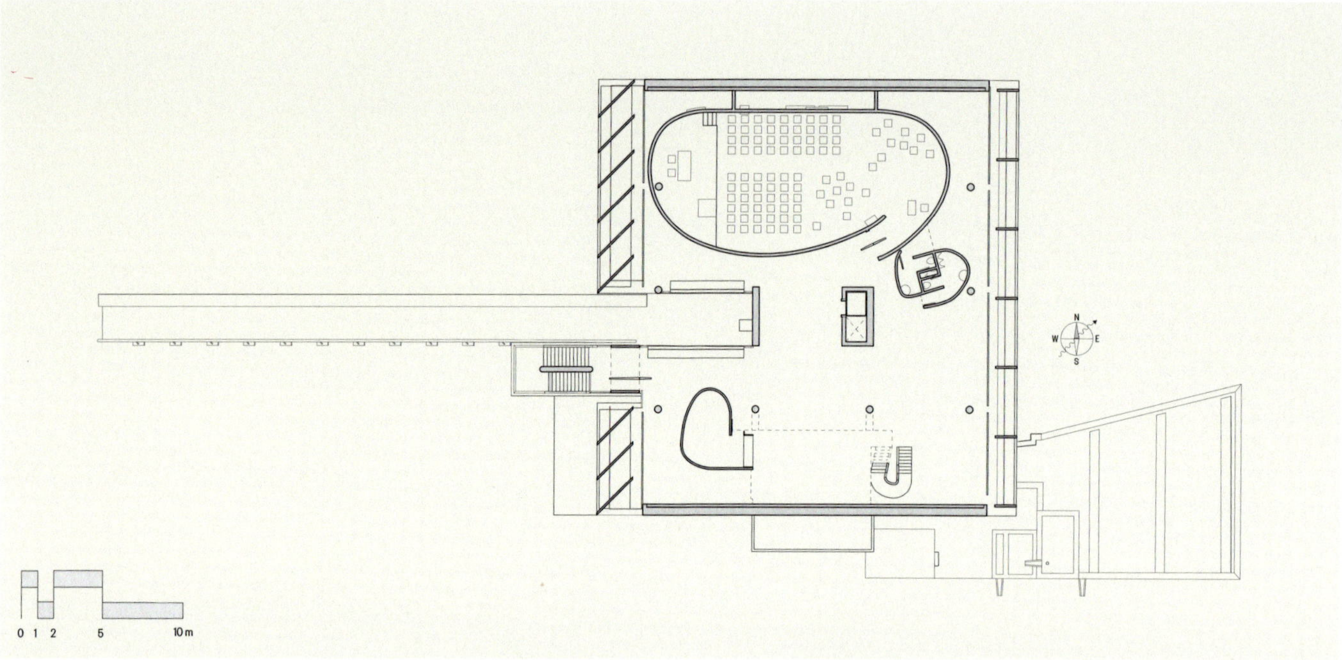

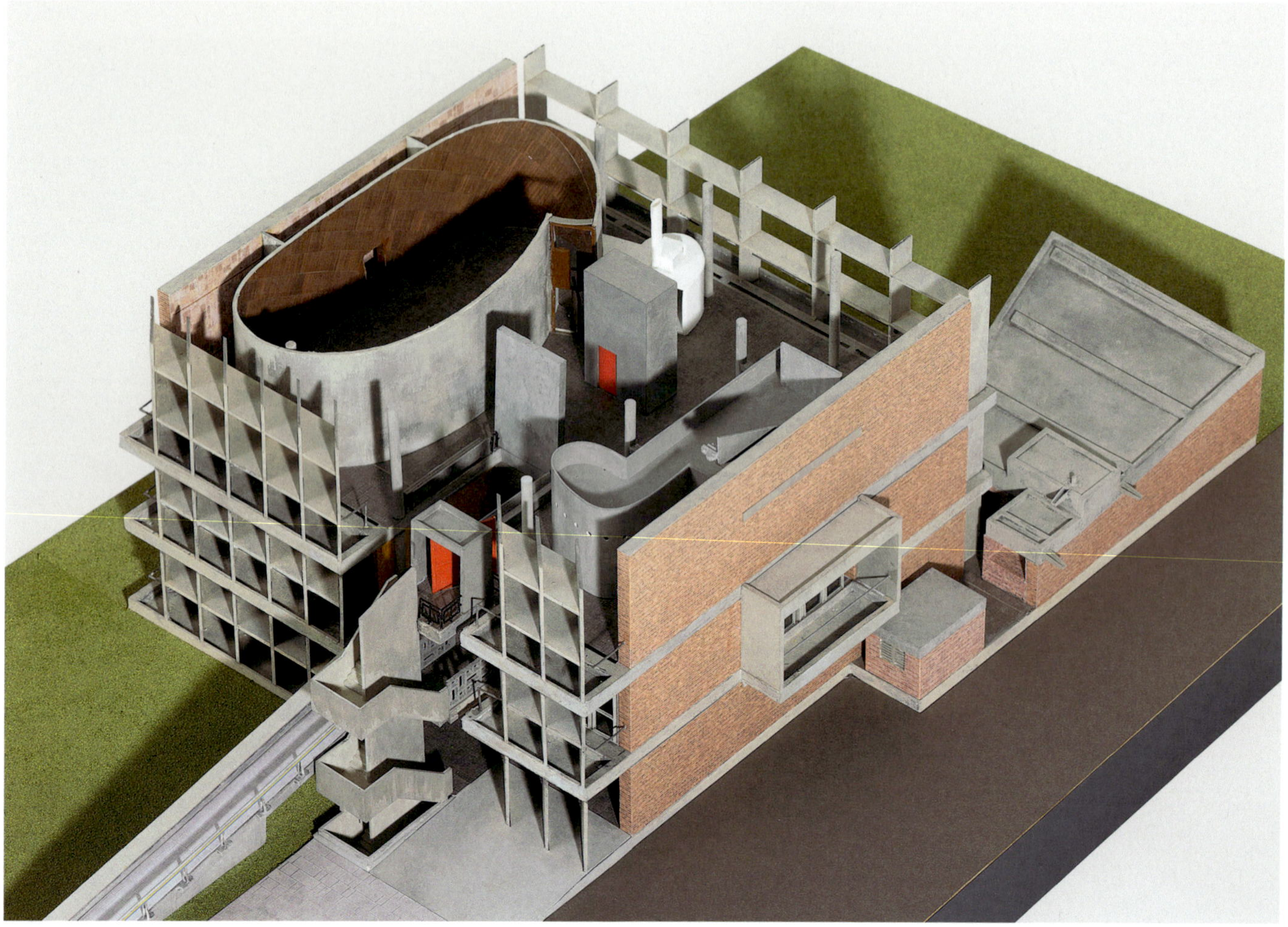

↑ Second floorplan showing the culmination of the main stair sequence, with kitchen and bar to the south and the meeting hall to the north. Plan as designed by Atelier Le Corbusier and constructed.

↓ Model of the second floor, southwest view, showing the meeting hall to the north and the kitchen/bar and mezzanine to the south. Between the two, the open breezeway can be seen.

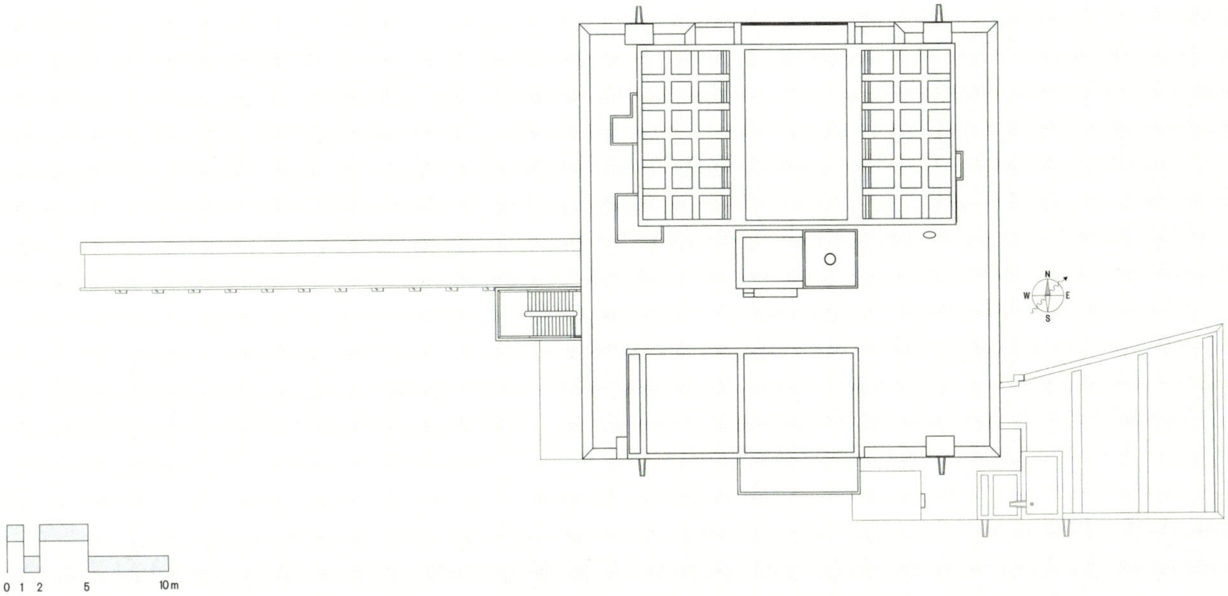

↑ Roof plan showing the elevated, inverted-arch roof to the north and the raised mezzanine roof to the south. Plan as designed by Atelier Le Corbusier and constructed.

↓ Model, southwest roof view. The model represents the building as it stood in 2024, including the addition of the lavatory in the 1970s to the south.

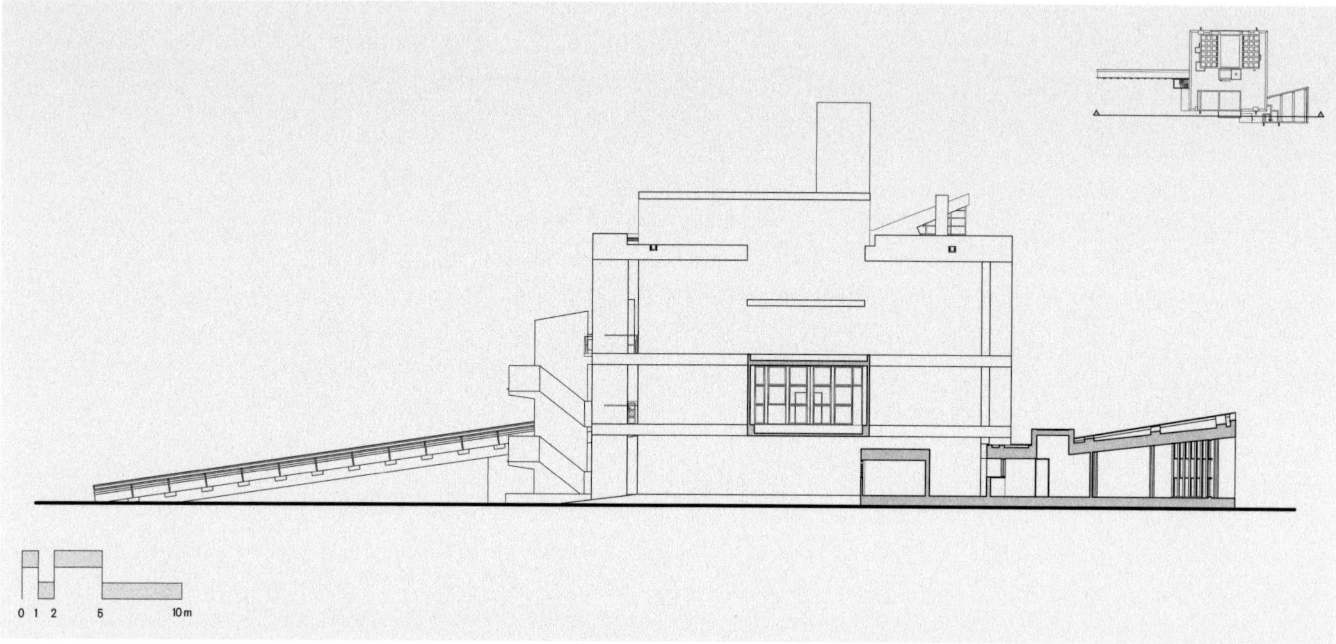

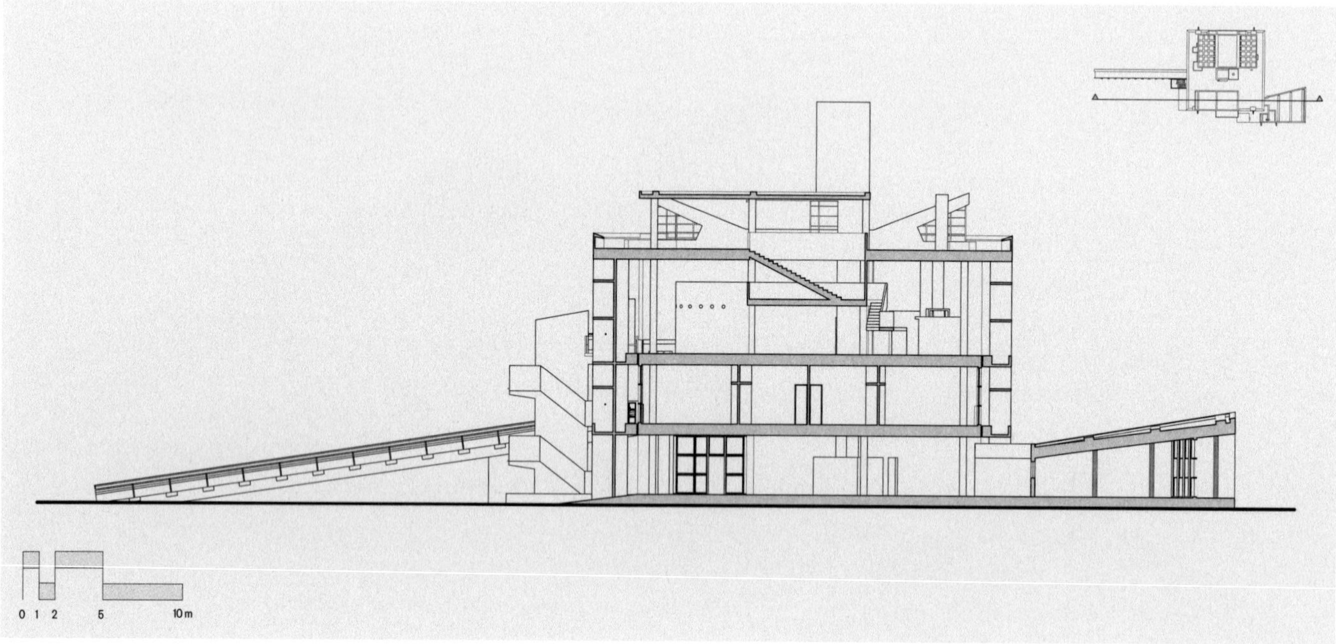

↑ East-west section A–A, cut through the cafeteria, as designed by Atelier Le Corbusier and constructed, with the addition of the lavatory in the 1970s.

↓ East-west section B–B, cut through the ground floor breezeway, cafeteria, first floor presidential office suite, second floor mezzanine, and the stairs to the roof. As designed by Atelier Le Corbusier and constructed.

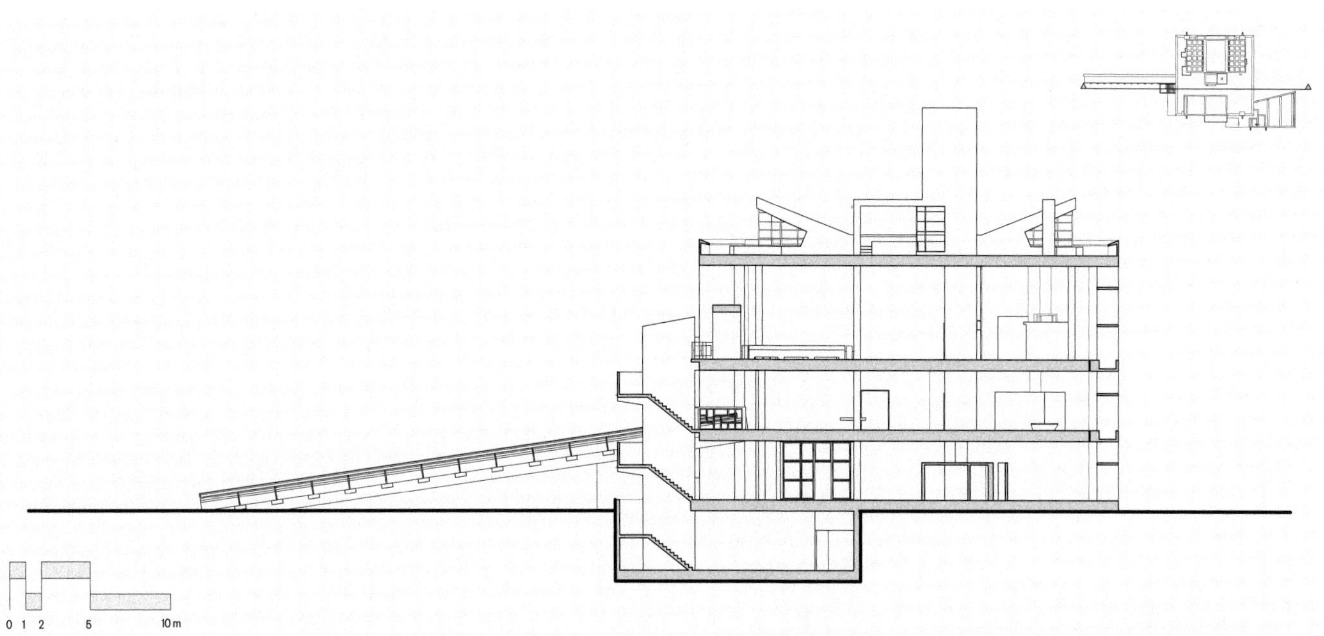

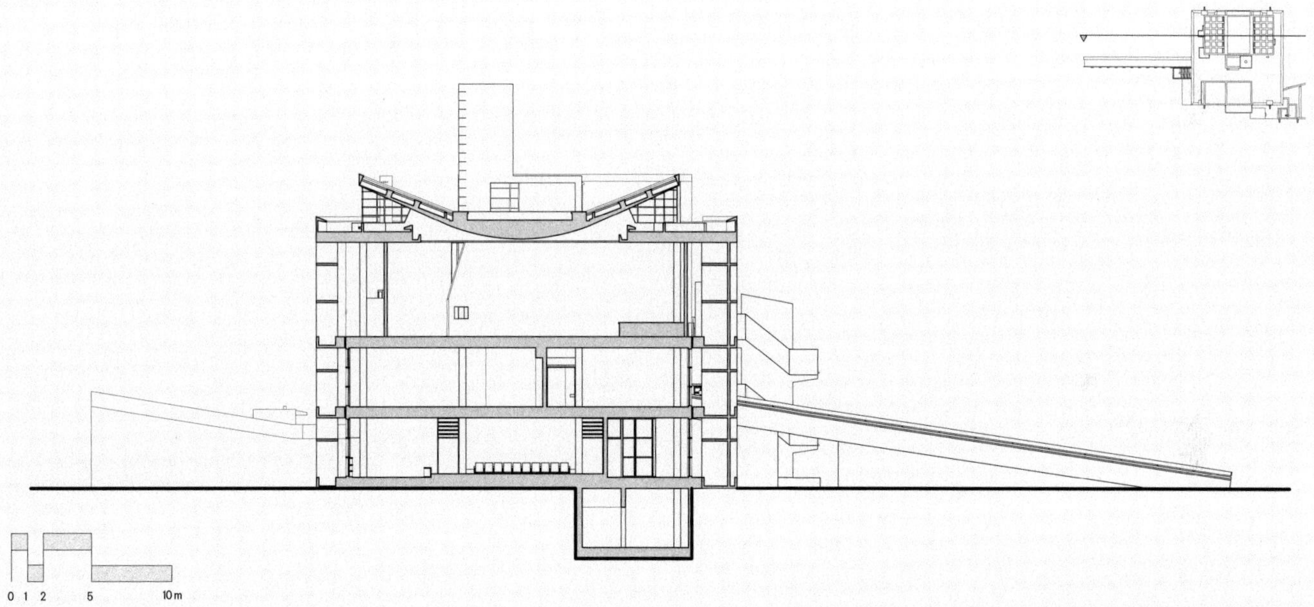

↑ East-west section C–C, as designed by Atelier Le Corbusier and constructed. Changes to the basement during construction are reflected.

↓ West-east section D–D, as designed by Atelier Le Corbusier and constructed. Changes to the basement during construction are reflected.

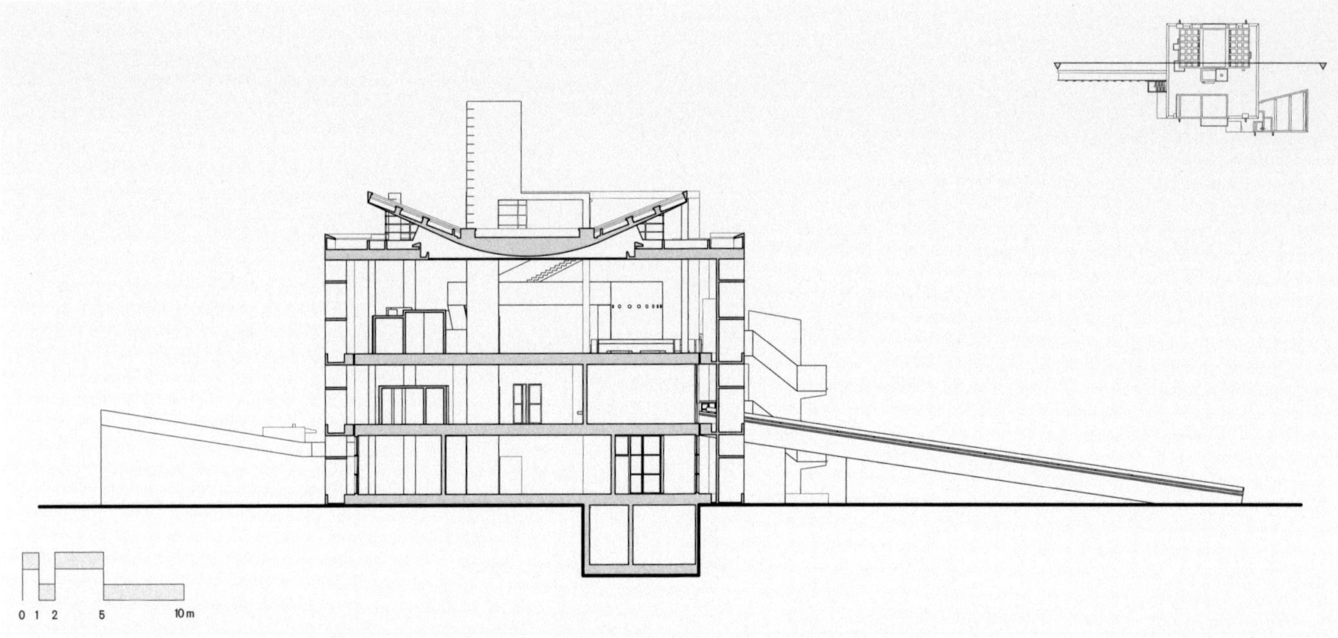

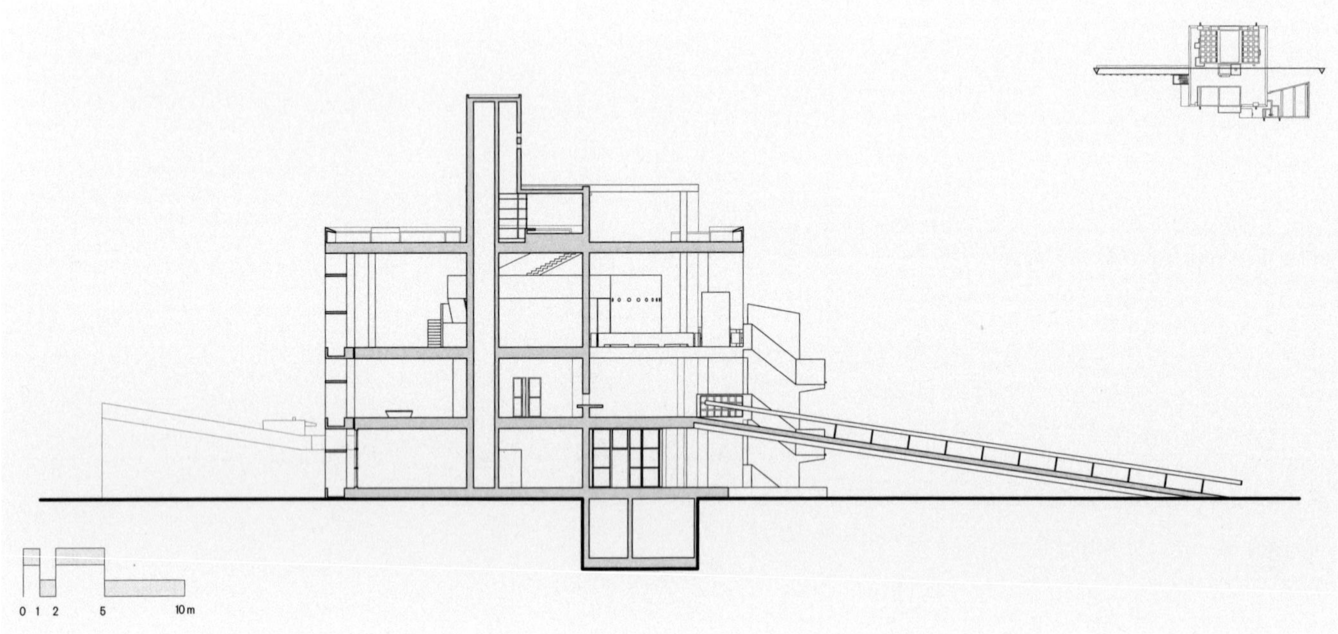

↑ West–east section E–E, cut through the basement, ground floor lecture hall, first and second floor breezeways and bathrooms. As designed by Atelier Le Corbusier and constructed. Changes to the basement during construction and the addition of the lecture hall are reflected.

↓ West–east section F–F, cut through the basement, the ramp and the entrance spaces/breezeways on all three floors. As designed by Atelier Le Corbusier and constructed. Changes to the basement during construction are reflected.

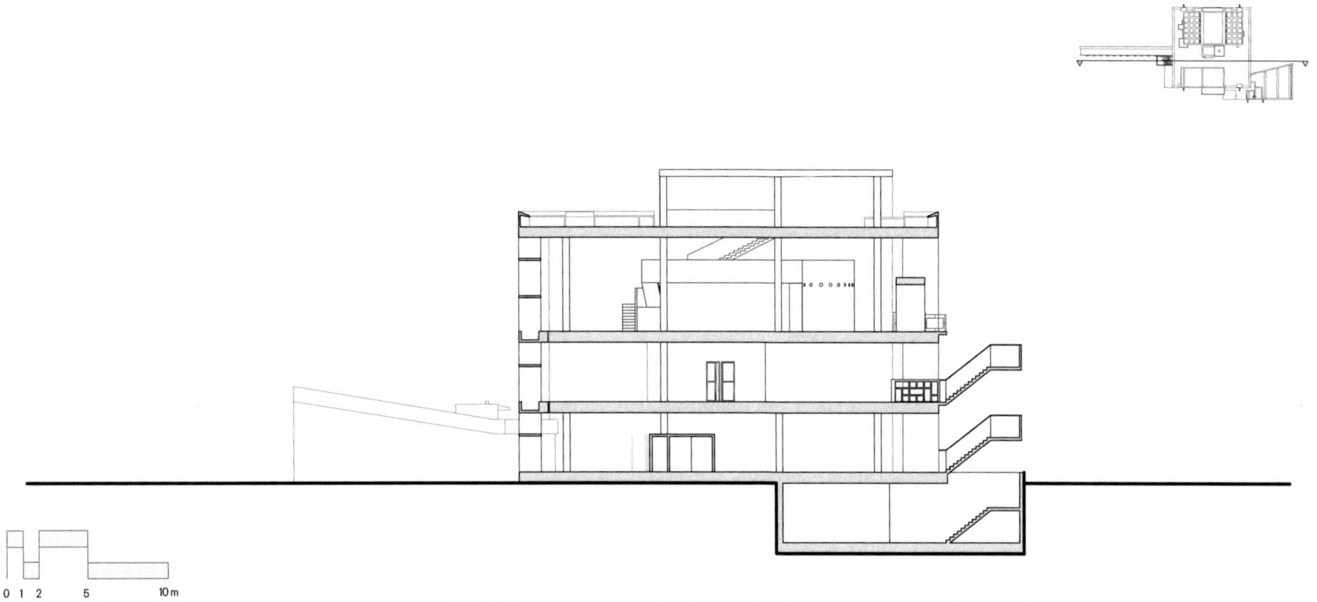

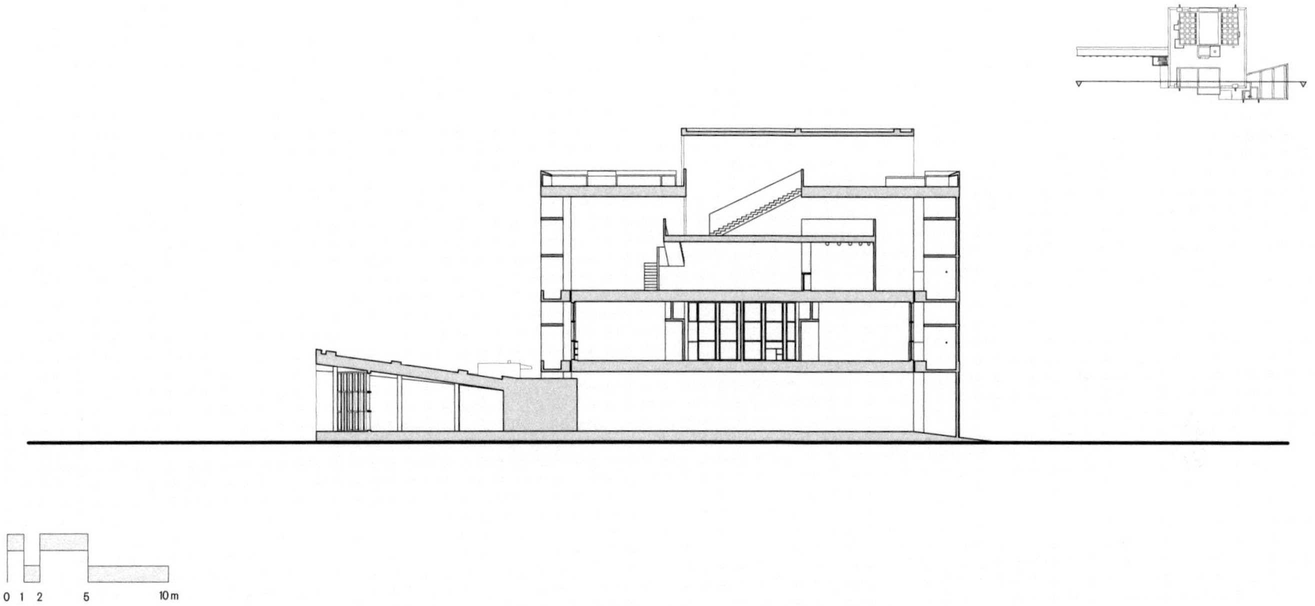

↑ West–east section G–G, cut through the stairs, basement access, ground floor breezeway and bathrooms, and first and second floor breezeways. As designed by Atelier Le Corbusier and constructed. Changes to the basement during construction are reflected.

↓ West–east section H–H, cut through the ground floor breezeway and cafeteria, first floor presidential office suite, second floor mezzanine, and the stairs to the roof. As designed by Atelier Le Corbusier and constructed.

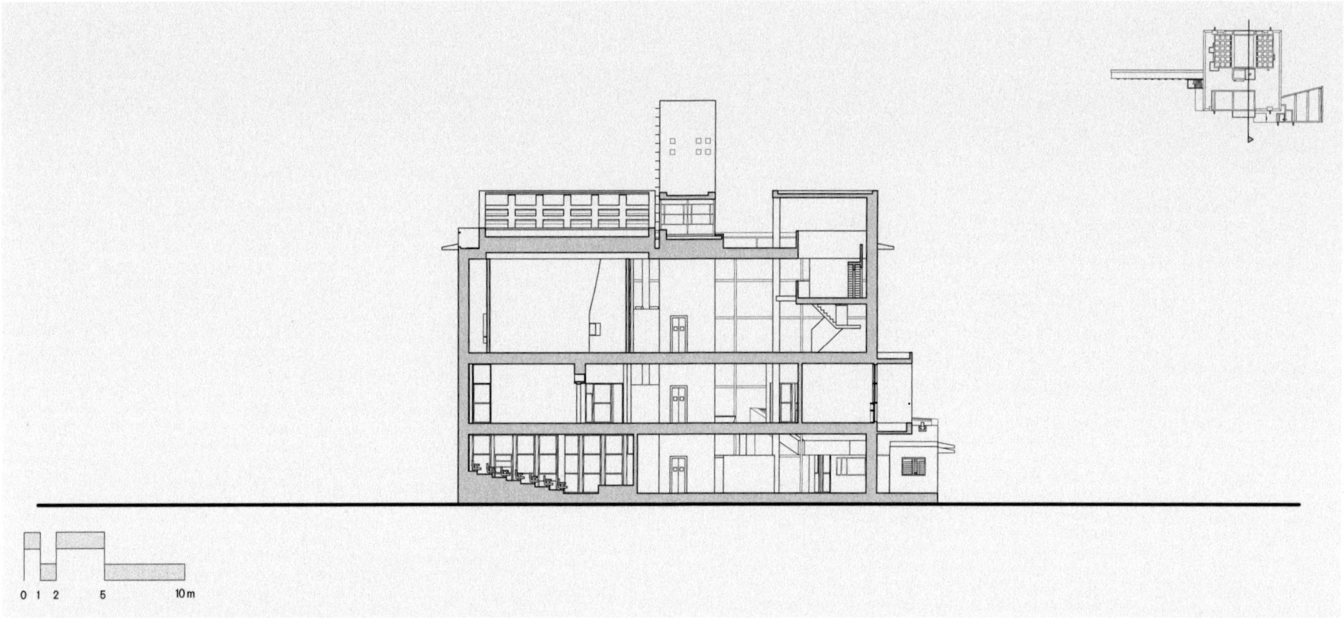

↑ South-north section I-I, cut through the ground floor lecture hall and breezeway, first floor conference room and presidential office suite, second floor meeting hall, breezeway, and mezzanine. As designed by Atelier Le Corbusier and constructed. Changes to the lecture hall and the addition of the lavatory during the 1970s are reflected.

↓ North-south section J-J cut through the ground floor lecture hall and breezeway, first floor conference room, bathrooms, and presidential office suite, second floor meeting hall, bathrooms, breezeway, and mezzanine. As designed by Atelier Le Corbusier and constructed. Changes to the lecture hall and the addition of the lavatory during the 1970s are reflected.

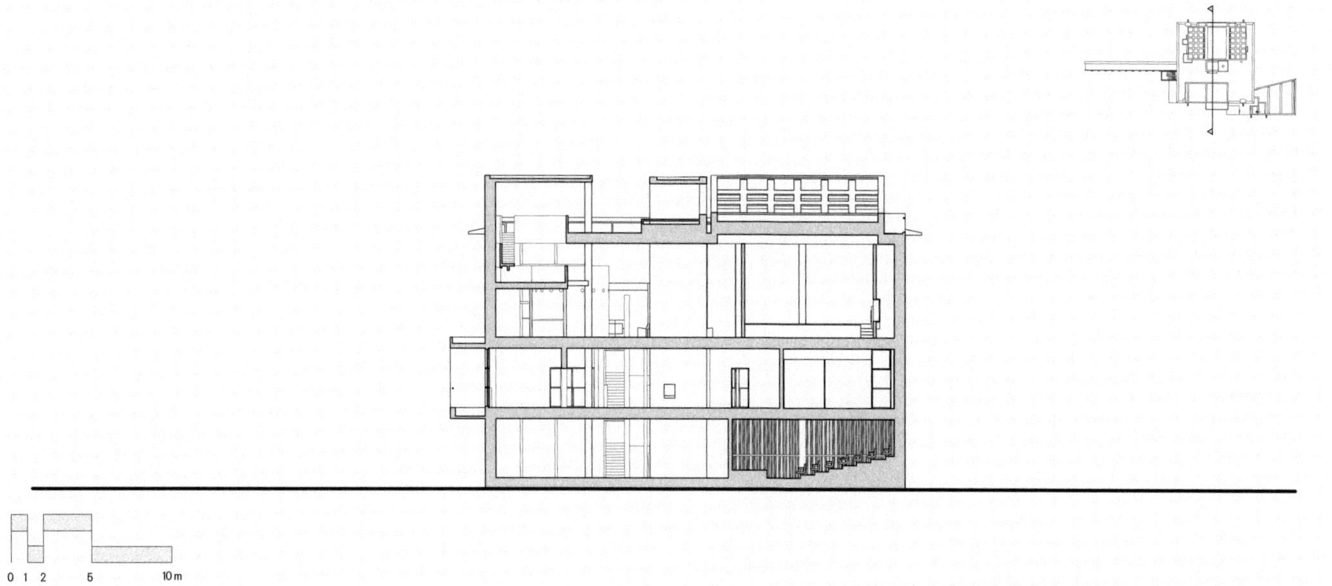

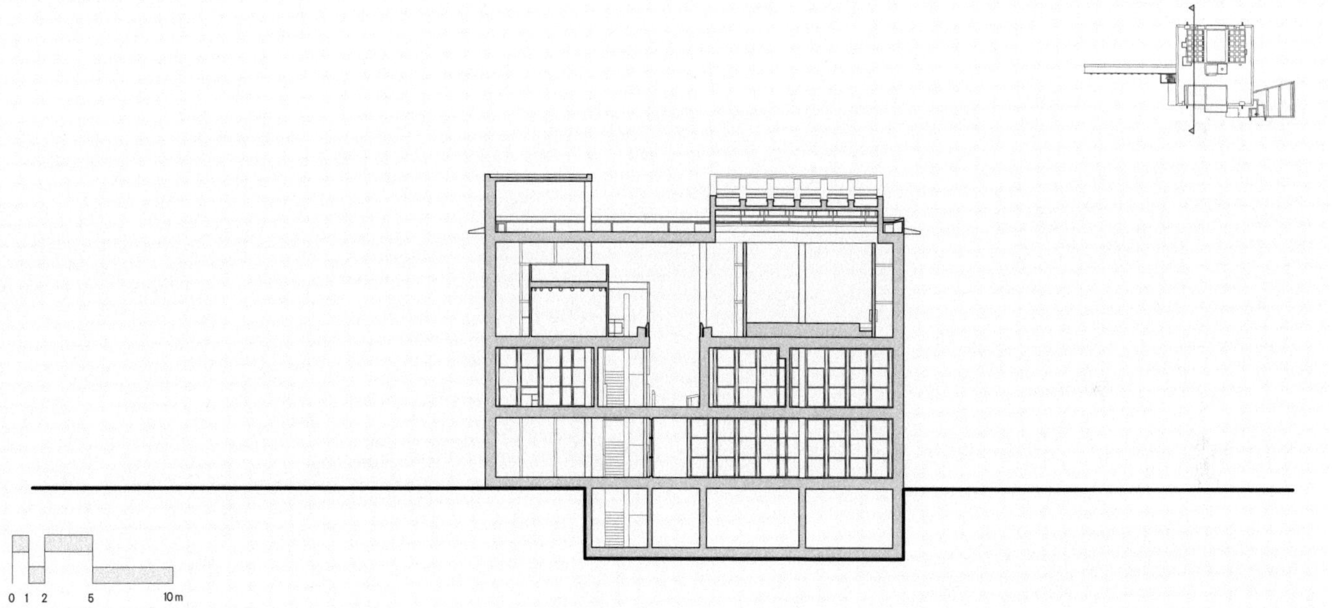

↑ North-south section K–K, cut through the ground floor lecture hall and breezeway, first floor conference room and presidential office suite, second floor meeting hall, breezeway, and mezzanine. As designed by Atelier Le Corbusier and constructed. Changes to the lecture hall during the 1970s are reflected.

↓ North-south section L–L, cut through the basement, ground floor gallery and breezeway, first floor conference room and presidential office suite, second floor meeting hall, breezeway, and mezzanine. As designed by Atelier Le Corbusier and constructed. Changes to the basement during construction are reflected.

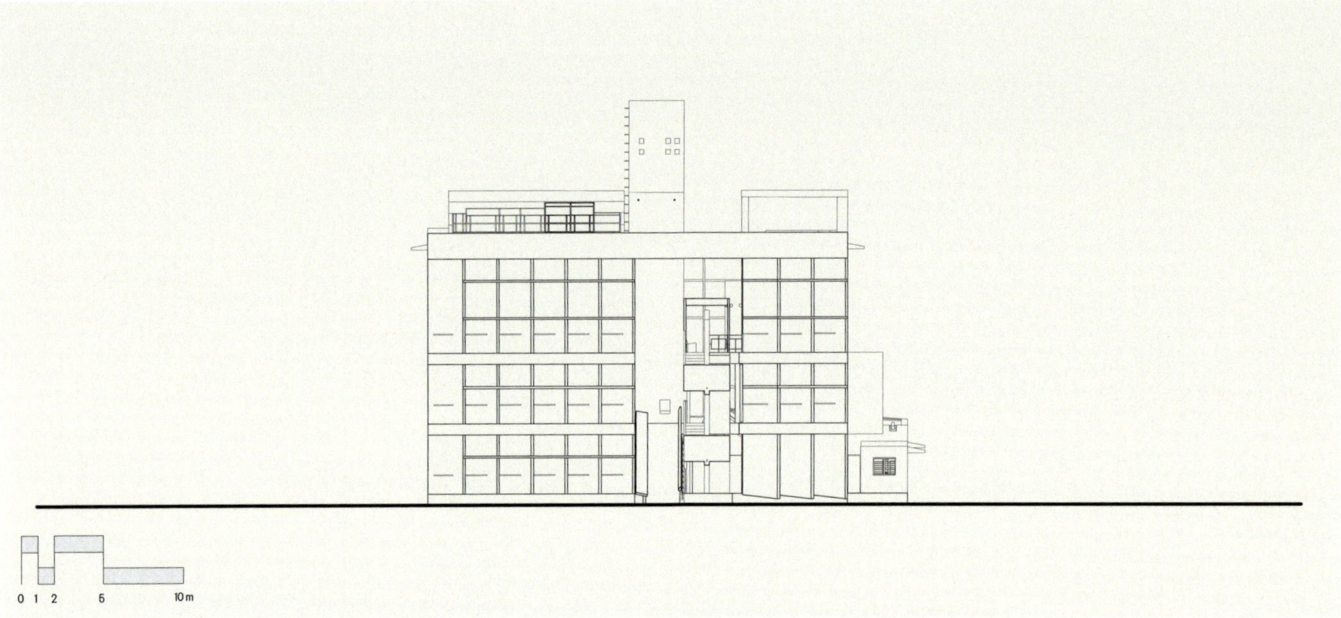

↑ West elevation showing the entrance ramp, stairs, and the brise-soleil. As designed by Atelier Le Corbusier and constructed, with the addition of the 1970s lavatory to the south.

↓ Model, west view, showing the entrance ramp and stairs, describing the entry sequence from Ashram Road onto the ramp, and the three-story open volume between the north and south brise-soleil.

↑ East elevation showing the glass-enclosed spaces on parts of the ground and first floors and the open breezeways on the upper floors. As designed by Atelier Le Corbusier and constructed.

↓ Model, east view, facing the Sabarmati River with the cafeteria volume to the lower left and the meeting hall to the upper right.

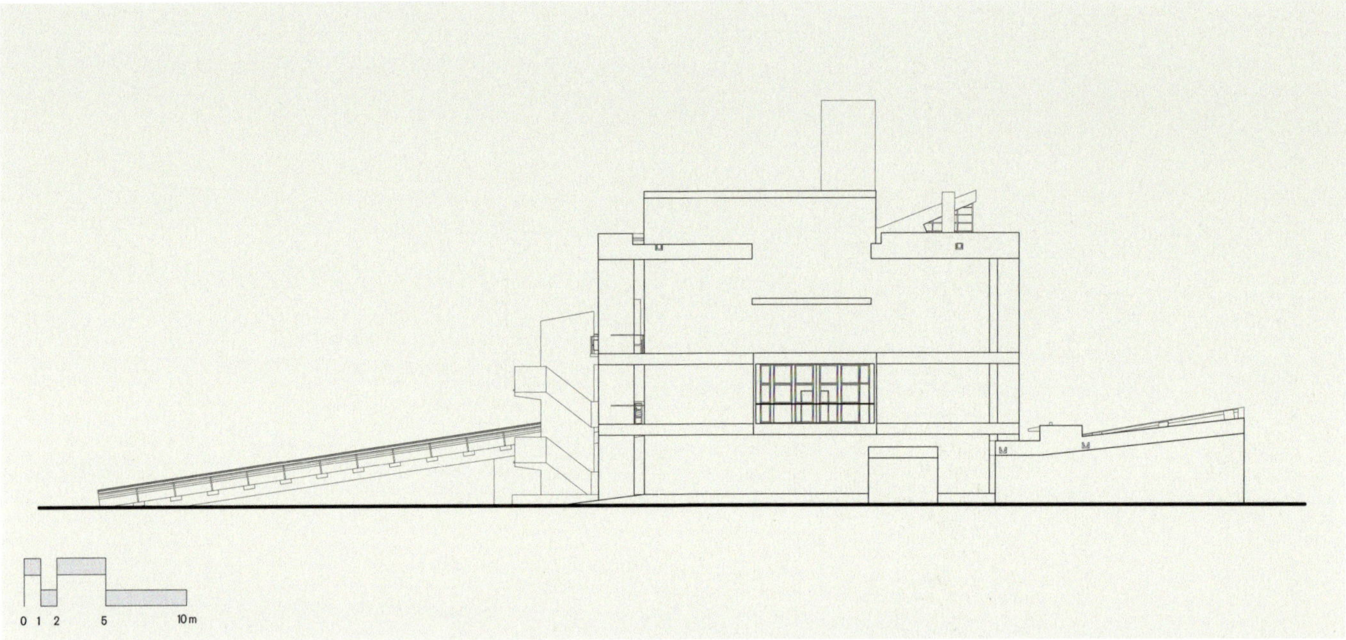

↑ South elevation showing the single-window volume in the blank brick party wall, punctuated by the concrete structural slabs. The ramp and the stair are visible to the west and the cafeteria to the east. As designed by Atelier Le Corbusier and constructed. The addition of the lavatory building to the south during the 1970s is reflected.

↓ Model, south view, with the main entrance ramp to the left and the cafeteria to the right. The volume projecting from the south brick party wall contains the windows of two offices.

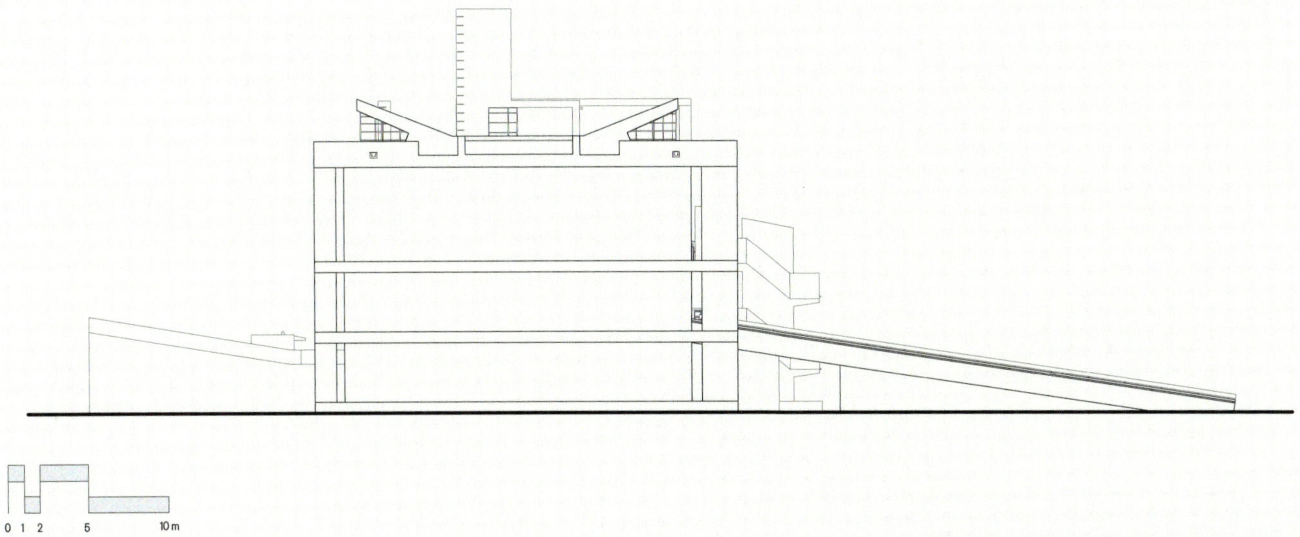

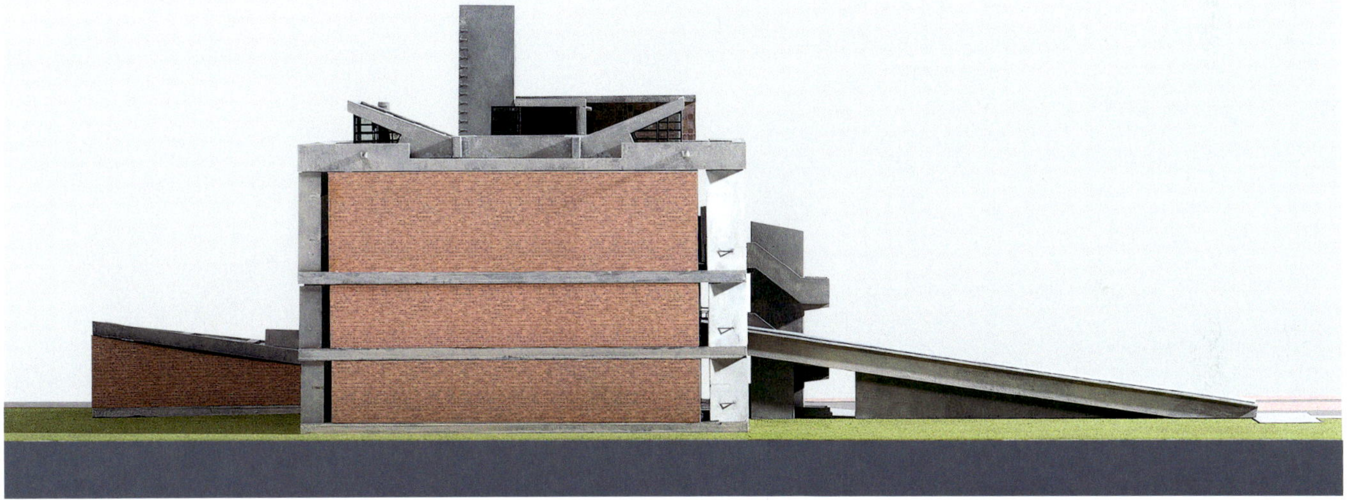

↑ North elevation showing the blank brick party wall, striated by the concrete structural slabs. The ramp and the stair are visible to the west and the cafeteria to the east. The roof projection of the meeting hall is also visible. As designed by Atelier Le Corbusier and constructed.

↓ Model, north view of the brick party wall, with the ramp and stair to the right and the cafeteria to the left of the building volume. Also visible is the inverted-arch roof of the meeting hall.

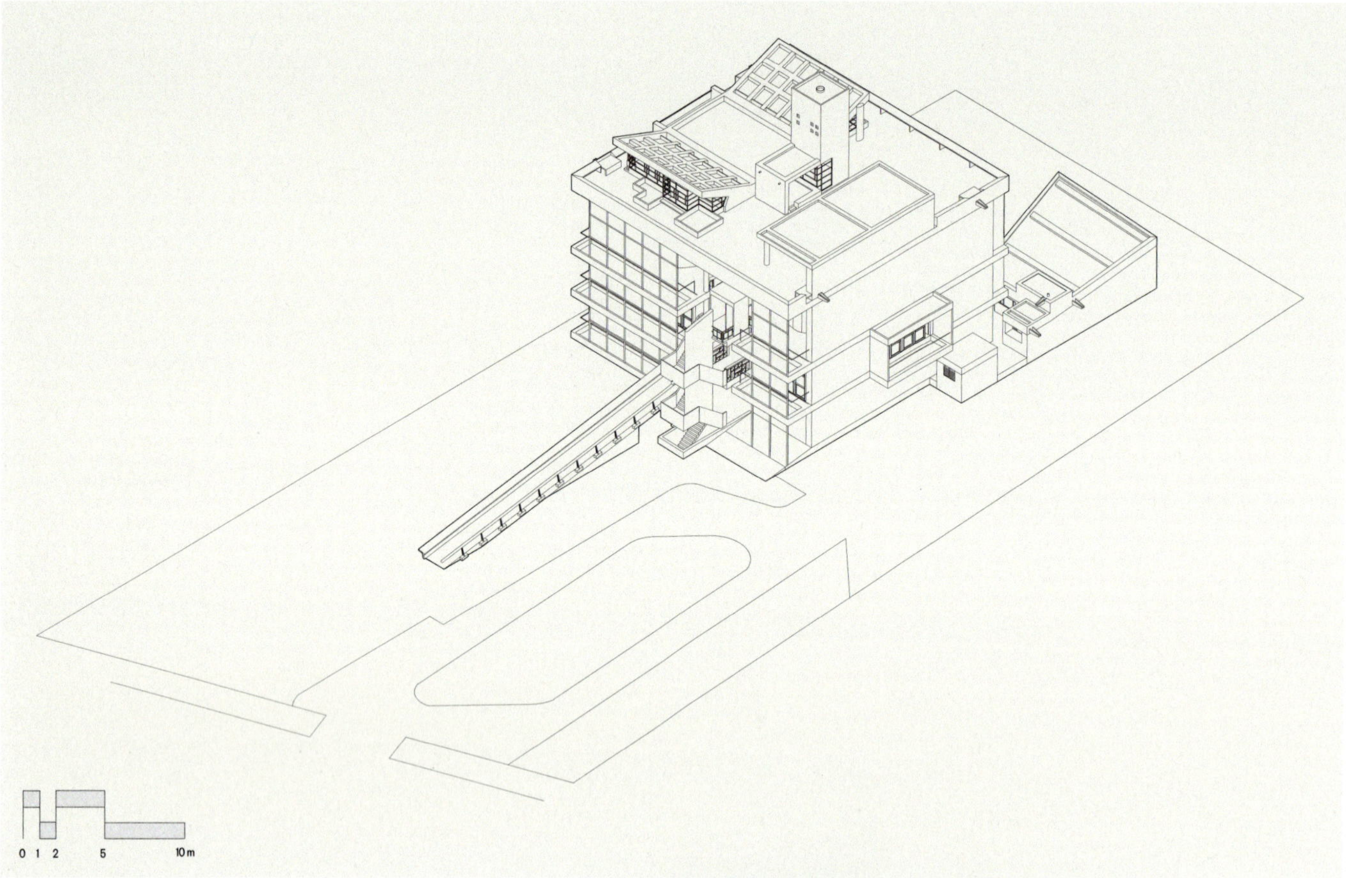

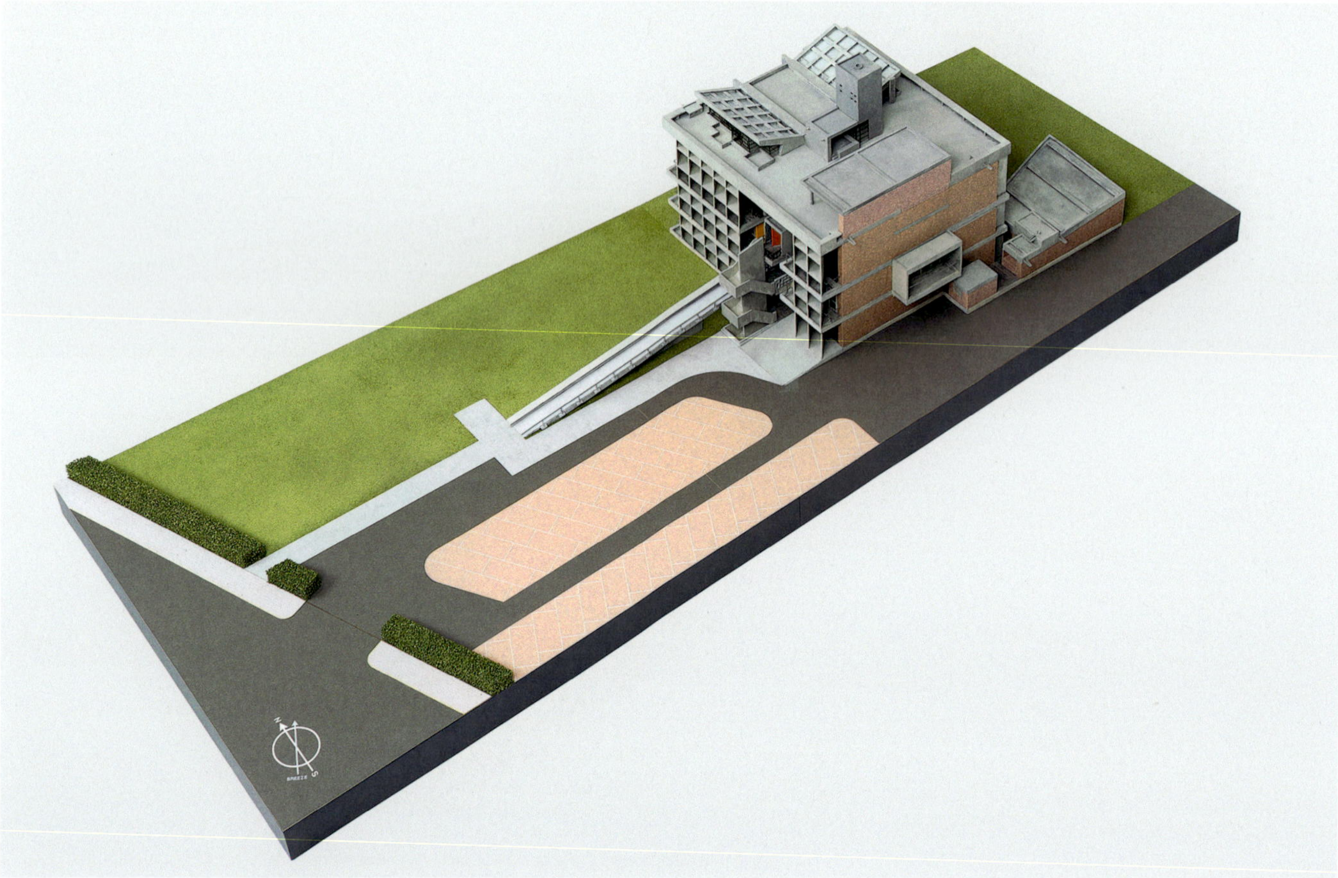

↑ Southwest isometric with all exterior building elements visible in one view. As designed by Atelier Le Corbusier and constructed, with the addition of the 1970s lavatory building to the south.

↓ Model, southwest view, including the entire site from Ashram Road to the Sabarmati River.

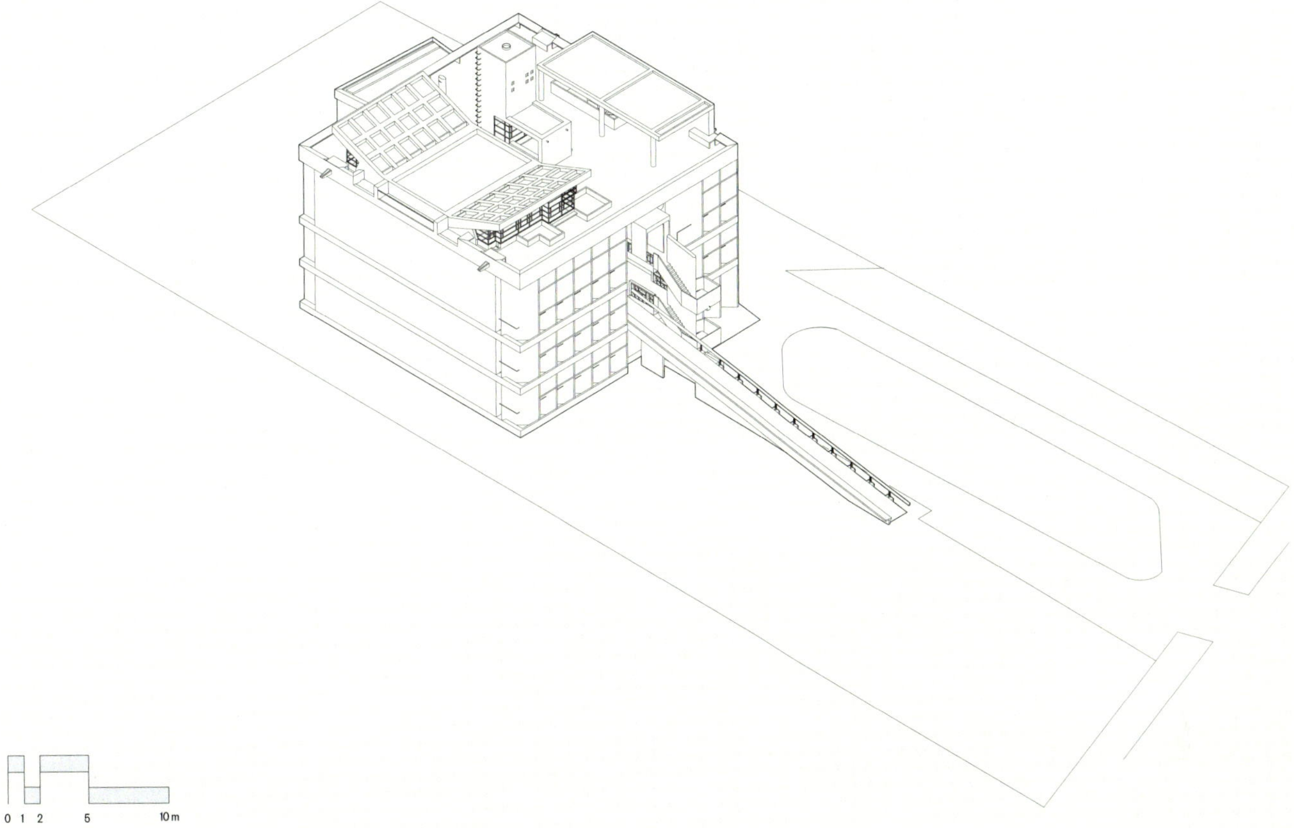

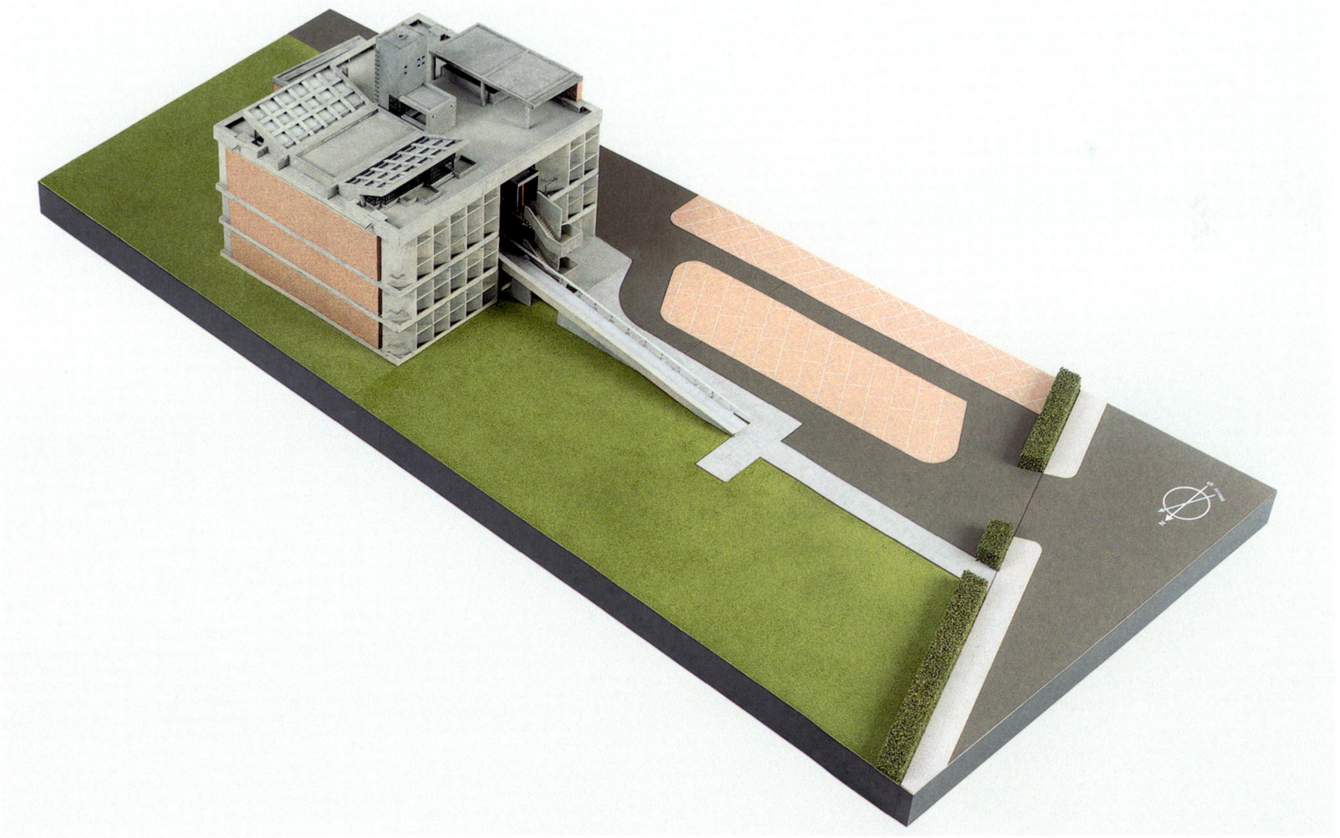

↑ West-north isometric, with the ramp reaching to Ashram Road. As designed by Atelier Le Corbusier and constructed.

↓ Model, west-north view, best describing the relationship of the ramp, stair, and the three-story open-air breezeway volume.

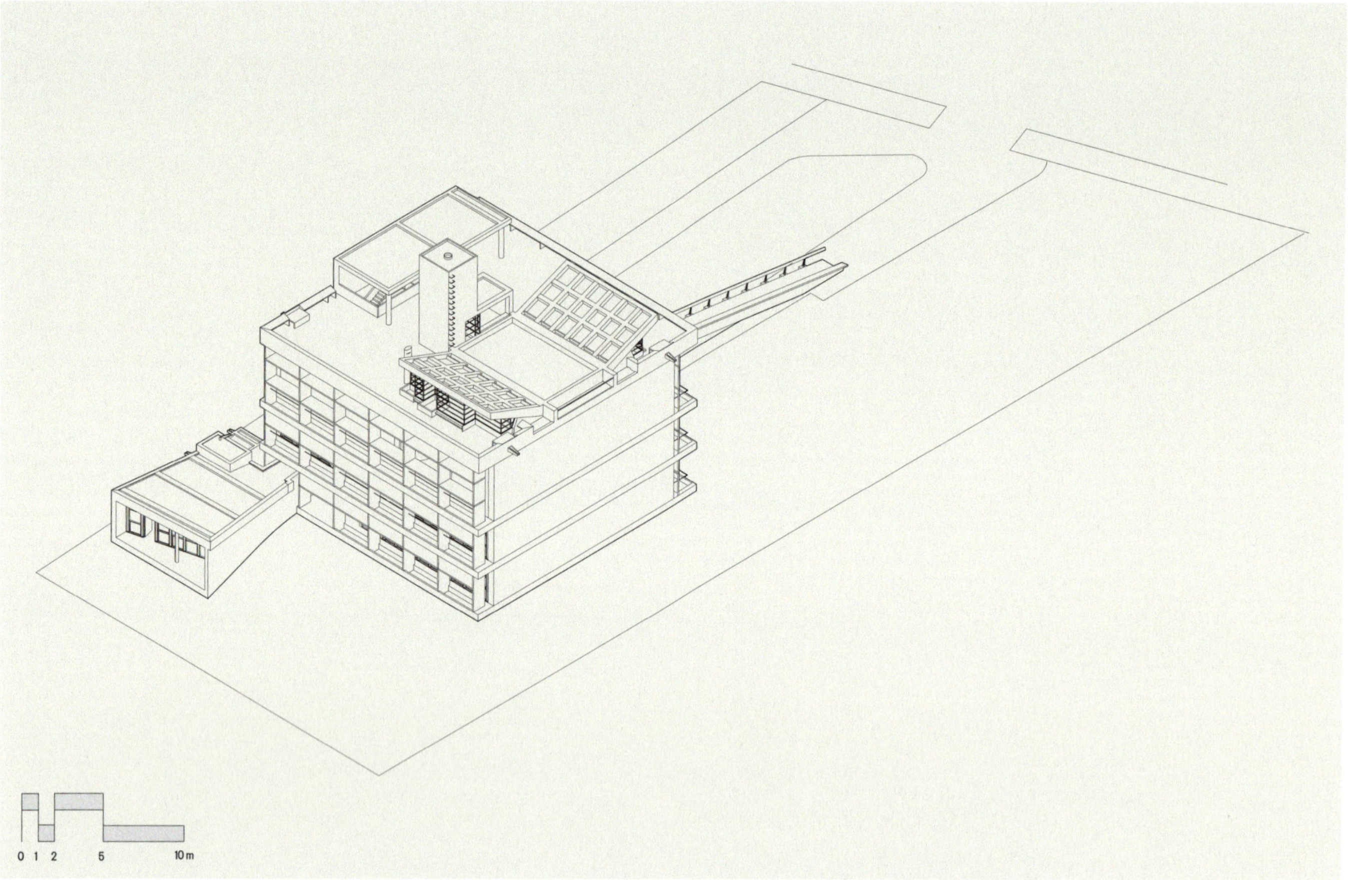

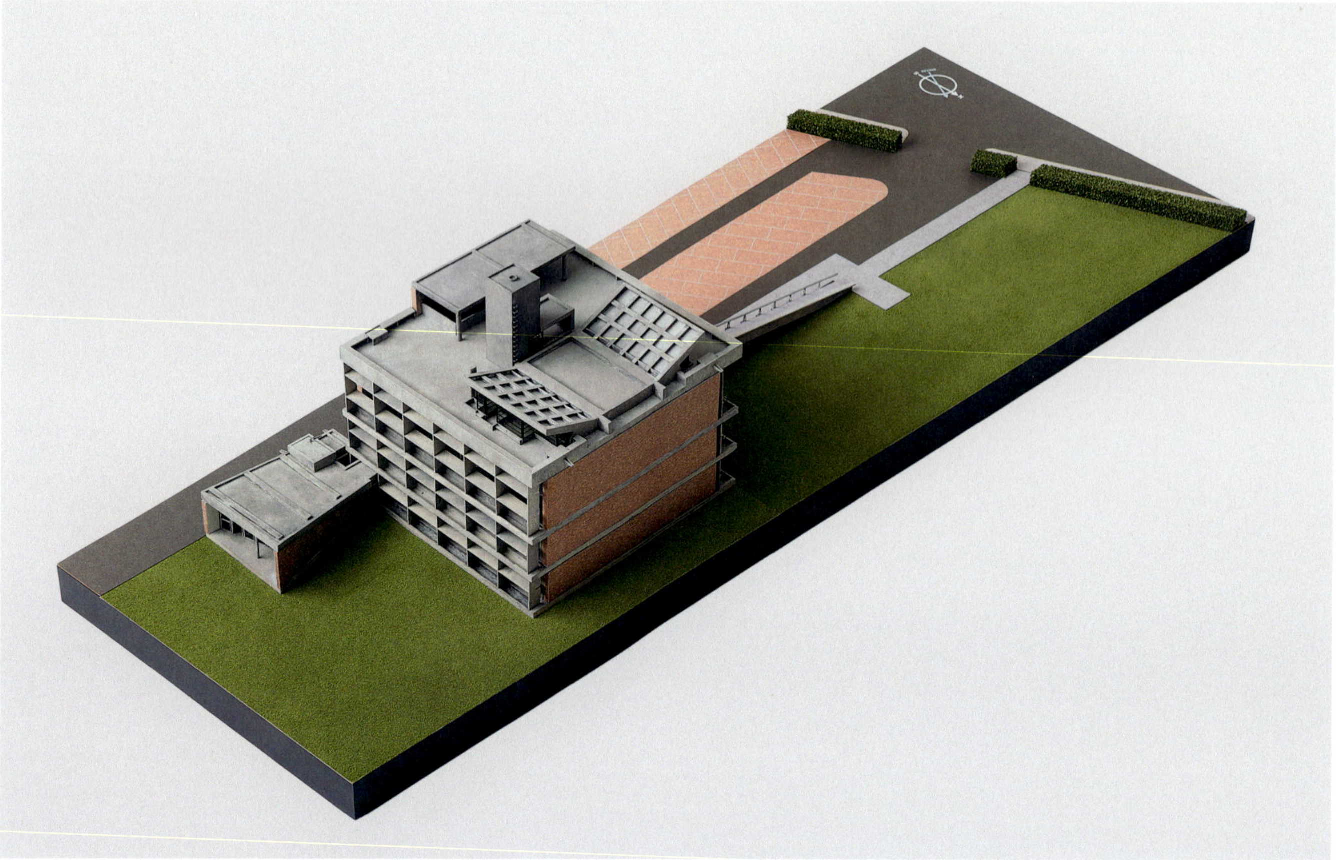

↑ North-east isometric, with the brise-soleil and the cafeteria facing the Sabarmati River. As designed by Atelier Le Corbusier and constructed.

↓ Model, northeast view.

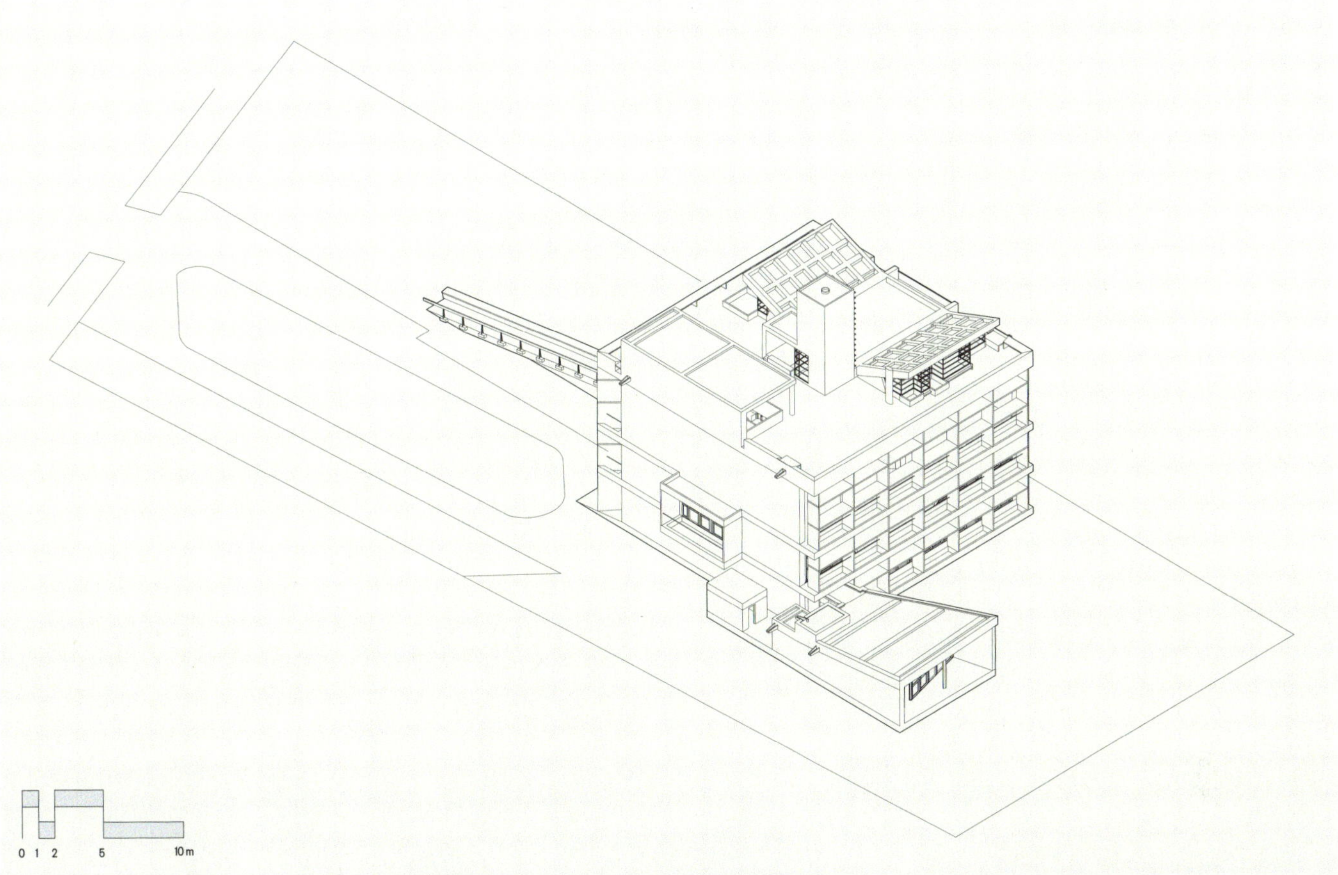

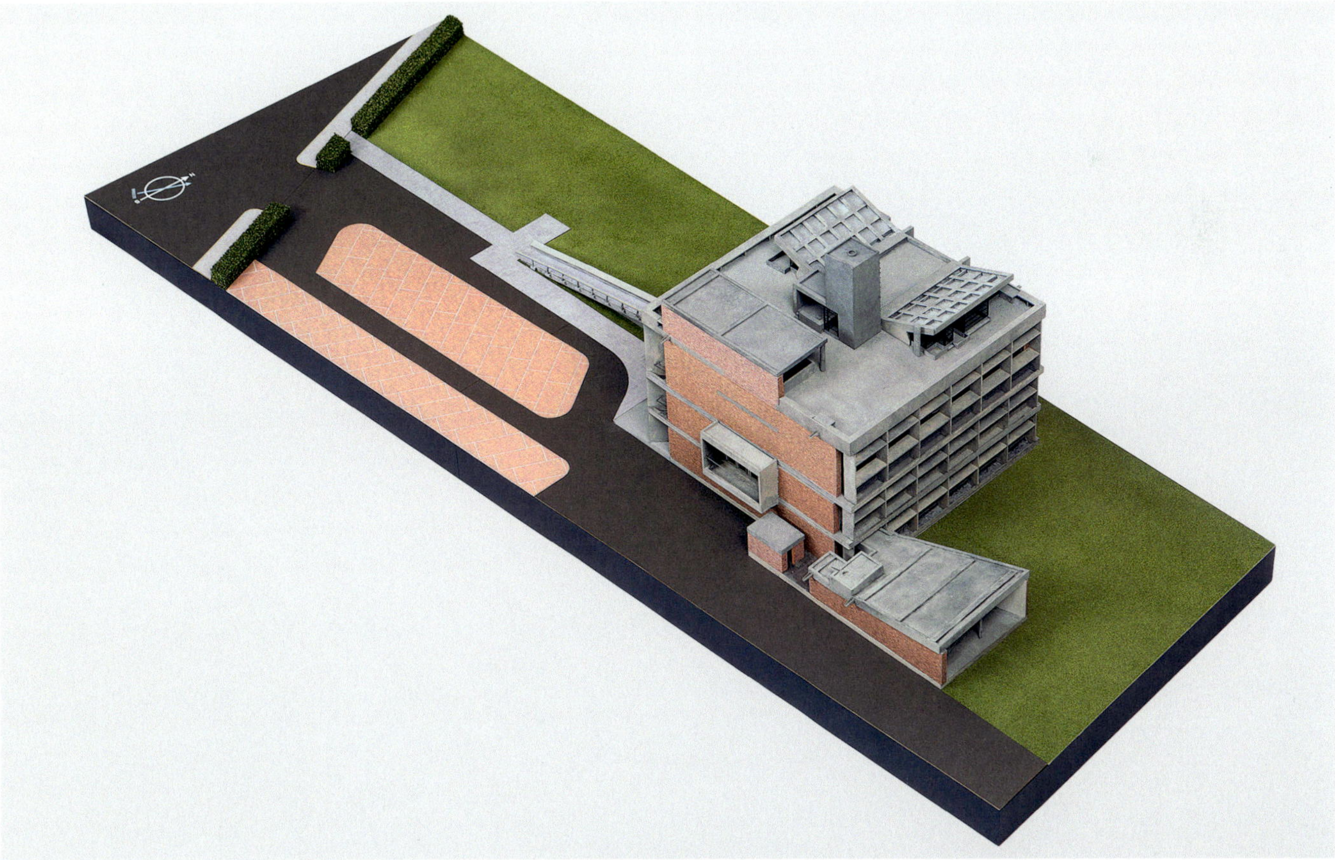

↑ East-south isometric, as designed by Atelier Le Corbusier and constructed, with the addition of the 1970s lavatory building, to the south.

↓ Model, east-south view, with the cafeteria, the east brise-soleil, and the inverted-arch roof of the meeting hall prominent.

↑ Model, west-view detail of the ramp, stair, brise-soleil, and the three-story breezeway volume.

↓ Model, northwest roof view, showing the inverted-arch roof of the meeting hall.

ACKNOWLEDGMENTS

Most often the last piece of writing – and always the most difficult – is the acknowledgments section. There are those that have contributed directly to the project, and those most centrally, but indirectly. The difficulty lies in registering everyone and acknowledging the full spectrum of their contribution, direct and indirect, in essence a book by itself, in parallel. Needless to say, this brief acknowledgment will be insufficient, but without it, I would be remiss.

The seeds of this project were planted many years ago in a class on Le Corbusier at Cornell University taught by the late Professor Lee Hogden. An invitation from Bruce Lindsey in 2013 to conduct a workshop as the "Laskey Design Challenge" at Washington University gave me a chance to think more analytically and didactically about Le Corbusier's paintings. Another workshop, along with a lecture and symposium in 2015, organized by "The Architect's Role" and Ramin Safari-Rad in Tehran, allowed me to write a lecture and prepare for a day-long symposium on the Millowners' Association Building. This started many years of critical thinking, documentation, measurement, research, and writing.

In the arena of documentation of the building, I am indebted to my Penn State student assistants, Marzena Viktoria Nowobilski, who worked with me between 2017 and 2021; Mia Gabrielle Fantasia, between 2021 and 2024; and John Martin, between 2021 and 2023. They know and modelled this building with millimetric precision. They helped prepare all the documents of the building that appear in the book. Based on their computational model, a physical model was prepared by Izzy Daing of Ryerson Studio, and photographed by Cody Godard at the College of Arts and Architecture at Penn State.

My colleague Arpan Johari opened so many doors for me in Ahmedabad that they would be impossible to list. He hosted me graciously during my visit (including homemade dinners) and connected me to people and places I needed to visit. He introduced me to the late Balkrishna Vithaldas Doshi, the 2018 Pritzker Prize winner, who served as the on-site architect for the Millowners' Association building. Doshi (as Le Corbusier used to call him) invited me to his studio and indulged me in a two-hour conversation about his experience in Le Corbusier's studio and on the building site. Arpan also introduced me to Abhinava Shukla, the then Secretary of the Millowners' Association, who greeted me with open arms and gave me free access to the building for measurements and photography on multiple occasions. Without him, none of the documentation would have been possible. I am grateful to Arpan and Abhinava for their friendship and support.

For research, I relied on the Fondation Le Corbusier in Paris, with Arnaud Dercelles and Delphine Studer tirelessly providing resources both for research and the production of the book. Virginia Mokslaveskas at the Getty Research Center was invaluable in locating archival images. The Penn State library system and the amazing librarians at the architecture library gave me access to resources that were unimaginable during the Covid pandemic 2020–2021. This allowed me to continue work without interruption.

The chapters on Valéry, Ruskin, and Nietzsche were studies towards my dissertation. I am grateful to Professors Shaun Irlam, Rodolphe Gasche, and David Johnson for their insights, direction, and support throughout the study. Their work has been and will remain inspirational to me.

One figure who was always in the picture – without me recognizing his significance initially – is Kenneth Frampton. I only understood how central Frampton was to the book when I was almost done, reading through the text. At that point, I shared the manuscript with him, and he graciously read, edited, corrected, and commented on multiple occasions. He then agreed to write a foreword to the book. I am forever indebted and honored.

Last, but not least, and most central is the support I received from the Stuckeman Chair of Integrative Design at the Stuckeman School at the Pennsylvania State University. Without the Stuckeman Family's financial support, neither the documentation, nor the research would have been possible. This book is an acknowledgement of the productive results of their philanthropy. In addition, I am grateful to Frank Jacobus, Head of Architecture at Penn State, for providing financial support.

A project that has been brewing for as long as this one, and of this scale and complexity, conducted across the globe, has, undoubtedly, involved many more that I have not named. I am grateful to all those who have helped shape this work, whether directly or indirectly.

BIBLIOGRAPHY

Abel, C. "Rationality and Meaning in Design," *Design Studies* 1, pt. 2 (October 1979): 69–76.

Alberti, Leon Battista. *De re aedificatoria*. Translated by Joseph Rykwert, Neil Leach, and Robert Tavernor as *On the Art of Building in Ten Books.* Cambridge, Massachusetts, and London: The MIT Press, 1988.

Allison, Peter. "Le Corbusier: Architect or Revolutionary?" *Architectural Association Quarterly* 3, no. 2 (April–July 1971): 10–20.

Aoki, J. "Theory of Formalized Space," *Japan Architect* 56 (November–December 1981): 9.

Aristotle. *The Complete Works of Aristotle* (Revised Oxford Translation). Edited by Jonathan Barnes. Princeton, New Jersey: Princeton University Press, 1984. Vols. 1 and II.

Atwood, Sara. "Imitation and Imagination: John Ruskin, Plato, and Aesthetics," *Carlyle Studies Annual,* no. 26 (2010): 141–164.

Bahga, Sarbjit and Surinder Bahga. *Le Corbusier and Pierre Jeanneret: Footprints on the Sands of Indian Architecture.* New Delhi: Galgotia Publishing Company, 2000.

Banham, Peter Reyner. "The Last Formgiver," *Architectural Review* 140 (August 1966): 86, 97–108.

Banham, Peter Reyner. *Theory and Design in the First Machine Age.* Cambridge, Massachusetts: The MIT Press, 1980.

Banham, Peter Reyner. *A Concrete Atlantis.* Cambridge, Massachusetts: The MIT Press, 1989.

Bataille, George. *The Accursed Share. Vol I: Consumption.* Translated by Robert Hurley. New York: Zone Books, 1991.

Benjamin, Walter. "The Work of Art in the Age of Mechanical Reproduction," in Hannah Arendt, ed. *Illuminations.* New York: Schocken Books, 1969.

Benton, Tim. *Le Corbusier Secret Photographer.* Zurich: Lars Müller Publishers, 2013.

Benton, Tim. *The Painter Le Corbusier: Eileen Gray's Villa E 1027 and Le Cabanon.* Basel: Birkhäuser, 2023.

Besset, Maurice. *Le Corbusier.* Translated by Robin Kemball. New York: Rizzoli, 1976.

Blake, Peter. *Le Corbusier: Architecture and Form.* The Master Builders series. New York: Knopf, 1960, Pelican edition, Baltimore, Maryland: Penguin Books, 1966.

Boesiger, Willy. *Le Corbusier: Last Works.* Translated by Henry A. Frey. New York: Praeger; London: Thames & Hudson, 1970.

Boudon, Philippe. *Lived-In Architecture: Le Corbusier's Pessac Revisited.* Preface by Henri Le Febvre. Translated by Gerald Onn. Cambridge, Massachusetts: The MIT Press, 1971.

Brooks, H. Allen, ed. *Le Corbusier.* Princeton, New Jersey: Princeton University Press, 1987.

Burke, Edmund. *A Philosophical Inquiry into the Origin of our Ideas of the Sublime and Beautiful.* New York: Garland, 1971.

Cohen, Jean-Louis. *Le Corbusier: An Atlas of Modern Landscapes.* New York: Museum of Modern Art, 2013.

Colquhoun, A. "Displacement of Concepts," *Architectural Design* 43, no. 42 (April 1972): 239–240.

Constant, Caroline. *The Modern Architectural Landscape.* Minneapolis: University of Minnesota Press, 2012.

Cresti, Carlo. *Le Corbusier.* London, New York, Sydney, Toronto: Hamlyn Publishing Group, 1970 (Twentieth-Century Masters series).

Curtis, William J. R. *Le Corbusier: Ideas and Form.* New York and London: Phaidon, 2015.

Derrida, Jacques. "Architecture Where the Desire May Live," interview with E. Meyer, *Domus* 671 (1986).

Derrida, Jacques. "Point de Folie – maintenant l'architecture," translated by Kate Linker, *AA Files,* no. 12 (Summer 1986).

Derrida, Jacques. "Why Peter Eisenman Writes Such Good Books," translated by Sarah Whiting, *Architecture and Urbanism* (August 1988).

Derrida, Jacques. "Khōra," in *On the Name.* Stanford, California: Stanford University Press, 1995.

Derrida, Jacques and Peter Eisenman. *Chora L Works.* New York: The Monacelli Press, 1997.

Donner, P. F. R. "Criticism: Architecture for Art's Sake," *Architectural Review* 90 (October 1941): 124–126.

Doshi, Balkrishna. V. "The Unfolding of an Architect," *G. A.* (A.D.A. Edita, Tokyo) 32 (1974): unpaginated.

Eisenman, Peter. "Aspects of Modernism: Maison Dom-ino and the Self-Referential Sign," *Oppositions,* no. 15/16 (Winter/Spring 1979): 118–128.

Etlin, Richard A. "Le Corbusier, Choisy, and French Hellenism: The Search for a New Architecture," *The Art Bulletin* 69, no. 2 (1987).

Flusser, Vilém. *The Shape of Things: A Philosophy of Design.* London: Reaktion Books, 1999.

Forster, Kurt W. "Antiquity and Modernity in the La Roche-Jeanneret Houses of 1923." *Oppositions,* 15/16 (Winter/Spring 1979): 130–153.

Frampton, Kenneth. "The Humanist vs. the Utilitarian Ideal," *Architectural Design* 38 (1968): 134–136.

Frampton, Kenneth. "City of Dialectic," *Architectural Design* 39 (October 1969): 541–546.

Frampton, Kenneth. "Le Corbusier and the Dialectical Imagination," in Yukio Futagawa, ed. *Le Corbusier: Millowners' Association Building 1954. Carpenter Center for Visual Arts, Harvard University, Cambridge Massachusetts, USA, 1961–64.* Tokyo: A.D.A. EDITA Tokyo Publishing Co., 1975.

Frampton, Kenneth. "Apres le Purisme," *Oppositions,* 15/16 (Winter/Spring 1979): 155.

Frampton, Kenneth. *Modern Architecture: A Critical History.* London: Thames & Hudson, 2007.

Futagawa, Yukio, ed. *Le Corbusier: Sarabhai House 1955, Shodhan House 1956.* Tokyo: A.D.A. EDITA Tokyo Publishing Co., 1974.

Futagawa, Yoshio and Yukio Futagawa. *Le Corbusier: Shodhan House.* Tokyo: A.D.A. EDITA Tokyo Publishing Co., 2014.

Gargiani, Roberto and Anna Rosellini. *Le Corbusier: Béton Brut and Ineffable Space, 1940–1965.* Lausanne: EPFL Press, 2011.

Gast, Klaus-Peter. *Le Corbusier. Paris – Chandigarh.* Basel: Birkhäuser, 2000, 172–177.

Giedion, Sigfried. *Space, Time and Architecture.* 5th edition. Cambridge, Massachusetts: Harvard University Press, 1967.

Gutheim, Frederick. "The New Corbusier," *Architectural Record* 118 (November 1955): 180–187.

Haas, F. "Dada and Architecture," *Architectural Review* 145 (April 1969): 288.

Hegel, Georg Wilhelm Friedrich. "Architecture," in *Hegel's Aesthetics,* Vol. II. Oxford: Oxford University Press, 1975.

Heidegger, Martin, *Poetry, Language, Thought.* Translated by Albert Hofstadter. New York, Hagerstown, San Francisco, London: Harper & Row Publishers, 1975.

Hervé, Lucien. *Le Corbusier: As Artist, As Writer.* Translated by Haakon Chevalier. Neuchatel, Switzerland: Editions du Griffon, 1970.

Hitchcock, Henry-Russell, Jr. "Abstract Pictures Make Concrete Houses; Tracing the Dual Career of Le Corbusier as Painter and Architect Through the Boston Institute's Exhibition," *Art News* 47 (April 1948): 36–38, 55.

Jeanneret, Charles-Édouard (Le Corbusier). "L'Esprit Nouveau en Architecture," in *Almanach d'architecture moderne.* (Paris: Éditions Crès, 1925)

Jeanneret, Charles-Édouard (Le Corbusier). *The Decorative Art of Today.* Translated by James Dunnett. Cambridge, Massachusetts: The MIT Press, 1987. (First published under the title *L'Art décoratif d'aujourd'hui.* Paris: Éditions G. Crès, 1925.

Jeanneret, Charles-Édouard (Le Corbusier). *Une Maison - Un Palais.* Paris: Éditions G. Crès, Collection de "L'Esprit Nouveau", 1928.

Jeanneret, Charles-Édouard (Le Corbusier). "Architecture, the Expression of the Materials and Methods of our Times," *Architectural Record* no. 66 (August 1929): 123–128.

Jeanneret, Charles-Édouard (Le Corbusier). *Towards a New Architecture.* Translated by Frederick Etchells. New York, Toronto, London, Sydney: Holt, Reinhart and Winston, 1946.

Jeanneret, Charles-Édouard (Le Corbusier). *When the Cathedrals Were White, A Journey to the Country of Timid People.* Translated by Francis E. Hyslop, Jr. New York: Reynal and Hitchcock, 1947.

Jeanneret, Charles-Édouard (Le Corbusier). "Tools of Universality," *Trans/Formation* 1, no. 1 (1950): 40–42.

Jeanneret, Charles-Édouard (Le Corbusier). *The Modulor 2.* Cambridge, Massachusetts: Harvard University Press, 1958.

Jeanneret, Charles-Édouard (Le Corbusier). *Creation Is a Patient Search.* Translated by James Palmes. New York: Frederick, A Praeger Publishers, 1960.

Jeanneret, Charles-Édouard (Le Corbusier). *My Work.* Translated by James Palmes. London: The Architectural Press, 1960.

Jeanneret, Charles-Édouard (Le Corbusier). *Textes et dessins pour Ronchamp.* Paris: Forces-Vives, 1965.

Jeanneret, Charles-Édouard (Le Corbusier). *Œuvre Complète, Le Corbusier 1910–1965.* Zurich: Les Editions d'Architecture Zurich, 1967.

Jeanneret, Charles-Édouard (Le Corbusier). *The Radiant City.* New York: The Orion Press, 1967 (Originally published as *La Ville Radieuse* in 1933).

Jeanneret, Charles-Édouard (Le Corbusier). *The City of Tomorrow.* Translated by Frederick Etchells. Cambridge, Massachusetts: The MIT Press, 1971.

Jeanneret, Charles-Édouard (Le Corbusier). *The Modulor.* Cambridge, Massachusetts: The MIT Press, 1977.

Jeanneret, Charles-Édouard (Le Corbusier) and Fondation Le Corbusier. *Le Corbusier Sketchbooks.* New York: The Architectural History Foundation and Cambridge, Massachusetts: The MIT Press, 1981. 4 volumes.

Jeanneret, Charles-Édouard (Le Corbusier) and Fondation Le Corbusier. *The Le Corbusier Archive.* Garland Architectural Archive Series. New York, London: Garland Publishing; Paris: Fondation Le Corbusier, 1982–1984. 32 volumes.

Jeanneret, Charles-Édouard (Le Corbusier) and Amédée Ozenfant. "After Cubism," in Carol S. Eliel, ed. *L'Esprit Nouveau: Purism in Paris, 1918–1925.* Los Angeles and New York: LA County Museum of Art and Harry Abrams, 2001.

Jeanneret, Charles-Édouard (Le Corbusier). *Journey to the East.* Translated by Ivan Zaknic. Cambridge, Massachusetts: The MIT Press, 2007.

Jencks, Charles. *Le Corbusier and the Tragic View of Architecture.* Cambridge, Massachusetts: Harvard University Press, 1973.

Jordan, Robert Furneaux. *Le Corbusier.* London: Dent; New York: Lawrence Hill, 1972.

Koetter, Fred. "Le Corbusier at Work: Review," *Oppositions,* no. 19/20 (Winter/Spring 1980): 215–221.

Koolhaas, R. "Dali and Le Corbusier: The Paranoid-Critical Method," *Architectural Design* 48, no. 2–3 (1978): 152–163.

Krauss, R. "Leger, Le Corbusier and Purism," *Art Forum* 10 (April 1972): 50–53.

Lahiji, N. "The Gift of the Open Hand: Le Corbusier Reading George Bataille's 'La Part Maudite'," *Journal of Architectural Education* 50, no. 1 (September 1996): 50–67.

Lionni, L. "Corbu in India," *Architectural Forum* 106 (April 1957): 142–147.

Lowman, Joyce. "Corb as Structural Rationalist: The Formative Influence of Engineer Max DuBois," *Architectural Review* 160, no. 956 (October 1976): 229–33.

Malabou, Catherine. "Nietzsche's *Ecce Homo,*" COL 711: Philosophy and Writing (Class Lecture at the University at Buffalo, Buffalo, New York, Spring 2011).

Malpas, Jeff. "Truth in Architecture," in V. Petridou, E. Constantopoulos, and P. Pagalos, eds. *The Significance of Philosophy in Architectural Education.* Athens: Michelis Foundation, 2012.

Moholy-Nagy, Sibyl. "The Achievement of Le Corbusier," *Arts Magazine* 40 (November 1965): 40–45.

Moore, Richard A. *Le Corbusier: Myth and Meta Architecture, the Late Period (1947–1965).* New York: Wittenborn, 1977.

Nietzsche, Friedrich. *Thus Spoke Zarathustra.* Translated by Walter Kaufman. New York: Modern Library Edition (Random House), 1995.

Nietzsche, Friedrich. *The Birth of Tragedy.* Translated by Douglas Smith. Oxford: Oxford University Press, 2008.

Pawley, Martin. *Le Corbusier.* Photographs by Yukio Futagawa. New York: Simon & Schuster, 1970.

Pevsner, Nikolaus. "Time and Le Corbusier," *Architectural Review* 125 (March 1959): 159–165.

Phaidon Editors, with an introductory essay by Jean-Louis Cohen. *Le Corbusier Le Grand.* New York and London: Phaidon, 2014.

Plato. *Plato: Complete Works.* Edited by John M. Cooper. Indianapolis, Indiana, and Cambridge, Massachusetts: Hackett Publishing Company, 1997.

Plato. *Selected Dialogues of Plato.* The Benjamin Jowett translation, revised, and with an introduction by Hayden Pelliccia. New York: The Modern Library, 2001.

Rousseau, Jean-Jacques. *The Social Contract and The Discourses.* Translated by G. D. H. Cole. New York, and Toronto: Alfred Knopf/Everyman's Library, 1993.

Rowe, Colin. "The Mathematics of the Ideal Villa," *Architecture and Urbanism,* no. 58 (October 1975): 29–40.

Ruskin, John. *Modern Painters.* London: John Wiley & Sons, 1843.

Ruskin, John. *The Works of John Ruskin.* Edited by E. T. Cook and Alexander Wedderburn. London: George Allen, 1903–1912. 39 volumes.

Ruskin, John. *The Seven Lamps of Architecture.* New York: Farrar, Straus and Giroux, 1979.

Semper, Gottfried. *The Four Elements of Architecture.* Translated by Harry Francis Malgrave and Wolfgang Herrmann. Cambridge: Cambridge University Press, 1989.

Serenyi, Peter. "Le Corbusier's Changing Attitude Toward Form," *Society of Architectural Historians Journal* 24, no. 1 (March 1965): 15–23.

Serenyi, Peter. "Timeless, but of its Time: Le Corbusier's Architecture in India," *Perspecta: The Yale Architectural Journal* 20 (1983): 91–118.

Serenyi, Peter, ed. *Le Corbusier, in Perspective.* Englewood Cliffs, New Jersey: Prentice-Hall, 1975.

Sert, Josep Luis. "Le Corbusier and the Image of Man," in *Four Great Makers of Modern Architecture: Gropius, Le Corbusier, Mies van der Rohe, Wright.* (The Verbatim Record of a Symposium Held at the School of Architecture, Columbia University, March–May, 1961) New York: Da Capo Press, 1970, 172–176.

Swenarton, Mark. "Ruskin and the Moderns," in *Artisans and Architects.* London: Palgrave Macmillan, 1989.

Tafuri, Manfredo. "The Crisis of Utopia: Le Corbusier at Algiers," in *Architecture and Utopia.* Cambridge, Massachusetts, and London: The MIT Press. 1976.

Turner, Paul. "The Education of Le Corbusier – A Study of the Development of Le Corbusier's Thought, 1900–1920," unpublished PhD dissertation. Harvard University, 1971.

Valéry, Paul. *Eupalinos ou L'Architecte*. Paris: Éditions de la Nouvelle Revue française, 1923.

Valéry, Paul. *Eupalinos, or The Architect,* in *Dialogues.* Princeton, New Jersey: Princeton University Press, 1989.

Vitruvius, Marcus V. Pollio. *On Architecture (Books 1–10).* Translated by Frank Granger. Cambridge, Massachusetts, and London: Harvard University Press, 1998, Volume 1 (Books 1–5), Volume 2 (Books 6–10).

Von Moos, Stanislaus. "Cartesian Curves," *Architectural Design* 43, no. 42 (April 1972): 237–239.

Von Moos, Stanislaus. *Le Corbusier: Elements of a Synthesis.* Translated by Beatrice Mock, Joseph Stein, and Maureen Oberil. Cambridge: The MIT Press, 1979.

Von Moos, Stanislaus and Arthur Rüegg, eds. *Le Corbusier Before Le Corbusier.* New Haven, Connecticut, and London: Yale University Press, 2002.

Whitman, Walt. "Song of Myself, 51," in *Leaves of Grass.* Brooklyn, New York: Rome Brothers, 1855.

INDEX

ILLUSTRATION CREDITS

p. 8, 10 Paul Valéry, *Eupalinos ou L'Architecte* (Paris: Éditions de la Nouvelle Revue Française, 1923), front matter, p. 90 and 100. Image courtesy of the Fondation Le Corbusier.

p. 11 Lucien Hervé, photographs of architecture and artworks by Le Corbusier, 1949–1965, The Getty Research Institute, Los Angeles, California. Accession no. 2002.R.41.

p. 13 top Charles-Édouard Jeanneret, *Study of Pine Trees,* 1905–1906, black gouache and pencil on paper. FLC_DE_2520_R. Image courtesy of the Fondation Le Corbusier.

p. 13 bottom Charles-Édouard Jeanneret, *Pine Forest Ornament,* 1911, gouache on paper. FLC_DE_1764_R. Image courtesy of the Fondation Le Corbusier.

p. 14 left Le Corbusier, *Vertical Still Life,* 1922, oil on canvas, 146.3 × 89.3 centimeters, Kunstmuseum, Basel. Peinture FLC 317. Image courtesy of the Fondation Le Corbusier.

p. 14 right *L'Esprit Nouveau 1,* Cover. Image courtesy of the Fondation Le Corbusier.

p. 15 Fonds Perret, CNAM/SIAF/CAPA/Archives d'architecture contemporaine/Auguste Perret/UFSE/SAIF/2024. © 2025 Artists Rights Society (ARS), New York/SAIF, Paris. Photograph courtesy of Alamy, stock photo #12.

p. 16 FLC L4(19)66. Image courtesy of the Fondation Le Corbusier.

p. 18 Le Corbusier, *Vers Une Architecture* (Paris: Éditions G. Crès, Collection de "L'Esprit Nouveau", 1923) Cover of the 3rd edition. Image courtesy of the Fondation Le Corbusier.

p. 22 Le Corbusier, letter to Jean-Jacques Duval, April 30, 1949. FLC: E1(20)465-466. Image courtesy of the Fondation Le Corbusier.

p. 24 Le Corbusier and Fondation Le Corbusier, *Le Corbusier Sketchbooks,* Volume 2, E18, 361. FLC_CA_E18_361. Image courtesy of the Fondation Le Corbusier.

p. 31 Le Corbusier and Fondation Le Corbusier, *Le Corbusier Sketchbooks,* Volume 2, E18, 336. FLC_CA_E18_336. Image courtesy of the Fondation Le Corbusier.

p. 35 Peter Reyner Banham. Image courtesy of the Getty Research Institute, Los Angeles, CA. R2017144_910009_b3_f2_001. Image appears in Reyner Banham, *A Concrete Atlantis*, Introduction, page 5.

p. 38 Le Corbusier, *Bottle of Red Wine,* 1922, oil on canvas, 60 × 73 centimeters. Peinture FLC 311. Image courtesy of the Fondation Le Corbusier.

p. 39 Charles-Édouard Jeanneret, *Stylized Ornaments,* 1905, black ink, gouache and pencil on paper, 24.3 × 31.7 centimeters. FLC_D_1765-R. Image courtesy of the Fondation Le Corbusier.

p. 44 Le Corbusier, *The Parthenon,* Athens, 1911, watercolor and pencil on paper, 21 × 13.7 centimeters. FLC_DE_2851-R. Image courtesy of the Fondation Le Corbusier.

p. 45 John Ruskin, "Sketch after Rain," WA.RS.ED.209, 27 May 1846. Image courtesy of Ashmolean Museum, University of Oxford. Image appears on the title page of *Stones of Venice.*

p. 46 top Le Corbusier, *Study of column capital,* Saint Vital, Ravenne, 1907, watercolor and pencil on paper, 20 × 19 centimeters. FLC_DE_1970-R. Image courtesy of the Fondation Le Corbusier.

p. 46 bottom John Ruskin, *Study of the column capital of Torcello Cathedral,* Venice. *The Stones of Venice,* page 60.

p. 47 top Le Corbusier, sketch of the Jura Mountains, 1914. *Le Corbusier Sketchbooks,* Volume 1, A1, 4. FLC_CA_A1_4. Image courtesy of the Fondation Le Corbusier.

p. 47 bottom *L'Esprit Nouveau 2.* Cover. Image courtesy of the Fondation Le Corbusier.

p. 49 John Ruskin, Part of the façade of the destroyed Church of San Michele in Foro, Lucca, Italy, sketched in color. WA.RS.ED.084, 30 June–1 July 1846. Partial black-and-white version included in *The Seven Lamps of Architecture,* Plate VI. Image courtesy of Ashmolean Museum, University of Oxford.

p. 51 Le Corbusier, *Towards a New Architecture,* pages 134–135. Image courtesy of the Fondation Le Corbusier.

p. 53 top Peter Behrens, Sketch of AEG Hochspannungsfabrik-Berlin,1909; Image courtesy of Heritage Image Partnership Ltd / Alamy Stock Photo.

p. 53 bottom Peter Behrens, AEG Turbinenfabrik, Berlin, interior, 1910–1912. Dr. Franz Stoedtner Archive. Image courtesy of Bildarchiv Foto Marburg / Art Resource, NY.

p. 56 Le Corbusier, *Towards a New Architecture,* page 194.

p. 64 Yukio Futagawa, Image courtesy of Yoshio Futagawa /GA photographers. Image appears in: *Le Corbusier: Millowners Association Building Ahmedabad, India. 1954. Carpenter Center for Visual Arts, Harvard University, Cambridge Massachusetts, USA, 1961–64.* Tokyo: A.D.A. Edita, 1975. Page 9.

p. 66 top Le Corbusier sketchbook E18, FLC_CA_E18_couv-R. Image courtesy of the Fondation Le Corbusier.

p. 66 bottom Le Corbusier sketchbook E19, FLC_CA_E19_couv. Image courtesy of the Fondation Le Corbusier.

p. 67 Le Corbusier and Fondation Le Corbusier, *Le Corbusier Sketchbooks,* Volume 2, 358. FLC_CA_E18_358. Image courtesy of the Fondation Le Corbusier.

p. 69 Le Corbusier and Fondation Le Corbusier, *Le Corbusier Sketchbooks,* Volume 2, 350. FLC_CA_E18_350. Image courtesy of the Fondation Le Corbusier.

p. 71 Le Corbusier and Fondation Le Corbusier, *Le Corbusier Sketchbooks,* Volume 2, 675. FLC_CA_E25_675. Image courtesy of the Fondation Le Corbusier.

p. 72 Atelier Le Corbusier, AMOA 4389, FLC 06781A. Image courtesy of the Fondation Le Corbusier.

p. 73 top Atelier Le Corbusier, AMOA 5120, FLC 6838. Image courtesy of the Fondation Le Corbusier.

p. 73 bottom Atelier Le Corbusier, AMOA 4482, FLC 6795A. Image courtesy of the Fondation Le Corbusier.

p. 74 Atelier Le Corbusier, AMOA 4489, FLC 6806A. Image courtesy of the Fondation Le Corbusier.

p. 77 Atelier Le Corbusier, AMOA 4394, FLC 6789. Image courtesy of the Fondation Le Corbusier.

p. 78 top Atelier Le Corbusier, AMOA 4490, FLC 6808. Image courtesy of the Fondation Le Corbusier.

p. 78 bottom Atelier Le Corbusier, AMOA 4478, FLC 6790. Image courtesy of the Fondation Le Corbusier.

p. 80 Atelier Le Corbusier, FLC 6776. Image courtesy of the Fondation Le Corbusier.

p. 85 Atelier Le Corbusier. FLC 6905. Image courtesy of the Fondation Le Corbusier.

p. 86 top Atelier Le Corbusier, FLC 6849. Image courtesy of the Fondation Le Corbusier, highlights by author.

p. 86 bottom Atelier Le Corbusier, AMOA 4389, FLC 6781. Image courtesy of the Fondation Le Corbusier, highlights by author.

p. 87 bottom Atelier Le Corbusier, FLC 6876. Image courtesy of the Fondation Le Corbusier, highlights by author.

p. 89 top Atelier Le Corbusier, AMOA 4592, FLC 6818. Image courtesy of the Fondation Le Corbusier, highlights by author.

p. 90 Atelier Le Corbusier, FLC 6879. Image courtesy of the Fondation Le Corbusier, highlights by author.

p. 93 bottom Atelier Le Corbusier, AMOA 4482, FLC 6795. Image courtesy of the Fondation Le Corbusier, highlights by author.

p. 108 Atelier Le Corbusier, AMOA 5117, FLC 6837. Image courtesy of the Fondation Le Corbusier, highlights by author.

p. 109 top Atelier Le Corbusier, AMOA 4592, FLC 6818. Image courtesy of the Fondation Le Corbusier.

p. 109 bottom Atelier Le Corbusier, AMOA 4594, FLC 7098. Image courtesy of the Fondation Le Corbusier.

p. 110 top Atelier Le Corbusier, AMOA 4482, FLC 6795A. Image courtesy of the Fondation Le Corbusier.

p. 113 top Atelier Le Corbusier, AMOA 5120, FLC 6838. Image courtesy of the Fondation Le Corbusier, highlights by author.

p. 113 bottom Atelier Le Corbusier, FLC 6849. Image courtesy of the Fondation Le Corbusier, highlights by author.

p. 118 Le Corbusier, *Apollo and Medusa*, 1945, black ink on paper. Image courtesy of the Fondation Le Corbusier. Cited in Charles Jencks, *Le Corbusier and the Tragic View of Architecture*, page 183.

p. 124 left View from the Sabarmati River, FLC L3(8)5, Lucien Hervé photographs of architecture and artworks by Le Corbusier, 1949–1965, The Getty Research Institute, Los Angeles, California. Accession no. 2002.R.41.

p. 132 left Le Corbusier, Maison Dom-ino, sections, FLC 19204. Image courtesy of the Fondation Le Corbusier.

p. 132 right Le Corbusier, Maison Dom-ino, perspective view, FLC 19209A. Image courtesy of the Fondation Le Corbusier.

p. 144 Paranjay Bhawsinghka, Rounak Panchal, 2024.

p. 146 top left Yukio Futagawa, 1975. Image courtesy of Yoshio Futagawa /GA photographers.

p. 146 top right and bottom, 149 top and bottom, 150 M. Gandhi, MKG, 2024.

p. 152 Atelier Le Corbusier. Field instructions. P3-6-239-003 FLC. Image courtesy of the Fondation Le Corbusier.

p. 153 top Atelier Le Corbusier, AMOA 4594, FLC 6785. Image courtesy of the Fondation Le Corbusier, highlights by author.

p. 153 bottom Atelier Le Corbusier, FLC 6903. Image courtesy of the Fondation Le Corbusier.

The physical model was fabricated by Ryerson Studio, and photographed by Cody Goddard.

IMPRINT

Cover photos: Mehrdad Hadighi
Graphic design concept, cover:
Ondine Pannet, Bureau Est
Layout and typesetting: Amelie Solbrig
Copy editing: Ian McDonald
Project management: Ria Stein
Production: Amelie Solbrig

Paper: Magno Volume, 135g/m^2
Lithography: prints professional, Berlin
Printing: Grafisches Centrum Cuno, Calbe

Library of Congress Control Number: 2025902405
Bibliographic information published by the German National Library
The German National Library lists this publication in the Deutsche Nationalbibliografie; detailed bibliographic data are available on the Internet at http://dnb.dnb.de.

ISBN 978-3-0356-2869-2
e-ISBN (PDF) 978-3-0356-2870-8

Im Westfeld 8, 4055 Basel, Switzerland
Part of Walter de Gruyter GmbH, Berlin/Boston

Printed on acid-free paper produced from chlorine-free pulp. TCF ∞
Printed in Germany

MIX
Paper | Supporting responsible forestry
FSC® C043106

9 8 7 6 5 4 3 2 1
www.birkhauser.com

Questions about General Product Safety Regulation:
productsafety@degruyterbrill.com